The Per[illegible]
Irelar[illegible]
Ch[illegible]ip
200[illegible]

The All-Ireland Hurling andGaelic Football Championships

Damian Cullen

PENGUIN BOOKS

PENGUIN IRELAND

Published by the Penguin Group

Penguin Ireland,
25 St Stephen's Green, Dublin 2, Ireland
(a division of Penguin Books Ltd)

Penguin Books Ltd,
80 Strand, London WC2R 0RL, England

Penguin Group (USA) Inc.,
375 Hudson Street, New York, New York 10014, USA

Penguin Group (Australia),
250 Camberwell Road, Camberwell, Victoria 3124, Australia
(a division of Pearson Australia Group Pty Ltd)

Penguin Group (Canada),
90 Eglinton Avenue East, Suite 700, Toronto, Ontario, Canada M4P 2Y3
(a division of Pearson Penguin Canada Inc.)

Penguin Books India Pvt Ltd,
11 Community Centre, Panchsheel Park, New Delhi – 110 017, India

Penguin Group (NZ),
cnr Airborne and Rosedale Roads, Albany, Auckland 1310, New Zealand
(a division of Pearson New Zealand Ltd)

Penguin Books (South Africa) (Pty) Ltd,
24 Sturdee Avenue, Rosebank 2196, South Africa

Penguin Books Ltd. Registered Offices: 80 Strand, London WC2R 0RL, England

www.penguin.com

First published 2006

Photo credits:
p. 1: Damien Eagers / SPORTSFILE
p. 37: Damien Eagers / SPORTSFILE
p. 113: Damien Eagers / SPORTSFILE
p. 125: David Maher / SPORTSFILE
p. 183: David Maher / SPORTSFILE
p. 203: Brian Lawless / SPORTSFILE

Designed by Richard Marston
Printed in Italy by LegoPrint S.p.A

ISBN-13: 978-1-844-88102-4
ISBN-10: 1-844-88102-4

Contents

Introduction

It's become something of a misnomer to speak of a GAA 'season' as, in recent years, the club and county fixture congestion has become faintly ridiculous. After the final blows of the inter-county championship season, almost every county board invariably rushes to squeeze numerous club ties into an insufficient number of weekends, before attention turns to the club battles at provincial level. For the eight teams left standing after the four regional finals, even Christmas becomes part of the GAA season. The inter-county cup competitions begin at the turn of the year, before the leagues take over. And by the end of spring, fans are already impatiently waiting for the opening shots of another championship campaign.

No matter how congested the other three seasons are, though, it's the summer that football, hurling and camogie supporters live for. And with the new championship formats, the primary road to the All-Ireland finals has been upgraded to a multi-lane motorway. In 1995, only 17 senior hurling ties were required to complete the championship. Ten years later, and despite the top tier of the championship being limited to just twelve counties, there were 36 clashes among hurling's elite. Including the Christy Ring Cup and Nicky Rackard Cup competitions, the total number of hurling matches last summer rises to 84. Add the football championship – including the eight Tommy Murphy Cup ties – and the number of inter-county ties in 2005 hits 157. And we haven't even mentioned camogie and women's football yet, with the extra 46 entries taking the total number of senior championship ties over the 200 mark. So sit back and get ready: the summer months have never been so jam-packed with action.

In this, the second annual edition of this guide, we get straight to the live action in Chapter 1, with an explanation of how the three-tier hurling championship works (and sometimes doesn't), as well as county-by-county previews, analysis, squad lists and historical data, and a fill-in table for match results in the Liam MacCarthy Cup, Christy Ring Cup and Nicky Rackard Cup competitions. The following chapter does the same for the somewhat less complicated, but equally busy, football championship.

It's no coincidence that the modern growth in profile for the national games has been in tandem with an incredible boost in support and playing numbers in the women's games. Camogie and women's football have forced themselves on to the national media stage, not because of any ideas of gender balance, but because the quality and interest demands it. In recognition of this, Chapter 3 previews the upcoming season in both codes, as well as detailing past and reigning champions.

As last season's championship already seems such a long time ago, Chapter 4 gives the full details of the 2005 Liam MacCarthy and Sam Maguire competitions. Chapter 5 provides background on the GAA's history and its complicated structure, as well as details of the rules of the games, past All-Ireland finals, reigning champions and website links. And Chapter 6 provides information on many of the most popular summer destinations in all four provinces – including some new additions – for GAA fans before they hit the road again.

This guide's primary function is to answer all the questions that a GAA supporter might ask during the championship season. Whether it's trying to remember the past, such as which teams were promoted and relegated in the inaugural three-tier hurling championship, or the future, such as where a team will stand if they win or lose their next championship tie, or even settling a bet, such as when Kerry went 16 consecutive seasons without even appearing in an All-Ireland football final – whatever the question, hopefully, we'll give you the answer.

Because our aim is not only to inform but to provoke, here follows our annual pre-season ranking of the twelve counties competing in Tier One of the hurling championship, and of the thirty-three counties participating in the football championship:

Hurling

1. Galway
2. Cork
3. Kilkenny
4. Waterford
5. Tipperary
6. Clare
7. Wexford
8. Limerick
9. Offaly
10. Laois
11. Dublin
12. Westmeath

Football

1. Kerry
2. Tyrone
3. Laois
4. Armagh
5. Dublin
6. Mayo
7. Cork
8. Derry
9. Galway
10. Donegal
11. Down
12. Meath
13. Fermanagh
14. Wexford
15. Limerick
16. Offaly
17. Kildare
18. Roscommon
19. Westmeath
20. Monaghan
21. Cavan
22. Sligo
23. Clare
24. Louth
25. Longford
26. Carlow
27. Wicklow
28. Leitrim
29. Antrim
30. Tipperary
31. Waterford
32. London
33. New York

1 Hurling Championship 2006

1
Hurling Championship 2006

Championship Format

With one full running of the new senior hurling championship format now completed, it's perhaps a little easier for GAA supporters to understand and assess its merits. (See below for a full account of the structure of the hurling championship.)

One of the strongest arguments for the rejigged format – which will run until at least the end of 2007 – was that too many counties were not playing enough competitive matches each summer. For that reason alone, the new three-tier system – which involves round-robin play followed by a knock-out tournament and guarantees a minimum of three dates for each team during the summer – was generally welcomed by hurling fans and players in 2005. But the new championship system also threw up some rather unwelcome side-effects during its inaugural season.

Proponents of the new format pointed to the annual collection of one-sided ties. However, despite several weaker counties being dropped from the provincial championships in Munster and Leinster last season, crushing defeats and predictable contests have not been eradicated. In fact, almost half of the Tier One matches played last season were decided by seven points or more.

The uneven playing level was most evident in the Qualifiers, with predictable results and massive winning margins turning supporters off and hitting the GAA where it hurts the most – in the pocket. Last season, each of the two Qualifier groups contained two teams that were clearly much stronger than the other two, which meant there was little doubt as to who would claim the four available spots in the All-Ireland quarter-finals. With hurling supporters spared a 'group of death', they were also deprived of a group of interest. Meanwhile, the bizarre rule forcing teams finishing third and fourth in each group to partake in a relegation play-off – rather than just the two bottom teams fighting it out – resulted in group matches between the weaker counties counties becoming of little importance, as a victory couldn't in itself save a team from a relegation match. Hopefully this season's hurling championship will produce more than the 2005 total of one win by an underdog in 12 Qualifier games (and even that result, Clare beating Waterford in Ennis, can hardly be considered a major shock).

Probably the biggest disappointment for supporters was the realization that, for all the extra matches, the championship has become even more predictable. The eight teams qualifying for the All-Ireland quarter-finals will surely change little in the foreseeable future. After 25 championship games last season – 13 provincial ties (including Ulster) and 12 Qualifier matches – the number of teams challenging for the Liam MacCarthy Cup had been whittled down from 12 to, erm, eight. Only Offaly look capable of challenging last year's top eight for a place at the knock-out table.

While Cork, Westmeath and Louth all had very satisfying campaigns in 2005, the biggest loser was undoubtedly Ulster hurling, with Antrim being stripped of Tier One membership, Down missing out on reaching the top flight at the final hurdle and Derry surprising everyone by falling through the Tier Two trap-door. Tier One will therefore have no representation from the northern half of Ireland this season, with Westmeath, winners of the second tier, being the new addition to the exclusive 12-member club. Antrim's relegation does make the championship a little less complicated, with the mix-match Ulster championship – which last season involved counties from the first, second and third tiers, as well as no tier at all – no longer boasting a member of Tier One.

The same five Tier One teams that competed for the Munster title last season will battle it out again this summer. Leinster has gained a Tier One side and so requires an additional first-round match. With no Connacht championship, Galway gains automatic entry to the Qualifiers.

Tier One

Clare, Cork, Dublin, Galway, Kilkenny, Laois, Limerick, Offaly, Tipperary, Waterford, Westmeath, Wexford

Provincial Championships

Organized on a knock-out basis in Munster, Ulster and Leinster. There is no provincial championship in Connacht; Galway, as a member of Tier One, is the sole county from that province that will compete for the All-Ireland title. While the Munster and Leinster championships will include only Tier One members, the Ulster championship will include Antrim, London and Down from Tier Two, Derry from Tier Three, and New York.

All-Ireland Qualifiers

Eight counties take part in the All-Ireland Qualifiers: the first-round losers in the Munster (one team) and Leinster (two teams) championships, losing semi-finalists in the Leinster and Munster championships (four teams), and Galway.

- The eight teams are organized into two groups of four
- Groups are selected by open draw, apart from the provision that there can be no more than two teams from any province in each group
- Each county plays the other three teams in the same group once
- A county designated as 'weak' (by the National Games Administration Committee) may have two home games in the

group stage, provided the home venue reaches required standard (decided by the National Games Administration Committee and the National Safety Council)
- A team's finishing position in the group will be based first on points total (two points for a win, one for a draw), then scoring difference, then highest score, then result of the game(s) between counties that are level by all other measures

All-Ireland Quarter-finals

Pairings (a draw will be required) for All-Ireland quarter-finals are:
- Leinster champions v runner-up in one Qualifier group
- Munster champions v runner-up in other Qualifier group
- Leinster runner-up v winner of one Qualifier group
- Munster runner-up v winner of other Qualifier group

All-Ireland Semi-finals

Leinster and Munster champions (or the teams that defeated them in the quarter-final) will not be drawn against each other – therefore the earliest the Munster and Leinster champions could meet in the 2006 All-Ireland championship would be in the All-Ireland final.

Relegation and Promotion

The third- and fourth-placed teams in Group One and Group Two of the Qualifiers will play in a relegation play-off as follows:
- Third-placed team in Group One v fourth-placed team in Group Two
- Third-placed team in Group Two v fourth-placed team in Group One
- The two losing teams to play in a relegation final
- Losing team in the relegation final will be relegated to Tier Two for 2007 season

Tier Two

Antrim, Carlow, Down, Kerry, Kildare, London, Mayo, Meath, Roscommon, Wicklow

Group Stage

- Ten counties, organized into two groups of five.
- Each county plays the other four teams in its group once.
- A team's finishing position in the group will be based first on points total (two points for a win, one for a draw), then scoring difference, then highest score, then result of the game(s) between counties that are level by all other measures.

Semi-finals

The winner of Group One plays runner-up of Group Two, and the winner of Group Two plays runner-up of Group One.

Final

The winning team will be promoted to Tier One for 2006 season.

Relegation and Promotion

The fourth- and fifth-placed teams in Group One and Group Two will play in a relegation play-off as follows:

- Fourth-placed team in Group One v Fifth-placed team in Group Two
- Fourth-placed team in Group Two v Fifth-placed team in Group One
- The two losing teams to play in a relegation final
- The losing team in the relegation final will be relegated to Tier Three for 2006 season

Tier Three

Armagh, Cavan, Derry, Donegal, Fermanagh, Leitrim, Longford, Louth, Monaghan, Sligo, Tyrone, Warwickshire

- Twelve teams, organized into three groups of four
- Each team plays the other teams in the same group once
- The three first-placed teams in each group plus the best runner-up qualify for the semi-finals
- The Tier Three champion will be promoted to Tier Two for 2006 season

Provincial Championship Fixtures 2006

Leinster Senior Hurling Championship

Round	Date	Teams	Venue
Quarter-final (1)	May 21	Dublin v Westmeath	Portlaoise
Quarter-final (2)	May 21	Offaly v Laois	Portlaoise
Semi-final	June 10	Kilkenny v QF1 winner	Parnell Park or Cusack Park
Semi-final	June 11	Wexford v QF2 winner	Kilkenny
Final	July 2		Croke Park

Munster Senior Hurling Championship

Round	Date	Teams	Venue
Quarter-final	May 14	Tipperary v Limerick	Thurles
Semi-final	May 28	Clare v Cork	TBC
Semi-final	June 3	Waterford v QF winner	Thurles TBC
Final	June 25		TBC

Ulster Senior Hurling Championship

Round	Date	Teams	Venue
Quarter-final	May 14	Antrim v London	Ruislip
Semi-final	May 21	Down v QF winner	Belfast
Semi-final	May 21	Derry v New York	New York
Final	June 4		TBC

Connacht Senior Hurling Championship

No provincial championship; Galway go straight into All-Ireland qualifying group.

Tier One

Clare An Clár

Colours: **Yellow and blue**
Stadium: **Cusack Park, Ennis**
Capacity: **24,000**
GAA clubs: **88**

Munster SHC: **6**
1889, 1914, 1932, 1995, 1997, 1998

All-Ireland SHC: **3**
1914, 1995, 1997

National Hurling League: **3**
1946, 1977, 1978

Last five years:

2001: Unlucky to be beaten by a single point by Tipperary in the provincial semi-final.

2002: Fell yet again to Tipperary before going on a successful 'back door' run with wins over Dublin, Wexford, Galway and Waterford to reach the All-Ireland final. Kilkenny, however, proved too strong on the day.

2003: Gained some measure of revenge for recent years, beating Tipperary in provincial quarter-final. Failed to build on that win, losing to Cork in Munster semi-final and Galway in Qualifier series.

2004: Knocked out of Munster by Waterford. Beat Laois and Offaly in Qualifier series before falling to Kilkenny in replayed All-Ireland quarter-final.

2005: Entered the provincial championship against a Tipperary team that had two games already under its belt – and how it showed. After another struggling performance against Offaly, the summer was turned on its head when Waterford were sent home from Ennis empty-handed. Clare had woken up – and Wexford would feel the county's power before the rip-roaring All-Ireland semi-final clash with Cork, which ended in a narrow defeat.

Outlook

Hard to believe Clare beat Dublin, Offaly, Waterford and Wexford, before losing by a single point to Cork, and yet they did not merit a single outfield player on the 2005 All Stars selection. Perhaps it was a reflection of the strength throughout the side. This season Cork are first up and Clare will have to hit the ground running to fulfil any ambitions in Munster. Hopes and dreams in the All-Ireland championship may be more achievable.

Top player: **Davy Fitzgerald**

Supporters from Clare love him, supporters from other counties hate him. The driving force behind the Banner men for many years, his commitment to the cause is unrelenting.

Penguin Ireland Guide ranking: **6**

Clare squad 2006

Clare squad 2006	v **Tipperary** lost 0–14 2–14	v **Dublin** won 1–23 0–9	v **Offaly** won 1–12 1–11	v **Waterford** won 4–14 0–21	v **Wexford** won 1–20 0–12	v **Cork** lost 0–15 0–16
Davy Fitzgerald	●	●	●	●	●	●
Frank Lohan	●	●	●	●	●	●
Brian Lohan	●	●	●	●	●	●
Gerry O'Grady	●		●	●	●	●
Alan Markham	●	●	●	●	●	●
Seanie McMahon	●	●	●	●	●	●
Gerry Quinn	●	●	●	●	●	●
Brian O'Connell	●	●	●	●	●	●
Colin Lynch	●		●	●	●	●
Diarmuid McMahon	●	●	●	●	●	●
Tony Griffin	●	●	●	●	●	●
Barry Nugent	●		●		●	
Tony Carmody	●	●	●	●	●	●
Niall Gilligan	●	●	●	●	●	●
Andrew Quinn	●	○	○	●	○	●
David Forde	○	●	○	○		
Daithi O'Connell	○	●	○	○	○	
Conor Plunkett	○	○		○	○	
Colm Forde	○	●	●			
Brian Quinn		●				
David Hoey		○	○	●	●	●
Darragh Clancy		○				
Declan O'Rourke		○	○	○	○	○
Brian Lynch				○		
Jonathan Clancy					○	○
Philip Brennan						
Ken Kennedy						
Tomas Holland						
John Coen						
Tyrone Kearse						

● Played from start ○ Substituted on

Cork Corcaigh

Colours: **Red and white**
Stadium: **Páirc Uí Chaoimh, Cork**
Capacity: **42,000**
GAA clubs: **259**

Munster SHC: 48

1890, 1892, 1893, 1894, 1901, 1902, 1903, 1904, 1905, 1907, 1912, 1915, 1919, 1920, 1926, 1927, 1928, 1929, 1931, 1939, 1942, 1943, 1944, 1946, 1947, 1952, 1953, 1954, 1956, 1966, 1969, 1970, 1972, 1975, 1976, 1977, 1978, 1979, 1982, 1983, 1984, 1985, 1986, 1990, 1992, 1999, 2000, 2003, 2005

All-Ireland SHC: 29

1890, 1892, 1893, 1894, 1902, 1903, 1919, 1926, 1928, 1929, 1931, 1941, 1942, 1943, 1944, 1946, 1952, 1953, 1954, 1966, 1970, 1976, 1977, 1978, 1984, 1986, 1990, 1999, 2004, 2005

National Hurling League: 14

1926, 1930, 1940, 1941, 1948, 1953, 1969, 1970, 1972, 1974, 1980, 1981, 1993, 1998

Last five years:

2001: Surprised by Limerick in Munster quarter-final, losing by a single point.

2002: Lost to Waterford in provincial semi-final, but recovered temporarily to beat Limerick before crashing out to Galway in Qualifier series.

2003: Defeated Clare and Waterford to win Munster competition. Needed two hours to account for Wexford, before falling just short in All-Ireland final battle with Kilkenny.

2004: Beat Kerry and Limerick, but surrendered provincial title to Waterford in decider. Recovered to end the campaigns of Tipperary, Antrim and Wexford before gaining revenge over Kilkenny in the All-Ireland final.

2005: Overcame the reigning Munster champions, a weakened Waterford side in a game that boded well for the quality of summer hurling. The Rebels had the provincial title in the bag halfway through the home decider with Tipperary, and only then did the focus shift to holding on to the Liam MacCarthy Cup – which they did, through victories over Waterford, Clare and Galway.

Outlook

The fact a few players have deferred retiring from inter-county hurling to help the push for three in a row must have come as depressing news for other counties. Clare are worthy opponents, and Cork will have to be at the top of their game to put together back-to-back provincial titles. This season, however, the main focus of attention will certainly be on a date in September.

Top player: John Gardiner

In a side full of stars, the Na Piarsaigh defender shone brightest in many of the Rebel County's ties last season. The most consistent player on the Cork side.

Penguin Ireland Guide ranking: **2**

Cork squad 2006

	v Waterford won 2–17 2–15	v Tipperary won 1–21 1–16	v Waterford won 1–18 1–13	v Clare won 0–16 0–15	v Galway won 1–21 1–16
Dónal Óg Cusack	●	●	●	●	●
Pat Mulcahy	●	●	●	●	●
Diarmuid O'Sullivan	●	●	●	●	●
Brian Murphy	●	●	●	●	●
John Gardiner	●	●	●	●	●
Ronan Curran	●	●	●	●	●
Seán Óg Ó hAilpín	●	●	●	●	●
Tom Kenny	●	●	●	●	●
Jerry O'Connor	●	●	●	●	●
Ben O'Connor	●	●	●	●	●
Niall McCarthy	●	●	●	●	●
Neil Ronan	●	○	○	○	○
Kieran Murphy (Sarsfields)	●	●	●	●	●
Brian Corcoran	●	●	●	●	●
John Deane	●	●	●	●	●
Kieran Murphy (Erin's Own)	○	○	○	○	○
Timmy McCarthy		●	●	●	●
Wayne Sherlock		○		○	
Jonathan O'Callaghan		○			
Cian O'Connor			○		
Martin Coleman					
Paul Morrissey					
John Browne					
Graham Callinan					
Peter Kelly					
Ronan McGregor					
Kevin Harnett					
Eamonn Collins					

● Played from start ○ Substituted on

Dublin Áth Cliath

Colours: **Dark blue and light blue**
Stadium: **Parnell Park, Dublin**
Capacity: **11,000**
Stadium: **Croke Park, Dublin**
Capacity: **82,300**
GAA clubs: **211**

Leinster SHC: **23**

1889, 1892, 1894, 1896, 1902, 1906, 1908, 1917, 1919, 1920, 1921, 1924, 1927, 1928, 1930, 1934, 1938, 1941, 1942, 1944, 1948, 1952, 1961

All-Ireland SHC: **6**

1889, 1917, 1920, 1924, 1927, 1938

National Hurling League: **2**

1929, 1939

Last five years:

2001: Made an early provincial exit, narrowly losing a quarter-final clash with Laois.

2002: Defeated Westmeath and Meath before losing their Leinster semi-final tie with Wexford. Lost heavily to Clare in qualifying round.

2003: Defeated Westmeath in first preliminary round tie, but again needed two hours to defeat rivals Laois. Lost to Kilkenny in provincial semi-final and to Offaly in Qualifier.

2004: Again topped Westmeath in their provincial clash, but a semi-final loss to Offaly was followed by an unfortunate pairing with Kilkenny, who were still smarting from defeat to Wexford.

2005: A loss to Laois in Leinster was followed by a trio of defeats – to Clare, Waterford and Offaly – in their Qualifier group, but Dublin saved their season with a revenge victory over Laois in the relegation play-off.

Outlook

Last season Dublin lost their first three championship games by an average of over 17 points each. But you don't need to have a good season to secure your position in the new Tier One – you just need to have a better season than one of the other 11 sides in the top flight. Putting last year behind them is the number-one priority for Dublin hurling this season: chasing the big guns has given way to simply halting the decline.

Top player: **David Sweeney**

One of the capital's most consistent performers, Sweeney is comfortable in the half-back line and midfield. Has been known to chip in regularly with a point or two.

Penguin Ireland Guide ranking: **11**

Dublin squad 2006

	v Laois lost 0–14 4–14	**v Clare** lost 0–9 1–23	**v Waterford** lost 1–3 4–17	**v Offaly** lost 2–14 2–15	**v Laois** won 3–13 1–10
Gary Maguire	●	●	●	●	●
Greg Bennett	●		○	●	●
Sean O'Shea	●		●		
Gerard O'Meara	●	●	●	●	●
David Sweeney	●	●		●	●
Ronan Fallon	●	●	●	●	●
Stephen Hiney	●	●	●	●	●
Tommy Moore	●	●	●	●	●
Stephen McDonald	●	●	●	○	
Michael Carton	●	●	●	●	●
David Curtin	●	●	●		●
Derek O'Reilly	●	●	●	●	●
Emmet Carroll	●	●	●	●	●
Maitias Breathnach	●		●		
Stuart Mullen	●	○	○		
Stephen Perkins	○				
Carl Meehan	○			○	○
Peadar Carton	○	○	○	○	
Simon Daly	○				
Aodhan de Paor	○				
John Cullen		●	●	●	●
Damien Russell		●	●	●	●
Liam Ryan		●		○	○
Kevin Flynn		●		●	●
Tim Sweeney		○			
Eoin Moran		○	○	●	●
Tomas McGrane			●		
John Kingston			○	●	
Trevor O'Donoghue					
Cormac O'Brien					

● Played from start ○ Substituted on

Galway Gaillimh

Colours: **Maroon and white**
Stadium: **Pearse Stadium, Galway**
Capacity: **35,000**
Stadium: **Tuam Stadium, Tuam**
Capacity: **30,000**
GAA clubs: **86**

Connacht SHC: **20**

1900, 1901, 1902, 1904, 1905, 1906, 1908, 1910, 1911, 1912, 1914, 1915, 1917, 1923, 1994, 1995, 1996, 1997, 1998, 1999

All-Ireland SHC: **4**

1923, 1980, 1987, 1988

National Hurling League: **8**

1931, 1951, 1975, 1987, 1989, 1996, 2000, 2004

Last five years:

2001: Defeated Derry and Kilkenny to qualify for the All-Ireland final, where they fell to Tipperary.

2002: Big victories over Down and Cork meant a place in All-Ireland quarter-final, where they were tripped up by Clare.

2003: Successive defeats by Clare and Tipperary prevented progress from qualifying series.

2004: An easy victory over Down was followed by a thrashing at the hands of Kilkenny in third Qualifier round.

2005: Beat Laois, Antrim and (narrowly) Limerick in Qualifiers. A tight win over Tipperary in the All-Ireland quarter-final was followed by a thrilling 5-18 to 4-18 triumph over Kilkenny in the semi-final. Cork were unstoppable in the final, however.

Outlook

For years – after suffering defeat at the All-Ireland semi-final (and more recently, All-Ireland quarter-final) stage of the championship – Galway officials and players and supporters would point to the lack of early-season top-level games as the reason for their failings. That excuse is no longer valid, with the Connacht championship a thing of the past and Galway entering the championship at Qualifier stage. While only two teams from each Qualifier section can claim a place in the All-Ireland quarter-finals, the Tribesmen require a tough group, with at least three potential qualifiers, to prime them for the knock-out stages. The glory days of the 1980s are now a distant memory, but Galway certainly showed last season they have the backbone and skill to lay down a new milestone.

Top player: **Damien Hayes**

Doesn't often rack up huge personal tallies, but has become a crucial target man for the Tribesmen, and was a big reason why Galway reached the All-Ireland final last season.

Penguin Ireland Guide ranking: **1**

Galway squad 2006

	v **Laois** won 2–22 2–11	v **Antrim** won 3–29 0–10	v **Limerick** won 1–18 2–14	v **Tipperary** won 2–20 2–18	v **Kilkenny** won 5–18 4–18	v **Cork** lost 1–16 1–21
Liam Donoghue	●	●	●	●	●	●
Damien Joyce	●	●	●	●	●	●
Shane Kavanagh	●	●	●	●	●	●
Colin Coen	●	●	●	○		
Ger Mahon	●	●				
Derek Hardiman	●	●	●	●	●	●
Ollie Canning	●	●	●	●	●	●
Tony Óg Regan	●	●	●	●	●	●
David Collins	●	●	●	●	●	●
Richie Murray	●	●	●	●	●	●
David Forde	●		●	●	●	●
David Tierney	●	●	●	●	●	●
Damien Hayes	●	●	●	●	●	●
Kevin Hayes	●	●	●	○		○
Ger Farragher	●	●	●	●	●	●
Fergal Healy	○	○	●	●	●	●
Niall Healy	○	●	○	●	●	●
Fergal Moore	○	○				
David Donoghue	○					
Alan Kerins		○	○	●	●	●
David Hayes		○				
Andy Smyth		○				
Kevin Broderick					○	○
Paul Dullaghan						
John Lee						
Aongus Callanan						
Noel Kenny						
Liam Hodgins						
Tom Tierney						
Andy Coen						

● Played from start ○ Substituted on

Kilkenny Cill Chainnigh

Colours: Black and amber
Stadium: Nowlan Park, Kilkenny
Capacity: 26,300
GAA clubs: 41

Leinster SHC: 61

1888, 1893, 1895, 1897, 1898, 1900, 1903, 1904, 1905, 1907, 1909, 1911, 1912, 1913, 1916, 1922, 1923, 1925, 1926, 1931, 1932, 1933, 1935, 1936, 1937, 1939, 1940, 1943, 1945, 1946, 1947, 1950, 1953, 1957, 1958, 1959, 1963, 1964, 1966, 1967, 1969, 1971, 1972, 1973, 1974, 1975, 1978, 1979, 1982, 1983, 1986, 1987, 1991, 1992, 1993, 1998, 1999, 2000, 2001, 2002, 2003, 2005

All-Ireland SHC: 28

1904, 1905, 1907, 1909, 1911, 1912, 1913, 1922, 1932, 1933, 1935, 1939, 1947, 1957, 1963, 1967, 1969, 1972, 1974, 1975, 1979, 1982, 1983, 1992, 1993, 2000, 2002, 2003

National Hurling League: 11

1933, 1962, 1966, 1976, 1982, 1983, 1986, 1990, 1995, 2002, 2003, 2005

Last five years:

2001: Beat Offaly and Wexford to retain Leinster title, but fell to Galway in All-Ireland semi-final.

2002: Again overcame Offaly and Wexford to remain divisional kingpins, and underlined their dominance by reclaiming the Liam MacCarthy Cup, defeating Tipperary and Clare along the way.

2003: Defeated Dublin and Wexford en route to the Leinster title, and Tipperary and Cork en route to another All-Ireland.

2004: Shocked by Wexford in opening championship tie, then recovered to defeat Dublin, Galway, Clare (after a replay) and Waterford to reach All-Ireland final. Surrendered crown to Cork.

2005: Reclaimed Leinster title via a demolition of Offaly and a narrower win over Wexford. A five-point All-Ireland quarter-final victory over Limerick was followed by a shock defeat to Galway in a 5-18 to 4-18 classic.

Outlook

Kilkenny supporters are only recently starting to get over the fact that last season was not a successful one. How many teams have scored 4-18 in one game and lost? The absence of full-back Noel Hickey only partly explains Kilkenny's defeat to Galway; perhaps the heavy beating handed out to the Tribesmen the year before provides another clue. Still, while the defence creaked under the pressure, the forwards, led by Henry Shefflin and Tommy Walsh, kept the score-board attendants busy all summer. With Westmeath or Dublin first up in Leinster, there's a 99.9 per cent chance Kilkenny will be in the provincial decider yet again – it will be the first chance to gauge the 2003 champions' prospects for the summer.

Top player: Tommy Walsh

The only question the gifted player poses is where to put him – defence, midfield or up front? One of the true giants of the game, his pace with the sliotar causes nightmares for other counties.

Penguin Ireland Guide ranking: **3**

Kilkenny squad 2006

	v **Offaly** won 6–28 0–15	v **Wexford** won 0–22 1–16	v **Limerick** won 0–18 0–13	v **Galway** lost 4–18 5–18
James McGarry	●	●	●	●
James Ryall	●	●	●	●
Noel Hickey	●	●		
Jackie Tyrell	●	●		○
Richard Mullally	●	●	●	●
Peter Barry	●	●	●	●
JJ Delaney	●	●	●	●
Bryan Barry	●	●	●	
Derek Lyng	●	●	●	●
Martin Comerford	●	●	●	●
Eoin Larkin	●	●	●	●
Tommy Walsh	●	●	●	●
Richie Power	●	●	●	○
DJ Carey	●		●	●
Henry Shefflin	●	●	●	●
Conor Phelan	○	●		
John Hoyne	○	○	○	●
Michael Kavanagh	○	○	●	●
Eoin McCormack	○	○	○	○
John Tennyson	○		●	●
Eddie Brennan		○	○	●
Brian Hogan				○
Sean Dowling				
Jimmy Coogan				
Ken Coogan				
Mark Phelan				
PJ Ryan				
James 'Cha' Fitzpatrick				
Aidan Fogarty				
John Maher				
Willie O'Dwyer				
Colin Herity				

● Played from start ○ Substituted on

Laois Laoighis

Colours: Blue and white
Stadium: O'Moore Park, Portlaoise
Capacity: 27,000
GAA clubs: 85

Leinster SHC: 3
1914, 1915, 1949
All-Ireland SHC: 1
1915
National Hurling League: 0
Last five years:

2001: Victories over Meath and Dublin brought them to the provincial semi-final, where a much stronger Wexford team were waiting.
2002: Lost to Meath after Leinster preliminary-round victory over Wicklow.
2003: Again opened Leinster campaign with victory over Wicklow, then beat Carlow. Another two-leg loss to Dublin was followed by a lesson in hurling from Tipperary in Qualifiers.
2004: Defeated Carlow and Meath before exiting Leinster competition at the hands of Offaly. A Qualifier victory over Westmeath was followed by a big loss to Clare.
2005: A comprehensive defeat of Dublin raised hopes of some respectable performances against stronger opposition, but the season soon descended into a more predictable fare. Wexford ended Laois's Leinster campaign, and Qualifier losses to Galway and Limerick – offset only by a victory over Antrim – left the county in a relegation dogfight, which became scary after Dublin gained revenge in the relegation semi-final. Fortunately, Antrim could not do the same in the relegation final.

Outlook

Apart from Laois, Dublin and Westmeath, the other nine Tier One counties are probably strong enough to beat one another on their day. Laois are not a hundred miles from joining that group. But a big scalp in the Qualifiers would be needed to convince many hurling supporters. A meeting with neighbours Offaly isn't exactly the easiest way to ease into a new hurling championship.

Top player: James Young

Can play at midfield, though most comfortable in the half-forward line. A dead-ball specialist, he consistently battles against the strong tide the county often finds itself up against.

Penguin Ireland Guide ranking: **10**

Laois squad 2006

	v **Dublin** won 4–14 0–14	v **Wexford** lost 1–10 0–24	v **Galway** lost 2–11 2–22	v **Limerick** lost 1–9 2–15	v **Antrim** won 0–21 1–16	v **Dublin** lost 1–10 3–13	v **Antrim** won 1–23 1–15
Patrick Mullaney	●	●	●	●	●		
Brian Campion	●	●	●			●	●
Pakie Cuddy	●	●	●	●	●	●	●
Michael McEvoy	●	●	●	●	●	●	●
Joe Fitzpatrick	●	●	●	●	●		
Darren Rooney	●	●		●			●
Seamus Dwyer	●	●	●	●	●	●	●
James Young	●	●	●	●	●	●	●
James Walsh	●	●	●	●	●	●	●
Joe Phelan	●	●		●	●		
John Rowney	●		●	●	●	●	●
Liam Tynan	●	●	●	●	●		●
Tommy Fitzgerald	●	●	●	●	●	●	●
Mark Rooney	●	○		●	●	●	●
Damien Culleton	●	●	●	●	●	●	●
Enda Meagher	○	●	○		○	●	○
Philip Russell	○		○		○	●	●
Cahir Healy	○	●	●		○	●	●
Cathal Brophy	○	○	○	○	○	○	○
Canice Coonan	○	○	●				○
Robert Jones		○	○				
Pat Mahon			●	○	●	○	
John Walsh			○	●	●	●	●
Alan Delaney				○		○	
Colm Clear				○		○	○
Kevin Galvin						●	
Damien Walsh						○	
Eamonn Jackman							
Rory Conroy							
Jack O'Shea							

● Played from start ○ Substituted on

Limerick Luimneach

Colours: Green and white
Stadium: Gaelic Grounds, Limerick
Capacity: 49,500
GAA clubs: 107

Munster SHC: 18

1897, 1910, 1911, 1918, 1921, 1923, 1933, 1934, 1935, 1936, 1940, 1955, 1973, 1974, 1980, 1981, 1994, 1996

All-Ireland SHC: 7

1897, 1918, 1921, 1934, 1936, 1940, 1973

National Hurling League: 11

1934, 1935, 1936, 1937, 1938, 1947, 1971, 1984, 1985, 1992, 1997

Last five years:

2001: Gained revenge over Cork, then defeated Waterford in provincial semi-final, but found Tipperary too strong in the final. Lost narrowly to Wexford in All-Ireland quarter-final.

2002: Lost to Tipperary in Munster semi-final and to Cork in first game of Qualifiers.

2003: Unlucky to be beaten by Waterford in provincial semi-final. Recovered somewhat to defeat Kerry in Qualifier series, before crashing out to Offaly in next round.

2004: Beaten by Cork and Tipperary in provincial and Qualifier competitions respectively.

2005: Two draws against Tipperary – the second ending in extra-time defeat – got Limerick nowhere in Munster. Qualifier victories over Antrim and Laois, and a loss to Galway, meant second place in the group and an All-Ireland quarter-final date with Kilkenny. A rousing second-half performance could not prevent a five-point defeat.

Outlook

It's tough being a Limerick supporter – having expectations regularly raised, only for them to be cruelly crushed each time. To many, 'potential' – as evidenced by good performances against Tipperary, Galway and Kilkenny – is just a euphemism for 'not worth a damn at the moment'. Limerick's ambitions generally are radically altered on a month-to-month basis. A repeat first-round meeting with Tipperary in Thurles shouldn't intimidate the visitors after last season. Still, Limerick may have to seek their fortune once again in the Qualifier series, and then hope to progress beyond the All-Ireland quarter-final stage.

Top player: Peter Lawlor

When the half-back line clicked, so did the whole team. Lawlor dominated his area for most of last season and his excellent displays were recognized with an All Star nomination.

Penguin Ireland Guide ranking: **8**

Limerick squad 2006

Player	v **Tipperary** drew 2–14 2–14	v **Tipperary** lost 0–18 2–13	v **Antrim** won 4–25 1–9	v **Laois** won 2–15 1–9	v **Galway** lost 2–14 1–18	v **Kilkenny** lost 0–13 0–18
Timmy Houlihan	●	●	●	●	●	●
Stephen Lucey	●	●	●	●	●	●
Damien Reale	●	●	●	●		●
Mark Foley	●	●			●	●
Ollie Moran	●	●	●	●	●	●
Brian Geary	●	●	●	●	●	●
Peter Lawlor	●	●	●		●	●
Paul O'Grady	●	●	●	●	●	●
Donal O'Grady	●	●	●	●	●	
Conor Fitzgerald	●	●	○	●	○	
Niall Moran	●	●	●	●	●	●
Andrew O'Shaughnessy	●	●	●	●	●	●
Donnacha Sheehan	●	●	●	●		
TJ Ryan	●	●	●	●	●	●
Donie Ryan	●	●	●	●	●	●
Pat Tobin	○	○	●	○	○	○
Mickey Cahill	○					●
Sean O'Connor		○	○			
Kevin Tobin		○	○	●	○	
Paudie O'Dwyer			●	●	●	
Pat Kirby			○	○	●	●
Alan O'Connor			○			○
James O'Brien				○		●
Michael Clifford				○	●	
David Breen						
Garreth Heagney						
Patrick Cahill						
John Meskell						
Ger O'Connor						
Pat Sheehan						
John Paul Sheehan						

● Played from start ○ Substituted on

Offaly Uíbh Fhailí

Colours: **Green, white and gold**
Stadium: **St Brendan's Park, Birr**
Capacity: **11,000**
Stadium: **O'Connor Park, Tullamore**
Capacity: **16,000**
GAA clubs: **85**

Leinster SHC: **9**
1980, 1981, 1984, 1985, 1988, 1989, 1990, 1994, 1995

All-Ireland SHC: **4**
1981, 1985, 1994, 1998

National Hurling League: **1**
1991

Last five years:

2001: Lost heavily to Kilkenny in Leinster semi-final.

2002: Fell to Kilkenny again at provincial semi-final stage. Had a better result against Meath in Qualifier series, but not against Tipperary in next round.

2003: Lost to Wexford at penultimate stage of Leinster competition. Defeated Dublin and Limerick in Qualifier series before again falling to Tipperary.

2004: Beat Laois and Dublin, but came up short in provincial decider against Wexford. Subsequently lost to Clare in round-three Qualifier.

2005: Opened by taking a 28-point beating against Kilkenny, then lost respectably in Qualifiers against Waterford and Clare. Victories against Dublin in the final Qualifier and Antrim in the relegation semi-final saved the season. The lopsided result in the latter match was symptomatic of the ridiculousness of forcing third-place finishers in Qualifier groups to enter relegation play-offs.

Outlook

The thrashing by Kilkenny at the beginning of last season's provincial championship demonstrated that Division Two league hurling is no way to prepare for Tier One championship hurling. This year can hardly be any worse than last for Offaly, who know they have the potential to beat any team on their day; unfortunately, it hasn't been 'their day' in quite a while. Laois provide a relatively modest early-summer challenge, and, presuming they emerge unscathed, Offaly can at least comfort themselves that they cannot meet Kilkenny until the provincial decider, though Wexford may save them the trouble of that pairing.

Top player: **Brian Carroll**

One of the better Offaly players during the demolition by Kilkenny last season. Carroll's presence makes a huge difference for Offaly's chances on the field – especially on the scoreboard.

Penguin Ireland Guide ranking: **9**

Offaly squad 2006

	v Kilkenny lost 0–15 6–28	**v Waterford** lost 1–15 1–26	**v Clare** lost 1–11 1–12	**v Dublin** won 2–15 2–14	**v Antrim** won 5–17 1 0–18
Brian Mullins	●	●	●	●	●
Barry Teehan	●		●	●	●
Ger Oakley	●	●	●	●	●
David Franks	●	●			●
Daniel Hoctor	●				●
Kevin Brady	●	●	●	●	●
Colm Cassidy	●				
Michael Cordial	●	●	●	●	●
Brendan Murphy	●	●	●	●	●
Gary Hannify	●	●	●	●	●
Rory Hannify	●	●	●	●	●
Dylan Hayden	●	●	●	●	
Brian Carroll	●	●	●	●	●
Joe Brady	●	●	○	○	●
Damien Murray	●	●	○	○	○
Paul Cleary	○		●	●	○
Stephen Browne	○		●	●	
Aidan Hanrahan	○	○	●	●	●
Paul Molloy	○	●			
Cathal Parlon	○	○			○
Brian Whelahan		●	●	●	●
Barry Whelahan		●			○
Mick O'Hara		○	●	●	●
Neville Coughlan				○	
Martin Corcoran					○
Peter Healion					○
Niall Claffey					
Kevin Grogan					
Liam Bergin					
Andrew McRedmond					
Damien McDermott					
Paudie Mulhare					
Harry Ryan					
Conor Gath					

● Played from start ○ Substituted on

Tipperary Tiobraid Árann

Tiobraid Árann

Colours: Blue and gold
Stadium: Semple Stadium, Thurles
Capacity: 53,000
GAA clubs: 82

Munster SHC: 36

1895, 1896, 1898, 1899, 1900, 1906, 1908, 1909, 1913, 1916, 1917, 1922, 1924, 1925, 1930, 1937, 1941, 1945, 1949, 1950, 1951, 1958, 1960, 1961, 1962, 1964, 1965, 1967, 1968, 1971, 1987, 1988, 1989, 1991, 1993, 2001

All-Ireland SHC: 25

1887, 1895, 1896, 1898, 1899, 1900, 1906, 1908, 1916, 1925, 1930, 1937, 1945, 1949, 1950, 1951, 1958, 1961, 1962, 1964, 1965, 1971, 1989, 1991, 2001

National Hurling League: 18

1928, 1949, 1950, 1952, 1954, 1955, 1957, 1959, 1960, 1961, 1964, 1965, 1968, 1979, 1988, 1994, 1999, 2000

Last five years:

2001: Beat Clare and Limerick to claim provincial crown. Defeated Wexford in an All-Ireland semi-final replay, then overcame Galway in the final.

2002: Accounted for Clare and Limerick in Munster championship, but not Waterford in the final. Recovered to defeat Offaly and Antrim, but came up short in All-Ireland semi-final against Kilkenny.

2003: Lost to Clare in first round of provincial championship. Better news in Qualifier series, beating Laois, Galway and Offaly before bowing out to Kilkenny in All-Ireland semi-final.

2004: Beaten by Waterford in provincial semi-final and Cork in third-round Qualifier. Defeated Limerick in between the two defeats.

2005: Needed a replay, and extra time, to overcome Limerick, then beat Clare in the Munster semi-final before falling to Cork. A narrow All-Ireland quarter-final loss to Galway marked the beginning of that county's impressive progress to the final.

Outlook

The problem last season? Too many players didn't perform in too many games. In truth, Tipp should never have made it past the first round of the Munster championship. Clare's season false-started, and so the first fans saw of Tipperary's real potential was probably the second half of the Munster final – which was too late to make a difference. The last 15 minutes of the All-Ireland quarter-final with Galway will have haunted players and supporters from the Premier County for months. The new management regime is tasked with building on the strong foundations already in place. Meeting Limerick at home in round one isn't the worst of possible starting fixtures – but even if that meeting is negotiated, Waterford are lying in wait in the provincial semi-final. Nothing less than bettering last season's All-Ireland quarter-final appearance will do this summer.

Top player: Eoin Kelly

No other player has been the focus of such attention by other teams. The reason is simple – stop Kelly playing, and the battle against Tipperary is half won.

Penguin Ireland Guide ranking: **5**

Tipperary squad 2006

	v Limerick drew 2–14 2–14	**v Limerick** won 2–13 0–18	**v Clare** won 2–14 0–14	**v Cork** lost 1–16 1–21	**v Galway** lost 2–18 2–20
Brendan Cummins	●	●	●	●	●
Martin Maher	●				
Philip Maher	●	●		●	●
Paul Curran	●	●	●	●	●
Declan Fanning	●	●	●	●	●
David Kennedy	●	●	●	●	
Eamonn Corcoran	●	●	●	●	●
Colin Morrissey	●	●	●	●	●
Paul Kelly	●	●	●	●	●
John Devane	●	●	●	○	●
Francis Devanney	●	○	●	●	
Benny Dunne	●	●	●	●	●
Paddy O'Brien	●	○	○		
Eoin Kelly	●	●	●	●	●
Lar Corbett	●	●	●		
Ger O'Grady	○	○		○	○
Tommy Dunne	○	●	●	●	●
Diarmuid Fitzgerald	○	●	●	●	●
Micheal Webster	○	●	●	●	●
Darragh Egan	○				○
Mark O'Leary		○			
John Carroll		○		○	○
Conor O'Mahoney		○	○		○
Evan Sweeney		○	○	●	
Pa Morrissey		○			○
Hugh Maloney			○	○	●
Eddie Enright					●
Tom King					
Damien Young					
Tadhg Slevin					
Paul Ormonde					

● Played from start ○ Substituted on

Waterford Port Láirge

Colours: Blue and white
Stadium: Walsh Park, Waterford
Capacity: 16,600
GAA clubs: 55

Munster SHC: 7

1938, 1948, 1957, 1959, 1963, 2002, 2004

All-Ireland SHC: 2

1948, 1959

National Hurling League: 1

1963

Last five years:

2001: Lost Munster semi-final at the hands of Limerick.

2002: Beat Cork and Tipperary to claim the Munster title before being surprised by Clare in All-Ireland semi-final.

2003: Victories over Kerry and Limerick meant qualification for provincial decider again, but Cork won the day. Wexford rubbed salt into their wounds in Qualifier series.

2004: Reclaimed Munster title with victories over Clare, Tipperary and Cork. Again fell short at penultimate stage of All-Ireland championship, this time against Kilkenny.

2005: Beginning their campaign with a Munster semi-final against the reigning All-Ireland champions with a number of key players nursing injuries was never ideal, but the clash was a classic – and certainly encouraged supporters of the Deise to plan for a long summer. However, after Qualifier wins over Offaly and Dublin they got caught by Clare, which set up another match with Cork – this time in an All-Ireland quarter-final.

Outlook

Last season was a big step in the wrong direction. After 2002, winning the Munster title ceased to be the prime objective, but every season the team seems to be a player or two short of the real deal. This year they await the winner of Tipperary v Limerick and will fancy their chances of making it back into the provincial decider. If they do, they will also benefit from missing out on the Qualifier series – which clearly did nothing for the county's chances last season.

Top player: Ken McGrath

A rock for Waterford, McGrath is a fearless warrior at his best when the pressure is on. Still missed in the forwards, but his impact at centre-back over the past two seasons has been immense.

Penguin Ireland Guide ranking: **4**

Waterford squad 2006

	v **Cork** lost 2–15 2–17	v **Offaly** won 1–26 1–15	v **Dublin** won 4–17 1–3	v **Clare** lost 0–21 4–14	v **Cork** lost 1–13 1–18
Stephen Brenner	●	●	●	●	
Tom Feeney	●	●	●	●	●
Fergal Hartley	●	●	●	●	●
Eoin Murphy	●	●	●	●	●
Tony Browne	●	●	●	●	●
Ken McGrath	●	●	●	●	●
James Murray	●	●	●	●	●
Dave Bennett	●				●
Michael Walsh	●	●	●	●	●
Eoin Kelly	●	●	●	●	●
Dan Shanahan	●	●	●	●	●
Paul Flynn	●	●	●	●	●
John Mullane	●	●	●	●	●
Seamus Prendergast	●	●	●	●	●
Eoin McGrath	●	●	●	●	
Paul O'Brien	○		○	○	○
Brian Phelan	○	●	●	●	
Denis Coffey			○		
Jack Kennedy			○		●
Brian Wall			○		
Ger Power			○		
Clinton Hennessy					●
Paul Foley					○
Declan Prendergast					
Ian O'Regan					
Liam Lawlor					
John O'Leary					
Wayne Hutchinson					
Eddie Rockett					

● Played from start ○ Substituted on

Westmeath An Iarmhí

Colours: **Maroon and white**
Stadium: **Cusack Park, Mullingar**
Capacity: **15,000**
GAA clubs: **48**

Leinster SHC: **0**
All-Ireland SHC: **0**
National Hurling League: **0**
Last five years:

2001: Beaten by Carlow in Leinster.
2002: Defeated Kildare in Leinster preliminary tie before surrendering to Dublin.
2003: Beat Kildare again, and again lost to Dublin. Put up a decent challenge before bowing out against Kerry in Qualifier series.
2004: Comprehensively defeated Wicklow and Kildare before losing yet again to Dublin, and then to Laois in the Qualifiers.
2005: More than even Cork, Westmeath were the true winners of the new championship format, gaining promotion from Tier Two. After beating Roscommon, Derry and Down, and losing to Meath, in the group stage of the Christy Ring Cup, Westmeath beat Kildare comprehensively in the semi-final. The second defeat of Down, this time in the final – which was played at Croke Park and broadcast live on RTE television – was a fitting end to an excellent season.

Outlook

It may be unfair to suggest the easy part is now over, but Westmeath's Tier Two victory last season has propelled the county into a whole new world of hurling. They are now surrounded by giants of the game and many supporters will be interested to see how they cope. For the new structure to thrive, it's important that a team coming up from the Christy Ring Cup doesn't go straight back down with its tail between its legs. A first-round tie with Dublin should provide both a reasonable target and a chance to gauge what the season holds. In any case, it surely holds a relegation play-off date.

Top player: **Andrew Mitchell**

An outstanding player, Mitchell must be impatiently waiting for his chance to play on the big stage this season. Regularly one of the highest annual overall scorers in hurling.

Penguin Ireland Guide ranking: **12**

Westmeath squad 2006

Player	v **Roscommon** won 4–19 0–11	v **Meath** lost 2–10 3–16	v **Derry** won 1–14 2–8	v **Down** won 3–21 3–14	v **Kildare** won 7–14 1–12	v **Down** won 1–23 2–18
Mark Briody	●	●	●	●	●	●
Dermot Curley	●	●				○
Christo Murtagh	●	●	●	●	●	●
Conor Jordan	●		●	●	●	●
John Shaw	●	●	●	●	●	●
Brendan Murtagh	●	●	●	●	●	●
Darren McCormack	●	●	●	●	●	●
Enda Loughlin	●	●	●	●	●	●
Brian Connaughton	●	●	●	●	●	●
Ronan Whelan	●		○	●	●	●
Derek McNicholas	●	●	●		○	
Andrew Mitchell	●	●	●	●	●	●
Barry Kennedy	●	●	●	●	●	●
Blaine Lahart	●	●	○			
Joseph Clarke	●		●	●	●	●
Paddy Dowdall	○	●				
Noel Gavin	○	●	●		○	
Martin Williams	○	●	●	●	●	●
Michael Garvin	○	○				
Tony O'Keeffe		○				
Paul Williams		○				
Gerard Fagan		○			○	
Greg Gavin			●	●	●	●
Pat Clarke			○			
Killian Cosgrave				●	●	●
Daniel Carty					○	
Donal Devine					○	
Paul Greville						○
Brian Smyth						
Emmet Dalton						
Noel Boylan						
Niall Flanagan						
Mark Keane						
Ollie Fay						
Barry Williams						

● Played from start ○ Substituted on

Wexford Loch Garman

Colours: Purple and gold
Stadium: Wexford Park, Wexford
Capacity: 25,000
GAA clubs: 87

Leinster SHC: 20

1890, 1891, 1899, 1901, 1910, 1918, 1951, 1954, 1955, 1956, 1960, 1962, 1965, 1968, 1970, 1976, 1977, 1996, 1997, 2004

All-Ireland SHC: 6

1910, 1955, 1956, 1960, 1968, 1996

National Hurling League: 4

1956, 1958, 1967, 1973

Last five years:

2001: Fell in the provincial decider to Kilkenny, after passing Laois in semi-final. Recovered to defeat Limerick in the Qualifier series before finally surrendering to Tipperary in an All-Ireland semi-final replay.

2002: Again lost to Kilkenny in divisional final, this time after overcoming Dublin in semi-final. Qualifier series held no better luck, an encounter with Clare ensuring a quick championship exit.

2003: Third time unlucky, lost again to Kilkenny in Leinster final after dispatching Offaly. Defeated Waterford and Antrim to set up an All-Ireland semi-final meeting with Cork, where the Munster side needed two chances to proceed.

2004: Defeated Kilkenny and Offaly to become eastern kingpins again, then lost to eventual champions Cork in the All-Ireland semi-final.

2005: After Wexford defeated Laois in the Leinster semi-final, neutral fans were praying Kilkenny wouldn't record their second demolition job in succession. That Wexford again showed they are not intimidated by their star-studded neighbours was a welcome relief. Unusually, though, for a county that traditionally improves as the championship season progresses, Wexford's season ended there and then – they were subsequently steamrollered by Clare in the All-Ireland quarter-final.

Outlook

Only the brave tip the county for great things. It's simply impossible to know which Wexford will turn up – the one that can match Kilkenny in every position or the one that put up only token resistance in the 2005 All-Ireland quarter-final with Clare. This year's provincial draw was generous – a semi-final meeting with Offaly or Laois is certainly manageable. The prize for the winners, of course, is an almost certain repeat meeting with Kilkenny in the decider. With another All-Ireland quarter-final date a likelihood, Wexford will be hoping for a better performance this term.

Top player: Adrian Fenlon

Any midfielder who can control his patch while also getting forward regularly to assist the six forwards and chip in with a point or two is an invaluable asset.

Penguin Ireland Guide ranking: **7**

Wexford squad 2006

	v Laois won 0–24 1–10	**v Kilkenny** lost 1–16 0–22	**v Clare** lost 0–12 1–20
Damien Fitzhenry	●	●	●
David O'Connor	●	●	●
Darragh Ryan	●	●	●
Keith Rossiter	●	●	●
Malachy Travers	●	●	●
Declan Ruth	●	●	●
Diarmuid Lyng	●	●	●
Redmond Barry	●	○	○
Adrian Fenlon	●	●	●
Rory McCarthy	●	●	●
Eoin Quigley	●	●	●
Michael Jacob	●	●	●
Des Mythen	●	●	●
Mícheal Jordan	●	●	●
Rory Jacob	●	●	●
Nigel Higgins	○		
Paul Carley	○	●	●
Tomas Mahon	○	○	○
Darren Stamp	○		
Barry Lambert	○	○	
Willie Doran			○
Colm Kehoe			
Kevin Kavanagh			
Matty White			
John O'Connor			
MJ Furlong			
Chris McGrath			
David O'Brien			
Niall Maguire			

● Played from start ○ Substituted on

Hurling Championship Results Table

Munster

First Round			
Limerick			Tipperary
Replay:			

Semi-finals			
Clare			Cork
Replay:			
Waterford			Limerick/Tipperary
Replay:			

Final			
Replay:			

Ulster

Quarter-final			
Antrim			London
Replay:			

Semi-finals			
Down			Antrim/London
Replay:			
Derry			New York
Replay:			

Final			
Replay:			

Leinster

Quarter-finals			
Dublin			Westmeath
Replay:			
Laois			Offaly
Replay:			

Semi-finals			
Kilkenny			Dublin/Westmeath
Replay:			
Wexford			Laois/Offaly
Replay:			

Final			
Replay:			

All-Ireland Qualifiers

Group One – Round One			

Group Two – Round One			

Group One – Round Two			

Group Two – Round Two			

Group One – Round Three			

Group Two – Round Three			

Group One	P	W	D	L	F	A	Pts
1							
2							
3							
4							

Group Two	P	W	D	L	F	A	Pts
1							
2							
3							
4							

All-Ireland Quarter-finals

Replay:

Replay:

Replay:

Replay:

All-Ireland Semi-finals

Replay:

Replay:

All-Ireland Final

Replay:

Relegation Play-offs

Replay:

Replay:

Relegation Final			
Replay:			

Tier Two

Group One – Round One			

Group Two – Round One			

Group One – Round Two			

Group Two – Round Two			

Group One – Round Three			

Group Two – Round Three			

Group One – Round Four			

Group Two – Round Four			

Group One – Round Five			

Group Two – Round Five			

Group One	P	W	D	L	F	A	Pts
1							
2							
3							
4							
5							

Group Two	P	W	D	L	F	A	Pts
1							
2							
3							
4							
5							

All-Ireland Semi-finals			

All-Ireland Final			

Relegation Play-offs

Relegation Final			
Replay:			

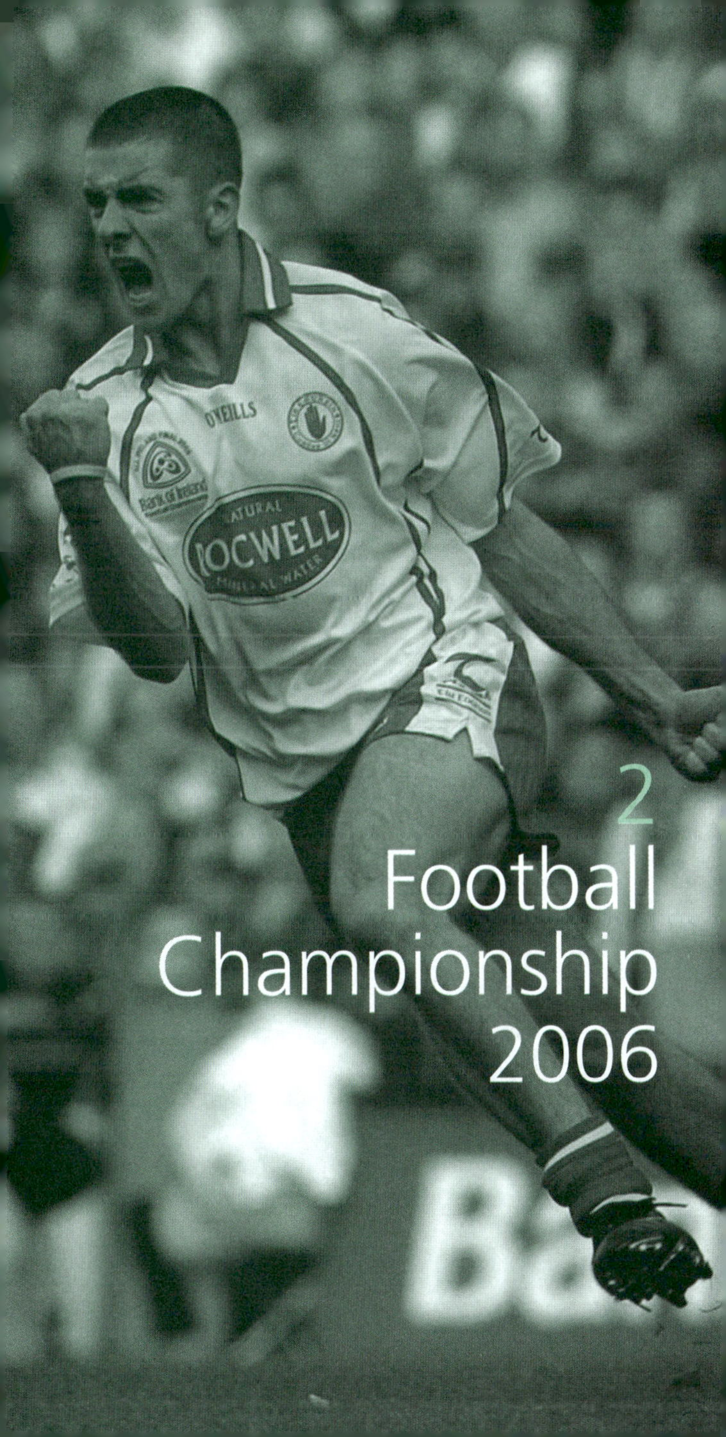

2
Football Championship 2006

2
Football Championship 2006

Championship Format

The Qualifier system traditionally throws up a dream cup-style run from an unlikely source, such as Fermanagh in 2004 and Roscommon in 2003. But last season there were no major surprise packets, with all four round-three winners – Cavan, Sligo, Monaghan and Derry – going on to be crushed by the losers of the provincial finals: Laois, Tyrone, Mayo and Cork.

It made for a unique situation in which all eight provincial finalists qualified for the All-Ireland quarter-finals – something which gives credence to the view that the gap between the best and the rest in senior inter-county football is widening considerably. And it may, in a small way, explain why the summer's secondary competition, the Tommy Murphy Cup, is being taken more seriously by counties knocked out in either of the first two rounds of the Qualifiers. A Declan Browne-inspired Tipperary took the honours last September at Croke Park.

Sixteen teams traditionally enter the first round of the senior football Qualifiers each season – with the long distance, high cost and visa difficulties preventing New York players from maintaining an interest in the championship after their annual first-round provincial exit, and general lack of interest from county officials stopping Kilkenny fielding a senior football team.

Provincial Championships

These shall be played on a knock-out basis in all four provinces, with the provincial winners qualifying for the All-Ireland quarter-finals.

All-Ireland Qualifiers

Counties designated as 'weak' (by the National Games Administration Committee) shall have home advantage in round one and round two – unless the home ground does not meet required standard. Home venues may be used in round three and round four, also provided the ground reaches the necessary standard. The draw for each round may have to be adjusted to prevent counties that have already met in the provincial championship from meeting again before the All-Ireland semi-final stage.

Round One

Involves all teams that did not qualify for their respective provincial semi-finals. Sixteen counties (assuming the non-participation of New York), eight games.

Round Two

Involves the eight winning teams from round one against the eight defeated sides from the provincial semi-finals. Sixteen counties, eight games.

Round Three

Involves the eight winning teams from round two. Eight counties, four games.

Round Four

Involves the four winning teams from round three, each playing against one of the four defeated provincial finalists. Eight counties, four games.

All-Ireland quarter-finals

Involving the four winning teams from round four, each playing against one of the four provincial champions. (Provincial champions cannot meet the team they defeated in the provincial final.) Eight counties, four games.

All-Ireland semi-finals

The draw is based on a provincial rota system. This season the draw will pit the Ulster champions against the Munster winners, and the champions of Connacht against the Leinster champions – provided, of course, that the provincial winners come through the quarter-finals. If any of these teams does not come through, the team that beat them in the quarters will occupy their slot in the rota.

Provincial Championship Fixtures 2006

Leinster SFC

Round	Date	Teams	Venue
First round	(A) May 14	Westmeath v Offaly	Croke Park
	(B) May 14	Meath v Louth	Croke Park
	(C) May 21	Wicklow v Carlow	Wexford
Quarter-finals	(D) May 28	Winner A v Kildare	Croke Park
	(E) May 28	Winner B v Wexford	Croke Park
	(F) June 4	Winner C v Laois	Carlow or Portlaoise
	(G) June 4	Longford v Dublin	Longford
Semi-finals	June 18	Winner D v Winner E	Croke Park
	June 25	Winner F v Winner G	Croke Park
Final	July 16		Croke Park

Munster SFC

Round	Date	Teams	Venue
Quarter-finals	(A) May 21	Kerry v Waterford	Killarney
	(B) May 21	Clare v Limerick	Limerick
Semi-finals	June 11	Winner A v Tipperary	Killarney TBC
	June 11	Winner B v Cork	Cork or Limerick
Final	July 9		TBC

Ulster SFC

Round	Date	Teams	Venue
Preliminary	May 7	Down v Cavan	TBC
Quarter-finals	(A) May 14	Armagh v Monaghan	Clones
	(B) May 21	Fermanagh v Antrim	Enniskillen
	(C) May 28	Tyrone v Derry	Omagh
	(D) June 4	Prelim. winner v Donegal	Ballybofey or Cavan
Semi-finals	June 11	Winner A v Winner B	TBC
	June 18	Winner C v Winner D	TBC
Final	July 9		TBC

Connacht SFC

Round	Date	Teams	Venue
Quarter-finals	(A) May 14	New York v Roscommon	New York
	(B) May 21	Galway v Sligo	Galway
	(C) May 28	London v Mayo	Ruislip
Semi-finals	June 18	Winner A v Winner B	Roscommon
	June 25	Winner C v Leitrim	Carrick-on-Shannon
Final	July 16		

Leinster

Carlow Ceatharlach

Colours: **Green, red and yellow**
Stadium: **Dr Cullen Park, Carlow**
Capacity: **19,000**
GAA clubs: **32**

Leinster SFC: **1**
1944
All-Ireland SFC: **0**
National Football League: **0**
Last five years:

2001: Lost to Wicklow, Wexford and Longford in preliminary stages of Leinster championship.

2001: Beat Wicklow at second attempt before losing to Kildare. Defeated Waterford in Qualifier series, then surrendered to Sligo.

2002: Beaten by Westmeath in preliminary round of provincial championship before collapsing to Laois by double scores in round one of Qualifier series.

2003: Lost to Westmeath, before scoring a rare victory – over Wicklow in the Qualifiers. Tripped up against Tipperary in the next round.

2004: Shocked Longford in first provincial round before giving Laois a good game. Down were waiting in the Qualifiers.

2005: After making something of a breakthrough in the early stages of the championship, Carlow were soon brought abruptly back to earth. The single-point provincial competition loss to Wexford, who are enjoying a high profile in recent years, should have served as a warning to Qualifier opponents Offaly. But it wasn't heeded and after the shock victory the visit of Limerick was welcomed rather than feared. Unfortunately for the home fans, the high point of the season had already passed.

Outlook

Forrest Gump should have compared life to Carlow football, rather than a box of chocolates. Carlow is one of several Leinster counties (including their first-round opponents Wicklow) to have improved significantly over the past few seasons, but consistency remains a major problem: you just never know what you're going to get.

Top player: **Simon Rea**

Usually scores about half of his team's total in each game. Stop Rea, stop Carlow.

Penguin Ireland Guide ranking: **26**

Carlow squad 2006

	v Wexford lost 2–10 3–12	v Offaly won 0–14 1–10	v Limerick lost 0–7 2–15
John Brennan	●	●	●
Brian Farrell	●		
Cormac McCarthy	●	●	●
Paul Cashin	●	●	●
John Hayden	●	●	●
Liam Murphy	●	●	●
Richard Sinnott	●	●	●
Patrick Walsh	●	●	●
Thomas Walsh	●	●	
Brian Carberry	●	●	●
Ray Walker	●	○	●
Patrick Hickey	●	●	○
Simon Rea	●	●	●
Mark Carpenter	●	●	●
Mark Brennan	●		●
Paul Kelly	○	○	○
Johnny Nevin	○		○
Willie Power	○	●	
Joe Byrne	○	●	●
Brian Kelly	○	●	●
John Kehoe		○	●
David Byrne			○
Willie Minchin			○
Stephen Murphy			
Bobby Daly			
David Nolan			
Johnny Kavanagh			
Kieran Pender			
Joe Waters			
John Murphy			

● Played from start ○ Substituted on

Dublin Áth Cliath

Colours: Dark blue and light blue
Stadium: Parnell Park, Dublin
Capacity: 11,000
Stadium: Croke Park, Dublin
Capacity: 82,300
GAA clubs: 211

Leinster SFC: 45

1891, 1892, 1894, 1896, 1897, 1898, 1899, 1901, 1902, 1904, 1906, 1907, 1908, 1920, 1921, 1922, 1923, 1924, 1932, 1933, 1934, 1941, 1942, 1955, 1958, 1959, 1962, 1963, 1965, 1974, 1975, 1976, 1977, 1978, 1979, 1983, 1984, 1985, 1989, 1992, 1993, 1994, 1995, 2002, 2005

All-Ireland SFC: 22

1891, 1892, 1894, 1897, 1898, 1899, 1901, 1902, 1906, 1907, 1908, 1921, 1922, 1923, 1942, 1958, 1963, 1974, 1976, 1977, 1983, 1995

National Football League: 8

1953, 1955, 1958, 1976, 1978, 1987, 1991, 1993

Last five years:

2001: Defeated Longford and Offaly to again make Leinster final, and again came up short, this time to Meath. Beat Sligo to set up All-Ireland quarter-final meeting with Kerry. Lost replay.

2002: Defeated Wexford, Meath and Kildare to win provincial title. Ended Donegal's interest in All-Ireland championship at second attempt to set semi-final date with eventual champions Armagh.

2003: Lost to Laois at Leinster semi-final stage, after first beating Louth. Similar story in Qualifier series, losing to Armagh after overcoming Derry.

2004: Disappointing start, losing to Westmeath, but favourable Qualifier draw resulted in wins over London, Leitrim, Longford and Roscommon. Quarter-final clash with Kerry proved a different story, though.

2005: So near and yet so far. Perhaps Dublin would have been better off losing by a single point, rather than drawing, in the first game against eventual All-Ireland champions Tyrone in the All-Ireland quarter-final: in the replay, the Ulster side exposed more weaknesses in the Leinster champions than supporters wanted to see. Still, regaining the provincial crown – with victories over heavyweights Meath and Laois – was a huge step.

Outlook

Dublin players and supporters don't begin any season merely hoping for success in Leinster. However, it is 11 years now since the biggest prize in football was captured by the county. Presuming they can account for Longford, a meeting with Laois in the provincial semi-final is more than likely. It's a game that will strongly indicate the immediate future of both teams.

Top player: Alan Brogan

Drove the county forward last season more than any other forward, scoring from play in each of the six championship ties.

Penguin Ireland Guide ranking: **5**

Dublin squad 2006

	v Longford won 2–23 0–10	v Meath won 1–12 1–10	v Wexford won 1–17 2–10	v Laois won 0–14 0–13	v Tyrone drew 1–14 1–14	v Tyrone lost 1–14 2–18
Stephen Cluxton	●	●	●	●	●	●
Paul Griffin	●	●	●	●	●	●
Paddy Christie	●	●	●	●	●	
Stephen O'Shaughnessy	●	●	●	●	●	●
Paul Casey	●	●	●	●	●	●
Barry Cahill	●	●	●	●	●	●
Coman Goggins	●	●	●	●	●	
Ciaran Whelan	●	●	●	●	●	●
Shane Ryan	●	●	●	●	●	●
Colin Moran	●	●	●	●	●	●
Alan Brogan	●	●	●	●	●	●
Bryan Cullen	●	●	●	●	●	●
Jason Sherlock	●	●	○	●	●	●
Conal Keaney	●	●	●	●	●	●
Tomas Quinn	●	●	●	●	●	●
Mark Vaughan	○	○	●			○
Declan O'Mahony	○					
David O'Callaghan	○					○
Darren Homan	○	○	○	○	○	
Senan Connell	○	○	○	○	○	○
Peadar Andrews		○	○	○	○	●
Darren Magee					○	●
Dessie Farrell					○	○
Declan Lally						○
David Henry						
Brian Murphy						
Ray Cosgrave						
Liam Óg Ó hEineacháin						
Ian Robertson						
Niall Cooper						
Kevin Leahy						
David Byrne						
Aidan Downes						
Eamon Fennell						

● Played from start ○ Substituted on

Kildare Cill Dara

Colour: **White**
Stadium: **St Conleth's Park, Newbridge**
Capacity: **13,000**
GAA clubs: **70**

Leinster SFC: **13**
1903, 1905, 1919, 1926, 1927, 1928, 1929, 1930, 1931, 1935, 1956, 1998, 2000

All-Ireland SFC: **4**
1905, 1919, 1927, 1928

National Football League: **0**

Last five years:

2001: Beat Carlow, then lost to Meath in provincial semi-final. Recovered to defeat Donegal by one point in Qualifier round two clash, before being on the other side of a single-point finish with Sligo.

2002: Beat Louth and, after a replay, Offaly to qualify for Leinster final. Defeat to Dublin was followed by heavy loss to Kerry in Qualifier series.

2003: Beat Longford and Meath to reach provincial final, but again fell at the last, this time to Laois. Lost to Roscommon in round four of Qualifiers.

2004: Disappointing season, losing to Wexford in the provincial championship and Offaly in round one of the Qualifiers.

2005: It was almost impossible to get a true reading of Kildare last season. The fright they got from Wicklow was widely attributed to the Garden County's improvement, and the defeat of reigning provincial champions Westmeath put down as proof of the Lake County's decline. However, nothing could have prepared supporters for the subsequent thumping by Laois, and Kildare failed to recover in time for the Qualifier clash with Sligo.

Outlook

With a new management on board and Kildare continuing a tradition of unveiling football stars with a proven track record in other counties, players and supporters are eager to move on. Despite being on the supposed easier side of the provincial draw, there are very few handy games left in Leinster competition, though Kildare could be luckier in the Qualifiers.

Top player: John Doyle

Whatever else Kildare lacks, it's not corner forwards. Doyle – along with Tadhg Fennin – is one of the best in the business. When he is at the top of his game, the Lilywhites have the scoring power to match most sides.

Penguin Ireland Guide ranking: **17**

Kildare squad 2006

	v **Wicklow** won 1–17 2–12	v **Westmeath** won 0–14 0–11	v **Laois** lost 0–9 0–21	v **Sligo** lost 1–10 1–11
Enda Murphy	●	●	●	●
Anthony Rainbow	●	●	●	●
Damien Hendy	●	○		●
Padraig Mullarkey	●	●		●
Michael Foley	●	●	●	●
Glenn Ryan	●	●	●	
David Lyons	●			●
Killian Brennan	●	●	●	●
Willy Heffernan	●	○	○	○
Eamonn Callaghan	●	●	○	
Padraig O'Neill	●			
Ronan Sweeney	●	●	●	●
Tadhg Fennin	●	●	●	●
Stuart McKenzie Smith	●	○	○	
John Doyle	●	●	●	●
Mark Hogarty	○			○
Karl Ennis	○	●	●	●
Dermot Earley	○	●	●	●
Ross Glavin	○	●	●	●
James Lonergan		●	●	
Mick Wright		●	●	○
Derek McCormack		○	●	
Andrew McLoughlin			●	●
Alan Barry			○	
James Kavanagh				●
Tomas O'Connor				○
Tommy O'Neill				○
Mark Herbert				
Aaron Flood				
Michael Conway				

● Played from start ○ Substituted on

Laois Laoighis

Colours: Blue and white
Stadium: O'Moore Park, Portlaoise
Capacity: 27,000
GAA clubs: 85

Leinster SFC: 6
1889, 1936, 1937, 1938, 1946, 2003

All-Ireland SFC: 0

National Football League: 2
1927, 1986

Last five years:

2001: After defeating Wexford, Offaly proved too strong in the Leinster quarter-final. Hopes were heightened again with victory over Clare in the Qualifiers, but Derry emerged from the round-two tie.

2002: Victory over Wicklow was followed by another defeat to Offaly in the provincial quarter-final. Big victories over Carlow and Clare in the Qualifiers were followed by an equally big third-round loss to Meath.

2003: Victory over Wexford was followed by another meeting with Offaly in the provincial quarter-final. This time Offaly were beaten, albeit after a replay, and this was followed by wins over Dublin and then Kildare in the final. Armagh ended the Laois campaign in the All-Ireland quarter-final.

2004: Defeated Carlow and Meath in another run to the Leinster final, where, after two hours, Westmeath emerged victorious. Tyrone rubbed salt into the wound in a round-four Qualifier.

2005: Laois looked to be heading for a long summer of football, only for their season to end suddenly. A false start against Offaly apart, the subsequent comprehensive victory over Kildare pointed to a provincial crown. Dublin, however, edged the tie – and Laois went back to an old tradition of not being able to put together a full 70 minutes of quality football. The second half against Derry bore no relation to the rather pitiful performance against the Ulster champions.

Outlook

Laois promise so much, and yet have not even come close to fulfilling their immense potential. Preparations for this season started even before last year's championship had been completed, with another big assault planned for this summer. Getting into the Leinster final this season will be difficult enough, never mind planning for anything beyond that.

Top player: Ross Munnelly

Usually operates around the half-forward line, but doesn't exactly subscribe to staying in position. He was the driving force behind Laois's provincial and All-Ireland campaigns: that they came up short in both last season wasn't for the lack of trying by Munnelly.

Penguin Ireland Guide ranking: **3**

Laois squad 2006

	v **Offaly** won 1–10 1–8	v **Kildare** won 0–21 0–9	v **Dublin** lost 0–13 0–14	v **Derry** won 1–11 0–11	v **Armagh** lost 1–11 2–17
Fergal Byron	●	●	●	●	●
Aidan Fennelly	●	●	●	●	●
Darren Rooney	●	●	●	●	●
Joe Higgins	●	●	●	●	●
Colm Begley	●	●	●	●	●
Tom Kelly	●	●	●	●	●
Padraig McMahon	●	●	●	●	●
Pauric Clancy	●	●	●	●	●
Noel Garvan	●	●	●	●	●
Ross Munnelly	●	●	●	●	●
Ian Fitzgerald	●				
Gary Kavanagh	●	○		○	○
Donal Brennan	●		○	●	●
Kevin Fitzpatrick	●	●	●	●	○
Chris Conway	●	●	●	●	○
Billy Sheehan	○	●	●	●	●
Stephen Kelly	○			○	●
Brian McDonald	○	●	●	○	●
Barry Brennan		●	●		●
Shane Cooke		○		●	
Paul McDonald		○			
Mark Dunne			○	○	○
Derek Conroy			○		
Michael Nolan					
Chris Bergin					
Kieran Kelly					
Paul Lawlor					
Tom McDonald					
Paul Begley					
Colm Kelly					

● Played from start ○ Substituted on

Longford An Longfort

Colours: Blue and gold
Stadium: Pearse Park, Longford
Capacity: 12,000
GAA clubs: 47

All-Ireland SFC: 0
Leinster SFC: 1
1968

National Football League: 1
1966

Last five years:

2001: Beat Louth, then lost to Dublin in the provincial quarter-final. The result was similar in the Qualifier against Wicklow.

2002: Surrendered to Louth in a replay in the first round of the Leinster championship. Beat Down in Qualifier round before bowing out to Derry.

2003: Lost in the Leinster quarter-final to Kildare, then in the Qualifier to Donegal.

2004: A shock first-round loss to Carlow was followed by a more credible Qualifier campaign, with victories over Monaghan and Waterford, before a defeat at the hands of Dublin.

2005: Running into a Dublin team with their eye on big things was never the way for a relative minnow to start a championship season, and Longford found it incredibly difficult to pick themselves up again after the big defeat. It was the second successive championship match with Dublin, Longford having met them in a third-round Qualifier in 2004. The defeat was much more emphatic in the second game. Still, Sligo were given a good run for their money in the Qualifiers before the Connacht side finally progressed.

Outlook

No prizes for guessing which team Longford drew for their opening game in the provincial championship. Still, despite the likelihood of a quick exit from senior competition in Leinster, this side has had Qualifier runs before – most recently in 2004.

Top player: Paul Barden

Often the link-man who turns defence into attack, the forward struggled against the tide in last season's championship – especially in the qualifier tie with Sligo.

Penguin Ireland Guide ranking: **25**

Longford squad 2006

	v Dublin lost 0–10 2–23	**v Sligo** lost 0–16 0–18
Damien Sheridan	●	●
Dermot Brady	●	●
Cathal Conefrey	●	●
Enda Ledwith	●	●
Dominic Glennon	●	
Declan Reilly	●	●
Arthur O'Connor	●	●
Paul O'Hara	●	
Bernard McElvaney	●	○
James Martin	●	●
Paul Barden	●	●
Paddy Dowd	●	●
Brian Kavanagh	●	●
Niall Sheridan	●	○
Padraic Davis	●	●
Stephen Lynch	○	
Mark Connor	○	
Trevor Glendenning	○	
Donnacha Corcoran	○	●
Mark Lennon	○	
Liam Keenan		●
Trevor Smullen		●
Kevin Mulligan		●
Kevin Smith		○
Shane Mulligan		○
Gavin Tonra		
Brian Sheridan		
Justin Nally		
David Blessington		
Thomas O'Rourke		
Enda Williams		
Shane Carroll		
Michael Kelly		
John Kenny		

● Played from start ○ Substituted on

Louth Lú

Colours: Red and white
Stadium: O'Rahilly's, Drogheda
Capacity: 7,500
GAA clubs: 51

Leinster SFC: 8
1909, 1910, 1912, 1943, 1948, 1950, 1953, 1957
All-Ireland SFC: 3
1910, 1912, 1957
National Football League: 0
Last five years:

2001: After losing to Longford in Leinster, beat Offaly and Tipperary in inaugural Qualifier competition. Westmeath emerged victorious from third-round tie.

2002: Took two games to get past Longford, then very unfortunate to fall to Kildare by a single point. Recovered to beat Monaghan at start of Qualifier series, before being unfortunate for a second time, this time against Meath.

2003: Victory over Wicklow was followed by a crushing defeat at the hands of Dublin. Respectable loss to Cavan in Qualifier series.

2004: Beaten by Wexford before surprising Antrim in the first round of the Qualifiers. Succumbed to Galway in second round after putting up a struggle.

2005: Despite losing half of their four championship games it was a relatively successful summer for the county's senior footballers – though nothing like what they are capable of achieving. After a comprehensive loss to Offaly and a stuttering defeat of Waterford, the season finally took a significant upswing with the scalp of Roscommon. A few seasons ago losing to Monaghan would have been viewed as a disaster, but losing to the Ulster side that were still on a high from winning the NFL Division Two title and the more recent win over Wexford was viewed more sympathetically last summer by Louth supporters.

Outlook

Louth have made several attempts to rebuild towards a significant breakthrough in the past decade, but have little to show for it. With a new manager on board this season expectations are at a reasonable level, though the best chance the county has for success probably rests in the Qualifiers, as Meath should prove too strong in the opening tie.

Top player: **Simon Gerrard**

A stalwart for the Wee County for several years, whether he's playing in the half-back or full-back line. Forwards very rarely get anything easy off the tigerish defender, who has also been know to get forward – and even score – on occasion.

Penguin Ireland Guide ranking: **24**

Louth squad 2006

	v **Offaly** lost 1–6 1–15	v **Waterford** won 1–12 1–8	v **Roscommon** won 0–11 0–10	v **Monaghan** lost 0–14 1–12
Shane McCoy	●	●	●	●
David Mackin	●			
Simon Gerrard	●	●	●	●
Jamie Carr	●	●	●	●
Conor Sheridan	●	●	●	●
Aaron Hoey	●		●	●
Alan Page	●	●	●	●
David Deveney	●	●	●	○
John Kermath	●	●	●	●
Paddy Keenan	●		●	●
Nicky McDonnell	●	○	○	●
Ronan Carroll	●	●		○
Mark Stanfield	●		●	○
JP Rooney	●	●	●	●
Darren Clarke	●	●	●	●
Trevor O'Brien	○	●		
Brendan Reilly	○	●	●	●
Paddy Matthews	○	●	●	●
Shane Lennon		●	●	●
Brian Keenan		●		
David Martin		○		
Christy Grimes			○	●
Ollie McDonnell			○	○
Ray Kelly			○	
Sean Connor				
Peter McGinnity				
Sean O'Neill				
Ronan Valentine				
Niall Sharkey				
Derek Shevlin				
Gavin Long				
John Neary				
Colin Goss				
Brian White				

● Played from start ○ Substituted on

Meath An Mhí

Colours: Green and gold
Stadium: Pairc Tailteann, Navan
Capacity: 29,000
GAA clubs: 153

Leinster SFC: 20
1895, 1939, 1940, 1947, 1949, 1951, 1952, 1954, 1964, 1966, 1967, 1970, 1986, 1987, 1988, 1990, 1991, 1996, 1999, 2001

All-Ireland SFC: 7
1949, 1954, 1967, 1987, 1988, 1996, 1999

National Football League: 7
1933, 1946, 1951, 1975, 1988, 1990, 1994

Last five years:

2001: Defeated Westmeath, Kildare and Dublin to claim provincial crown. Needed two attempts to see off challenge of Westmeath once again, before destroying Kerry to reach All-Ireland final. No match for on-song Galway.

2002: Again overcame Westmeath, then crashed out of Leinster championship to Dublin at semi-final stage. Recovered to claim victory over Louth and Laois before losing fourth-round Qualifier to Donegal.

2003: Defeated Westmeath, again after a replay, but lost provincial semi-final meeting with Kildare. Beat Monaghan in round two of Qualifier series, then lost to Fermanagh.

2004: Defeated Wicklow in Leinster quarter-final, but found Laois a much tougher challenge. Fermanagh again eliminated them from the Qualifier series.

2005: Even though Meath won the tie, Leitrim sounded the death knell of the Royal County's season. After a narrow defeat to a fancied Dublin in the provincial championship and the subsequent hammering of Antrim in Belfast, few expected Meath to need extra-time, and more than their fair share of lucky bounces, to ease past the Connacht side. The decline was obvious and irreversible, with Cavan finishing off the job.

Outlook

Meath are entering a new, wholly unfamiliar era, with the steady hand of Sean Boylan now no longer at the helm. While many viewed the change of management as necessary, an immediate revival is unlikely. The draw, however, was more than kind and a provincial final appearance is certainly within their grasp. Beware a Meath team with momentum.

Top player: Graham Geraghty

Entering a new era with a fresh management structure, Meath could do with the veteran forward giving it 100 per cent for at least another season.

Penguin Ireland Guide ranking: **12**

Meath squad 2006

	v **Dublin** lost 1–10 1–12	v **Antrim** won 5–12 0–13	v **Leitrim** won 1–12 1–8	v **Cavan** lost 1–6 1–8
David Gallagher	●	●	●	●
Mark O'Reilly	●		●	●
Kevin Reilly	●	●	●	●
Niall McKeigue	●	●	●	●
David Crimmins	●	●	●	●
Darren Fay	●	●	●	●
Caoimhín King	●	●	●	●
Nigel Crawford	●	●	●	●
Anthony Moyles	●	●	●	●
Niall Kelly	●	●	●	○
Peadar Byrne	●	●	●	●
Graham Geraghty	●	●	●	●
Joe Sheridan	●	○	○	●
Brian Farrell	●	●	●	
Stephen Bray	●	●	●	●
Paddy Reynolds	○	●		○
John Cullinane	○			
Daithi Regan	○			
Ollie Murphy	○		○	○
Tommy O'Connor		●	●	●
Ray Magee		○	○	●
Michael Burke		○	○	○
Niall McLaughlin		○	○	
Mark Ward		○		
Seamus Kenny			○	
Trevor Giles				
Brian O'Reilly				
Stephen MacGabhann				
Conor Brennan				
Charles McCarthy				
Denis Kealy				
Cian Ward				
Rory McGuire				

● Played from start ○ Substituted on

Offaly Uíbh Fhailí

Colours: Green, white and gold
Stadium: St Brendan's Park, Birr
Capacity: 11,000
Stadium: O'Connor Park, Tullamore
Capacity: 16,000
GAA clubs: 85

Leinster SFC: 10
1960, 1961, 1969, 1971, 1972, 1973, 1980, 1981, 1982, 1997

All-Ireland SFC: 3
1971, 1972, 1982

National Football League: 1
1998

Last five years:

2001: Beat Laois, then lost in Leinster semi-final to Dublin. Lost disastrously to Louth in second-round Qualifier.

2002: Defeated Laois in provincial quarter-final, but fell to Kildare after a replay. Lost to Limerick in Qualifier series.

2003: Took Laois to second match in Leinster quarter-final, but eventually surrendered. Favourable Qualifier draw resulted in wins over London and Clare before defeat to Roscommon.

2004: Single-point loss to Westmeath in first round of provincial championship, followed by hard-fought victory over Kildare, before Wexford ended their interest in the championship.

2005: Offaly supporters couldn't quite believe it when their season ended last year. It seemed one minute they were preparing for a strong assault on the championship, and the next they found themselves left with more free weekends than necessary to run their club competitions. Even though they gave Laois a huge fright in the provincial championship, the annoyance at having lost the game must have played on their minds. Smarting, they were dumped into the Qualifiers. From Carlow's point of view it was the perfect time to play Offaly, and they took full advantage.

Outlook

Rhode gained a small measure of revenge over the winter, beating Stradbally in the club football championship, but how the Offaly county team would like another crack at Laois. Unlikely to meet in the qualifiers, they'd have to make it all the way to the Leinster final to make that pairing a possibility in 2006. Unlikely, of course – but Offaly have the manpower to make last season a distant memory.

Top player: Karl Slattery

Very comfortable going forward, which is becoming almost a prerequisite for a successful defender in the modern game. Tried, successfully, to plug the gaps when Offaly began falling apart last season.

Penguin Ireland Guide ranking: **16**

Offaly squad 2006

	v **Louth** won 1–15 1–6	v **Laois** lost 1–8 1–10	v **Carlow** lost 1–10 0–14
Padraig Kelly	●	●	●
Cathal Daly	●	●	●
Conor Evans	●	●	●
Scott Brady	●	●	●
Barry Mooney	●	●	
Shane Sullivan	●	●	●
Karl Slattery	●	●	●
Ciaran McManus	●	●	●
Alan McNamee	●	●	●
John Reynolds	●	○	●
Damien Hunt	●		
Neville Coughlan	●	●	●
Colm Quinn	●	●	●
Niall McNamee	●	●	●
James Coughlan	●	●	○
Mark Daly	○	●	●
John Kenny	○	○	●
Pascal Kellaghan		●	●
James Grennan		○	
Thomas Deehan			○
Barry Malone			
Roy Malone			
Joe Quinn			
Thomas Coughlan			
Martin Gorman			
Ciaran Kiely			
James Keane			
Sean Casey			
Colin McNamara			

● Played from start ○ Substituted on

Westmeath An Iarmhí

Colours: Maroon and white
Stadium: Cusack Park, Mullingar
Capacity: 15,000
GAA clubs: 48

Leinster SFC: 1
2004

All-Ireland SFC: 0

National Football League: 0

Last five years:

2001: Lost to Meath twice, in the Leinster opening round and, after a replay, in the All-Ireland quarter-final. In between, chalked up victories over Limerick, Wexford (after a replay), Louth and Mayo.

2002: Again lost to Meath in Leinster quarter-final, after opening with a victory over Carlow. Defeated Antrim, but collapsed in the face of Fermanagh in the Qualifier series.

2003: Again opened with victory over Carlow, and yet again fell to Meath after a replay. Worse lay in store in round one of the Qualifiers, with Monaghan registering something of a surprise.

2004: Beat Offaly, Dublin and Wexford to qualify for decider, winning first provincial title after two hours of play with Laois. Derry halted their march in next round.

2005: After the heady days of 2004, last season Westmeath lost to Kildare and Clare, with a fortunate one-point victory over Tipperary in between. It wasn't so much coming back to earth with a bump as going into a vertical nosedive and crash-landing at the speed of light. The inability to build on the success of the previous year was a desperate disappointment to football followers in the county, but the pitiful displays against the two Munster teams in the Qualifiers were even worse.

Outlook

Another county that has brought in a new management structure in the hope of reliving recent glory days. The provincial championship looks much too difficult for any repeat of 2004, with four wins against four title contenders required to claim the Leinster crown. Still, Westmeath can at least start the process of bringing success back to the county by treating the Qualifiers a little more seriously this season.

Top player: Rory O'Connell

Tough, uncompromising midfielder with talent to burn. Injuries played a significant part in a below-par 2005.

Penguin Ireland Guide ranking: **19**

Westmeath squad 2006

	v Kildare lost 0–11 0–14	**v Tipperary** won 0–12 1–8	**v Clare** lost 0–9 0–12
Gary Connaughton	●	●	●
James Davitt	●		
Damien Healy	●	●	●
John Keane	●	●	●
Michael Ennis	●	●	●
Derek Heavin	●	●	●
David Kilmartin	●	○	○
Rory O'Connell	●	●	○
David O'Shaughnessy	●	●	●
Alan Mangan	●	●	●
Fergal Wilson	●	●	●
Patrick Mulvihill	●	●	●
David Glennon	●	○	●
Denis Glennon	●	●	●
Dessie Dolan	●	●	
Justin McAteer	○	●	●
Joe Fallon	○	○	●
Gary Dolan	○	○	
David Duffy	○		○
Paul Conway	○	●	
Donal O'Donoghue		●	●
Colin Galligan			●
Damien Gavin			○
David Martin			○
Daniel McDermott			
John Brennan			
David Mitchell			
Alan Lambden			
Martin Flanagan			
Peter Tormey			
Aidan Lennon			
Shane Colleary			
Padraig Walsh			

● Played from start ○ Substituted on

Wexford Loch Garman

Colours: Purple and gold
Stadium: Wexford Park, Wexford
Capacity: 25,000
GAA clubs: 87

Leinster SFC: 10
1890, 1893, 1913, 1914, 1915, 1916, 1917, 1918, 1925, 1945

All-Ireland SFC: 5
1893, 1915, 1916, 1917, 1918

National Football League: 0

Last five years:

2001: Exited provincial competition to Laois, then surrendered to Westmeath in first-round Qualifier after a replay.

2002: Narrowly beaten by both Dublin and Tyrone, in the Leinster quarter-final and Qualifier round one respectively.

2003: First-round Leinster loss to Laois, followed by equally disappointing first-round Qualifier defeat to Derry.

2004: Defeated Louth and Kildare to make Leinster semi-final, where they lost to Westmeath. Bounced back to dump Offaly out of Qualifiers before running into a Derry side that was growing in confidence.

2005: A small, though significant, step backwards in the progress of the team, with Dublin rather comfortably dealing with their challenge and Monaghan causing something of an upset in the Qualifiers. Even the first-round victory over Carlow wasn't as straightforward as it ought to have been.

Outlook

Wexford have been threatening to make a big breakthrough for the past few years, but so far supporters have had to make do with small, though significant, victories. The footballers have drawn a line under 2005 and have been preparing for this summer for a long time now. Management are determined to stop supporters and observers talking about the potential of the squad and start admiring their successes – beginning with the provincial championship. There are two way of viewing the likelihood of meeting Meath in a quarter-final: as an unfortunate draw, or as an opportunity to be grasped with both hands.

Top player: Matty Forde

Wexford are not a one-man team. However, that's not to suggest that Forde cannot win a game on his own, because the outstandingly talented forward can alter the whole direction of any game in just one moment of smooth, breathtaking movement on the ball.

Penguin Ireland Guide ranking: **14**

Wexford squad 2006

	v **Carlow** won 3–12 2–10	v **Dublin** lost 2–10 1–17	v **Monaghan** lost 0–12 0–17
John Cooper	●	●	●
Niall Murphy	●	●	●
Philip Wallace	●	●	
Colm Morris	●	●	●
Darragh Breen	●	○	●
David Murphy	●	●	●
Paraic Curtis	●	●	●
Nicky Lambert	●	●	●
David Fogarty	●	●	●
Redmond Barry	●	●	●
Darren Foran	●	○	
Shane Cullen	●	●	●
PJ Banville	●	●	●
Paddy Colfer	●	●	○
Matty Forde	●	●	●
Diarmuid Kinsella	○	●	●
Jim D'Arcy	○	○	
John Hegarty	○		○
Kieran Kennedy		●	●
John Hudson		○	●
Jason Lawlor			○
Darren Browne			○
Anthony Masterson			
Brendan Doyle			
Pat Forde			
Ciaran Deely			
Tom Byrne			
George Sunderland			
Graeme Molloy			
Robert Mageen			

● Played from start ○ Substituted on

Wicklow Cill Mhantáin

Colours: **Blue and yellow**
Stadium: **Aughrim**
Capacity: **7,000**
GAA clubs: **65**

Leinster SFC: **0**
All-Ireland SFC: **0**
National Football League: **0**
Last five years:

2001: Lost replayed first-round Leinster championship game to Carlow by one point. Beat Longford in Qualifier series before crashing out to Galway.
2002: Shipped too many goals to progress past Laois in opening round of provincial championship. Had an easy victory over London in Qualifier before surrendering meekly to Kerry.
2003: Crashed out of Leinster championship to Louth before equally disappointing performance against Carlow in Qualifier series.
2004: Defeated by Meath in provincial competition, then lost in a battling performance against Derry in round-one Qualifier.
2005: Wicklow again played two and lost two – versus Kildare and Donegal – but the mood among the players and supporters was totally different from that of 2004: last season there was a feeling that the county was making significant progress. Kildare certainly won't take Wicklow for granted again in a hurry.

Outlook

The calm before the storm. Wicklow have the chance to get a victory under their belts in their opening tie verses Carlow before running into the juggernaut of Laois. If they get that far then another promising display would raise the spirits, even if further progress would have to be sought in the Qualifiers.

Top player: Tommy Gill

Back after a long break from inter-county football, Gill missed Wicklow's breakthrough (of sorts) last season. The Rathnew forward has the skills to push the county that important bit further they need to go.

Penguin Ireland Guide ranking: **27**

Wicklow squad 2006

Player	v **Kildare** lost 2–12 1–17	v **Donegal** lost 0–12 0–16
Robert Hollingsworth	●	●
Ciaran Hyland	●	●
Brendan Daly	●	●
Thomas Burke	●	●
Kevin Manning	●	●
Dara Ó'hAnnaidh	●	
Brendan Ó'hAnnaidh	●	●
David Dillon	●	●
James Stafford	●	●
David Smullen	●	●
Leighton Glynn	●	●
Thomas Harney	●	●
Paul Earls	●	●
Wayne O'Gorman	●	●
Alan Ellis	●	●
Gary Duffy	○	○
John Paul Davis	○	
Darragh O'Sullivan	○	○
Jonathon Daniels	○	○
Wesley Callaghan		●
Clive Davis		○
Gary Doran		○
Ian Burke		
John McKeown		

● Played from start ○ Substituted on

Munster

Clare An Clár

Colours: **Yellow and blue**
Stadium: **Cusack Park, Ennis**
Capacity: **24,000**
GAA clubs: **88**

Munster SFC: **2**
1917, 1992
All-Ireland SFC: **0**
National Football League: **0**
Last five years:

2001: Fell to Cork in semi-final before Laois handed them a quick exit from the Qualifier series.

2002: Beat Waterford before drawing with Tipperary at Munster semi-final stage. Replay didn't go according to plan, and neither did Qualifier meeting with Laois.

2003: Heavily beaten by Limerick in provincial semi-final before again leaving the Qualifier series empty-handed after clash with Offaly.

2004: Defeated by Kerry, then registered a surprise victory over Sligo in round one of Qualifiers. Cork then ended their interest in championship.

2005: The season seemed to be over after Cork delivered a thumping defeat in the provincial semi-final. However, the Banner men recovered to take the scalp of Westmeath in the Qualifiers. Sligo, though, were lying in wait, intent on revenge for the defeat to Clare in 2004.

Outlook

A few years ago a first-round pairing with Limerick would have been welcomed in Clare. Not any more. Limerick are now a much stronger and more talented side than before, whereas Clare continue to slip from season to season without any obvious progress – even allowing for last season's defeat of Westmeath. Another Munster title is out of reach, but a few successful performances in the Qualifier series aren't.

Top player: **David Russell**

The Kilkee man is the central figure for both club and county, and most attacking movements from deep go through his hands at some stage. Capable of chipping in with big scores when needed.

Penguin Ireland Guide ranking: **23**

Clare squad 2006

	v **Waterford** won 2–14 2–10	v **Cork** lost 0–6 0–18	v **Westmeath** won 0–12 0–9	v **Sligo** lost 0–11 1–13
Dermot O'Brien	●	●	●	●
Padraig Gallagher	●	●	●	●
Kevin Dilleen	●	●	●	
Brendan Moloney	●			
Alan Clohessy	●	●	●	●
Darragh Kelly	●	●	●	●
Mark O'Connell	●	●	○	●
Ger Quinlan	●	●	●	●
David Russell (Kilkee)	●	●	●	●
Peter O'Dwyer	●	●	●	●
Enda Coughlan	●	●	●	●
Odran O'Dwyer	●	●	●	●
Rory Donnelly	●	●	●	●
David Nealon	●			
Michael O'Dwyer	●	●		○
Ger Tubridy	○	○	●	●
Stephen Hickey	○	●	●	●
Ronan Slattery	○	●		●
Michael O'Shea	○	○	○	●
Declan Callanan		○	●	
David Russell (Éire Óg)		○		
Sean O'Meara		○		
Shane Daniels			●	
Conor Whelan				○
John Moody				○
David McInerney				
Eoin Curtin				
Eoin Glynn				
Brian Considine				
Donal O'Sullivan				
Tommy Ryan				

● Played from start ○ Substituted on

Cork Corcaigh

Colours: **Red and white**
Stadium: **Páirc Uí Chaoimh, Cork**
Capacity: **42,000**
GAA clubs: **259**

Munster SFC: **34**
1890, 1891, 1893, 1894, 1897, 1899, 1901, 1906, 1907, 1911, 1916, 1923, 1928, 1943, 1945, 1949, 1952, 1956, 1957, 1966, 1967, 1971, 1973, 1974, 1983, 1987, 1988, 1989, 1990, 1993, 1994, 1995, 1999, 2002

All-Ireland SFC: **6**
1890, 1911, 1945, 1973, 1989, 1990

National Football League: **5**
1952, 1956, 1980, 1989, 1999

Last five years:

2001: Accounted for Waterford and Clare before succumbing to Kerry in Munster final. Lost to Galway in Qualifier series.

2002: Needed two hours to defeat Kerry, and another two to beat Tipperary in the provincial final. Beat Mayo in the All-Ireland quarter-final before losing to Kerry in semi-final.

2003: Disastrous season, losing to Limerick and Roscommon in the first rounds of the Munster championship and Qualifier series respectively.

2004: Lost to Kerry before recovering to account for Clare in Qualifier clash. Croke Park and Fermanagh, however, signalled the end of Cork's season.

2005: Was last year a success or not? We're not quite sure. Cork in an All-Ireland senior football semi-final can't be discounted, but they never threatened to make the final step – and if one defeat to Kerry is hard to stomach, two losses to the Kingdom in the same season is, well, enough for Cork to vote no to the Qualifier system. The victories over Clare and Sligo were both comprehensive, but by far the peak of last season was the display against Galway, which served to lull supporters into a false sense of optimism.

Outlook

Commentators are already talking about another Cork v Kerry provincial final, though Limerick especially will have something to say about that. Even if they do reach the provincial decider, the signs aren't promising for a successful final. A similar run to last season's – through the 'back door' – seems much more probable.

Top player: **Anthony Lynch**

A tower of strength in the Rebel County's defence. Without his willingness to step up to the plate, Cork would never have still been involved in inter-county football at the end of August last season.

Penguin Ireland Guide ranking: **7**

Cork squad 2006

	v **Clare** won 0–18 0–6	v **Kerry** lost 0–11 1–11	v **Sligo** won 3–13 0–11	v **Galway** won 2–14 2–11	v **Kerry** lost 0–9 1–19
Kevin O'Dwyer	●	●	●	●	●
Niall Geary	●	●	●	●	●
Sean Levis	●		○		
Gary Murphy	●	●	●	●	●
Eoin Sexton	●	●	●	●	●
Anthony Lynch	●	●	●	●	●
Martin Cronin	●		○		○
Graham Canty	●	●	●	●	●
Derek Kavanagh	●	●	●	●	●
James Masters	●	●	●	●	●
Conor McCarthy	●	●	●	●	●
Nicholas Murphy	●	●	●	●	●
John Hayes	●	●	●	●	●
Fintan Gould	●	●	●		
Micheál Ó Croinín	●	●			
Noel O'Leary	○	●	●	●	●
Kevin O'Sullivan	○	○	○		○
Alan Cronin	○	○	○	○	○
Dermot Hurley	○		○		
Kieran O'Connor	○	○		○	○
Kevin McMahon		●	●	●	●
Philip Clifford		○	○	●	●
Brendan Jer O'Sullivan		○	●	●	●
Alan Quirke					
Diarmuid Duggan					
Colin Crowley					
Cian O'Riordan					

● Played from start ○ Substituted on

Kerry Ciarraí

Colours: Green and yellow
Stadium: Fitzgerald Stadium, Killarney Capacity: 39,000
Stadium: Austin Stack Park, Tralee Capacity: 14,000
GAA clubs: 73

Munster SFC: 70

1892, 1903, 1904, 1905, 1908, 1909, 1910, 1912, 1913, 1914, 1915, 1919, 1924, 1925, 1926, 1927, 1929, 1930, 1931, 1932, 1933, 1934, 1936, 1937, 1938, 1939, 1940, 1941, 1942, 1944, 1946, 1947, 1948, 1950, 1951, 1953, 1954, 1955, 1958, 1959, 1960, 1961, 1962, 1963, 1964, 1965, 1968, 1969, 1970, 1972, 1975, 1976, 1977, 1978, 1979, 1980, 1981, 1982, 1984, 1985, 1986, 1991, 1996, 1997, 1998, 2000, 2001, 2003, 2004, 2005

All-Ireland SFC: 33

1903, 1904, 1909, 1913, 1914, 1924, 1926, 1929, 1930, 1931, 1932, 1937, 1939, 1940, 1941, 1946, 1953, 1955, 1959, 1962, 1969, 1970, 1975, 1978, 1979, 1980, 1981, 1984, 1985, 1986, 1997, 2000, 2004

National Football League: 17

1928, 1929, 1931, 1932, 1959, 1961, 1963, 1969, 1971, 1972, 1973, 1974, 1977, 1982, 1984, 1997, 2004

Last five years:

2001: Defeated Tipperary, Limerick and Cork en route to another Munster title. After overcoming Dublin at the second attempt, they fell to Meath in All-Ireland semi-final.

2002: Lost replayed Munster semi-final with Cork after defeating Limerick. Qualifier run threw up successful meetings with Wicklow, Fermanagh, Kildare, Galway and Cork before All-Ireland final meeting with Armagh resulted in a one-point defeat.

2003: Beat Tipperary and Limerick to win provincial crown. An All-Ireland quarter-final victory over Roscommon was followed by a heavy loss to Tyrone.

2004: Retained provincial crown with victories over Clare, Cork and, after a second attempt, Limerick. Followed wins over Dublin and Derry with All-Ireland final success against Mayo.

2005: GAA supporters have often surmised that the best time to face Kerry is early in the championship. Tipperary would beg to differ. Kerry laid down an early warning that they meant business in 2005, and went on to claim the provincial title for the 1,456th time (or thereabouts). After dismissing Mayo and Cork, the reigning All-Ireland champions came up against 2003 champions Tyrone, who looked more determined in the decider.

Outlook

In soccer cup competitions, the bigger teams often get a bye past the early rounds. Kerry supporters must find it very difficult to get excited about playing Waterford and Tipperary before (surely inevitably) reaching the 2006 Munster final. From there it's anyone's guess where they will end up, though few will be betting against a date in September. Tougher opposition in a few rounds before the All-Ireland final would probably be beneficial – provided they survived them.

Top player: Colm Cooper

Looks can be deceiving. Cooper may not look capable of humbling the most towering and muscular of defenders, but he has earned the right to be treated as one of the most feared forwards in the game.

Penguin Ireland Guide ranking: **1**

Kerry squad 2006

	v Tipperary won 2–22 0–13	**v Limerick** won 2–10 0–10	**v Cork** won 1–11 0–11	**v Mayo** won 2–15 0–18	**v Cork** won 1–19 0–9	**v Tyrone** lost 2–10 1–16
Diarmuid Murphy	●	●	●	●	●	●
Aidan O'Mahony	●	●	●	●	●	●
Michael McCarthy	●	●	●	●	●	●
Tom O'Sullivan	●	●	●	●	●	●
Tómás Ó Sé	●	●	●	●	●	●
Eamonn Fitzmaurice	●	●	○	○	○	○
Mark Ó Sé	●	●	●	●	●	●
Darragh Ó Sé	●	●	●	●	●	●
William Kirby	●	○	○	●	●	●
Paul Galvin	●	●	●	○	●	●
Eoin Brosnan	●	●	●	●	●	●
Liam Hassett	●	●	●	●	●	●
Colm Cooper	●	●	●	●	●	●
Declan O'Sullivan	●	●	●	●	●	●
Mike Frank Russell	●	●	●	●	○	○
Paddy Kelly	○	●				
Bryan Sheehan	○	○	○	○	●	○
Dara Ó Cinnéide	○	○	●	●	○	●
Brendan Guiney	○					
Declan Quill	○	○		○	○	
Seamus Moynihan		○	●	●	●	●
Kieran Donaghy			○	○	○	
Ronan O'Connor			○			
Darren O'Sullivan						○
Kieran Cremin						
Mossie Lyons						
Michael Quirke						
Noel Kennelly						
Padraig Reidy						
Tommy Griffin						

● Played from start ○ Substituted on

Limerick Luimneach

Colours: **Green and white**
Stadium: **Gaelic Grounds, Limerick**
Capacity: **49,500**
GAA clubs: **107**

Munster SFC: **1**
1896

All-Ireland SFC: **2**
1887, 1896

National Football League: **0**

Last five years:

2001: Beaten by Kerry in the Munster semi-final and then by Westmeath in the inaugural Qualifier series.

2002: Again defeated by Kerry, before recovering to upset Cavan in a replayed first-round Qualifier. Followed that fine win with victory over Offaly before finally bowing out to Mayo by a single point.

2003: Shocked Cork in first round of provincial competition before beating Clare to reach final. Kerry stood firm, however, as did Armagh in fourth Qualifier round.

2004: Beat Tipperary and Waterford to again set up provincial decider with Kerry. Again Kerry won the crown, though a replay was needed this time. Met a Derry side that was gathering momentum in Qualifier round four.

2005: It has become a dismal pattern for Limerick: after losing to Kerry in the provincial competition, their season falls apart, as if they have nothing to play for now that their primary targets (Kerry and Munster) are gone. Last year, after Kerry saw them off in their first match in Munster, they bucked the trend slightly by thumping Carlow in their first Qualifier. Then Derry knocked them out for the second season running.

Outlook

Limerick know they will never win the provincial title without meeting Kerry. And this season will be no different, even though they will have the small matter of getting past a formidable Cork before setting up such a pairing. Their first outing, against Clare, will probably go according to plan. If they can't ease past the Banner men they have no business comparing themselves to Kerry anyway.

Top player: Stephen Kelly

Although Limerick supporters thought they had lost the talented forward early last year, the former International Rules player, who has the ability to torment defences, played in all three championship ties.

Penguin Ireland Guide ranking: **15**

Limerick squad 2006

	v Kerry lost 0–10 2–10	v Carlow won 2–15 0–7	v Derry lost 0–9 0–13
Seamus O'Donnell	●	●	●
Tommy Stack	●	●	●
John McCarthy	●	●	●
Conor Mullane	●	●	●
Padraig Browne	●	●	●
Stephen Lucey	●	●	●
Stephen Lavin	●	●	
John Quane	●	●	●
John Galvin	●	●	●
Michael Crowley	●	●	●
Muiris Gavin	●	●	●
Stephen Kelly	●	●	●
Conor Fitzgerald	●	●	●
Jason Stokes	●	○	○
Seanie Buckley	●	●	●
Mark O'Riordan	○	○	●
Michael O'Brien	○	○	○
Johnny Murphy	○	○	
Michael Reidy		●	●
Damien Reidy		○	
Jim Donovan			○
Diarmuid Sheehy			
Johnny Murphy			
Mike Jones			
Brian Begley			
Colm Hickey			
Sean Kiely			
Andrew Lane			
John O'Connell			
Pat Fitzgerald			
Eoin Keating			
Shane Gallagher			
Ger Ahern			

● Played from start ○ Substituted on

Tipperary Tiobraid Árann

Colours: **Blue and gold**
Stadium: **Semple Stadium, Thurles**
Capacity: **54,000**
GAA clubs: **82**

Munster SFC: **9**
1888, 1889, 1895, 1900, 1902, 1918, 1920, 1922, 1935

All-Ireland SFC: **4**
1889, 1895, 1900, 1920

National Football League: **0**

Last five years:

2001: Heavy defeat by Kerry, followed by a more disappointing loss at the hands of Louth in opening Qualifier game.

2002: Successful replayed Munster tie with Clare set up provincial final clash with Cork. Lost chance for upset with draw in first game, then lost replay before exiting Qualifiers against Mayo.

2003: Defeated Waterford, but ran out of luck in provincial semi-final against Kerry. Lost third-round Qualifier against Donegal after beating Carlow.

2004: Disastrous championship season, beginning with loss to Limerick. Worse was to follow with club-versus-county row resulting in management and then players withdrawing and allowing Fermanagh a walk-over in Qualifier series.

2005: The emphatic victory by Kerry in the first game may have been as expected, but the huge struggle 2004 Leinster champions Westmeath had in Thurles in the subsequent Qualifier round wasn't. Tipperary then entered and won the second edition of the Tommy Murphy Cup, and few watching a delighted Declan Browne walking up the steps of the Hogan Stand after the final could be unconvinced by the merits of the secondary competition.

Outlook

Football in Tipperary may be on a steadier footing than two years ago – when strife within the county led to the side withdrawing from the championship at Qualifier stage – but that doesn't help much when the opening championship fixture is against Kerry. So Tipperary are spared any worry of how far they will progress in the provincial championship. No matter. A kinder draw in the Qualifier series is much more important.

Top player: **Declan Browne**

A giant of a player trapped in a small inter-county body. If one player could win a game on his own, Tipperary would have a chance of great things. Some of his target-shooting is breathtaking.

Penguin Ireland Guide ranking: **30**

Tipperary squad 2006

	v Kerry lost 0–13 2–22	v Westmeath lost 1–8 0–12
Paul Fitzgerald	●	●
Damien Byrne	●	●
Niall Curran	●	●
Peter King	●	●
Pa Morrissey	●	●
Brian Lacey	●	●
Robbie Costigan	●	●
Kevin Mulryan	●	●
Fergal O'Callaghan	●	●
Glen Burke	●	●
Liam English	●	●
Paul Cahill	●	
Benny Hickey	●	●
Declan Browne	●	●
Brian Mulvihill	●	●
Niall Fitzgerald	○	○
Damien O'Brien	○	○
Eamonn Hanrahan	○	
Cian Maher		●
Brian Enright		
Padraig Foley		
John Shanahan		
Ian Barnes		

● Played from start ○ Substituted on

Waterford Port Láirge

Colours: Blue and white
Stadium: Walsh Park, Waterford
Capacity: 16,600
GAA clubs: 55

Munster SFC: 1
1898
All-Ireland SFC: 0
National Football League: 0
Last five years:

2001: Heavy defeat to Cork in provincial championship, followed by ultimately fruitless battle with Carlow in Qualifier series.

2002: Ran Clare close in Munster competition and Roscommon a little less close in Qualifier round one.

2003: Tipperary's turn to end their interest in Munster, before a wounded and dangerous Armagh inflicted a cruel hammering in first-round Qualifier.

2004: Ran into a confident Limerick side in provincial competition and a Longford team with something to prove in Qualifier round.

2005: Two games, two defeats in 2004. Two games, two defeats in 2005. Progress? Well, actually, yes – of a sort. Unlike the previous championship, last summer Waterford put it up to both Clare and Louth. The Tommy Murphy Cup was made for counties such as Waterford, and last year they participated, losing to Longford in the first round up at Ballymahon.

Outlook

As many counties know, under-age success doesn't guarantee better fortunes for the senior team in the following years. Still, it certainly helps and there is some evidence that Waterford is benefiting from some recent victories at lower grades. That doesn't mean they are ready for a senior championship outing against Kerry, but teams are beginning to be wary of playing Waterford in the Qualifier series. There are now several counties that Waterford would fancy their chances against. At the very least, that's a change for the better.

Top player: Niall Curran

Generally operates in the full-forward line, and only a lack of supply keeps his scoring tally down. Extremely accurate at hitting the target, from placed ball and play.

Penguin Ireland Guide ranking: **31**

Waterford squad 2006

Waterford squad 2006	**v Clare** lost 2–10 2–14	**v Louth** lost 1–8 1–12
Tom Wall	●	●
Paul Ogle	●	●
Laurence Hurney	●	
Niall Hennessy	●	
Andrew Heffernan	●	●
Michael Ahern	●	●
Trevor Costelloe	●	●
Shane Briggs	●	●
Andrew Hubbard	●	●
Karl O'Keeffe	●	●
William Kavanagh	●	
Ger Power	●	
Niall Curran	●	●
Gary Hurney	●	●
Liam Ó Lionáin	●	●
Eamonn Walsh	○	●
John Wall	○	○
Stephen Cunningham	○	●
Francie Halpin	○	
Richie Hennessy		●
Shane Walsh		●
Sean Dempsey		○
Patrick Hurney		○
Eoin Cunningham		
Kieran Connery		
Michael Crotty		
Jason Ryan		
Wayne Hennessy		

● Played from start ○ Substituted on

Ulster

Antrim Aontroim

Colours: **Saffron and white**
Stadium: **Casement Park, Belfast**
Capacity: **32,500**
GAA clubs: **108**

Ulster SFC: **10**
1900, 1901, 1908, 1909, 1910, 1911, 1912, 1913, 1946, 1951
All-Ireland SFC: **0**
National Football League: **0**
Last five years:

- **2001:** Lost twice to Derry, initially in first round of provincial championship, and then in Round Two of Qualifier series. In between, they beat Leitrim by two points.
- **2002:** Squashed by Derry in quarter-final by ten points, before bowing out to Westmeath by just one in Round One of the Qualifier series.
- **2003:** After overcoming Cavan, they were stopped at Ulster semi-final stage by eventual All-Ireland champions Tyrone. Unlucky to then meet reigning All-Ireland champions Armagh in Qualifier series, losing by only three points.
- **2004:** Disappointing season, losing not only to Donegal in Ulster, but also to an unfancied Louth in Qualifier series.
- **2005:** An opening-round draw with Cavan, in Cavan, was enough to move some locals to hope the progress of 2003 could be recaptured, as opposed to the setbacks of the following season. The replay in Belfast didn't work out so well, however – and Antrim certainly didn't deserve to exit the championship to a five-goal Meath.

Outlook

Antrim should apply to be relocated to another province. No matter who they draw there seems little point in planning for anything other than a short Ulster campaign. Still, there are many counties from elsewhere in the country that they can match, and with any luck they'll be paired with one or two of them in the Qualifiers.

Top player: **Kevin Madden**

A decade of inter-county football under his belt, Madden regularly chips in with vital scores, from placed balls and from play. Antrim needs a few more like him.

Penguin Ireland Guide ranking: **29**

Antrim squad 2006

	v **Cavan** drew 0–11 0–11	v **Cavan** lost 2–6 1–15	v **Meath** lost 0–13 5–12
Paddy Murray	●	●	●
Colm Brady	●		●
Andy McClean	●	●	●
Damien Gault	●		●
Tony Scullion	●	●	●
Gearoid Adams	●	●	●
Sean Kelly	●	●	●
Joe Quinn	●	●	●
Martin McCarry	●		
Ciaran Close	●	●	●
Brendan Herron	●	○	
Terry O'Neill	●	●	●
Kevin Brady	●	●	●
Michael McCann	●	●	○
Kevin Madden	●	●	●
Shane Devlin	○	●	
Andy Gallagher	○		
Kevin Murray	○	●	
Paddy Logan		●	
Paul Doherty		●	
Kevin McGourty		○	●
Tony Convery		○	○
Ciaran McGourty		○	●
Mark McCrory		○	●
Niall Enright			○
Chris Lynch			○
Peter McCann			○
John Finucane			
Jonathan McAleese			

● Played from start ○ Substituted on

Armagh Ard Mhacha

Colours: **Orange and white**
Stadium: **Athletic Grounds, Armagh**
Capacity: **18,000**

Ulster SFC: **12**
1890, 1902, 1950, 1953, 1977, 1980, 1982, 1999, 2000, 2002, 2004, 2005
All-Ireland SFC: **1**
2002
National Football League: **0**
Last five years:

2001: Lost to Tyrone, before recovering to defeat Monaghan and Down in Qualifiers. Galway edged their clash, however, by one point.

2002: Needed two games to defeat Tyrone, but only two more (against Fermanagh and Donegal) to reclaim Ulster title. A replay was needed to account for Sligo in All-Ireland quarter-final, and then a single point win over Dublin was followed by a similar one-point victory in All-Ireland final over Kerry.

2003: Dumped into Qualifiers by Monaghan, then staged an impressive comeback to beat Waterford, Antrim, Limerick, Dublin, Laois and Donegal to make a second successive All-Ireland final appearance. Tyrone, however, were not to be denied their day.

2004: Beat Monaghan, Cavan and Donegal to emerge undefeated in Ulster Championship. But then tripped up by Ulster opposition – Fermanagh – in All-Ireland quarter-final.

2005: Took the Ulster title after an epic campaign in which they saw off Fermanagh, Donegal (after a replay), Derry and Tyrone (also after a replay). An impressive win against Laois was followed by a one-point loss, in the All-Ireland semi-final, to eventual champions Tyrone.

Outlook

It's incredible that after playing eight senior football championship games, as well as reclaiming the Ulster crown, Armagh's season in 2005 is not viewed as a success by many in the county. Armagh certainly hadn't planned on playing six matches before emerging from Ulster, and it probably didn't help. This has been one of the most settled teams in the country over the past number of years – 'giving it one more year' is a commonly heard motto – and another provincial final is within their grasp, but, as was the case last year, that will be viewed more as a launching point rather than an end in itself.

Top player: **Stephen McDonnell**

If Armagh are to scale the heights of 2002 again, it will be McDonnell who carries them a large part of the way. He's surrounded by gems, but the three-time All Star winner shines the brightest.

Penguin Ireland Guide ranking: **4**

Armagh squad 2006

Armagh squad 2006	v **Fermanagh** won 2–12 1–7	v **Donegal** drew 0–12 0–12	v **Donegal** won 3–11 1–10	v **Derry** won 1–11 0–10	v **Tyrone** drew 2–8 0–14	v **Tyrone** won 0–13 0–11	v **Laois** won 2–17 1–11	v **Tyrone** lost 1–12 1–13
Paul Hearty	●	●	●	●	●	●	●	●
Andy Mallon	●	●	●	●	●	●	●	●
Francie Bellew	●	●	●	●	●	●	●	●
Kevin McElvanna	●		○				○	
Aaron Kernan	●	●	●	●	●	●	●	●
Kieran McGeeney	●	●	●	●	●	●		●
Ciaran McKeever	●	●		○	●	●	●	●
John Toal	●	●	○	○	●			
Paul McGrane	●	●	●	●	●	●	●	●
Martin O'Rourke	●	●	●	●	●		●	●
John McEntee	●	●	●	●	○	●	●	○
Oisín McConville	●	●	●	●	●	●	●	●
Stephen McDonnell	●	●	●	●	●	●	●	●
Ronan Clarke	●	●	●	●	●	●	●	●
Brian Mallon	●	●	●	●	●	●	●	●
Philip Loughran	○	○	●	●	○	●	●	●
Andrew McCann	○	○	●			○	○	○
Aidan O'Rourke	○	○	○	●	●	●	●	●
Malachy Mackin	○		○	○	●		○	
Paul Duffy	○							
Paul McCormack		●						
Paddy McKeever		○			○	○		●
Enda McNulty			●	●	●	●	●	○
Tony McEntee			○	○	●		○	○
Stephen Kernan				○			○	
John Paul Donnelly								
Ciaran McKinney								
Gareth Swift								

● Played from start ○ Substituted on

Cavan An Cabhán

Colours: **Blue and white**
Stadium: **Breffni Park, Cavan**
Capacity: **20,000**
GAA clubs: **59**

Ulster SFC: **38**
1891, 1903, 1904, 1905, 1915, 1918, 1919, 1920, 1922, 1923, 1924, 1925, 1926, 1928, 1931, 1932, 1933, 1934, 1935, 1936, 1937, 1939, 1940, 1941, 1942, 1943, 1944, 1945, 1947, 1948, 1949, 1952, 1954, 1955, 1962, 1967, 1969, 1997

All-Ireland SFC: **5**
1933, 1935, 1947, 1948, 1952

National Football League: **1**
1948

Last five years:

2001: Beat Down and Monaghan on the way to Ulster final appearance, where they lost to Tyrone before meeting and losing to Derry in Qualifiers.

2002: Lost to Donegal, then engaged in two closely contested clashes with Limerick, eventually emerging on the wrong side.

2003: Shocked by Antrim in quarter-final. Recovered to account for Louth, before Fermanagh stepped in to end their interest in the championship.

2004: Needed two hours to defeat Down before running into Armagh's march to Ulster title. Then walked into a Derry side gearing up for an even stronger run.

2005: The unpredictable nature of championship football was perhaps best displayed by Cavan last season. They drew with minnows Antrim before comfortably winning the replay; then they drew with giants Tyrone before being comfortably disposed of in the replay. They bounced back from that 21-point mauling, however, to redeem their season with Qualifier victories over Donegal and Meath before falling to 2004 All-Ireland finalists Mayo.

Outlook

Who knows what Cavan are capable of – they're certainly able to rise (or fall) to the occasion. Unlucky to occupy the harder side of the provincial draw, they may already have one eye on another decent Qualifier campaign.

Top player: **James Reilly**

Desperately unlucky not to be awarded an All Star for his outstanding performances between the sticks last season. Cavan's number one in every sense of the word.

Penguin Ireland Guide ranking: **21**

Cavan squad 2006

	v **Antrim** drew 0–11 0–11	v **Antrim** won 1–15 2–6	v **Tyrone** drew 1–7 0–10	v **Tyrone** lost 0–7 3–19	v **Donegal** won 1–11 1–10	v **Meath** won 1–8 1–6	v **Mayo** lost 0–8 0–11
James Reilly	●	●	●	●	●	●	●
Michael Hannon	●	●	●	●	●	●	●
Darren Rabbitte	●	●	●	●	●	●	●
Keith Fannin	●	●	●	●			
Karl Crotty	●						
Peter Reilly	●	●	●	●	●	●	●
Martin Cahill	●	●	●	●	●	●	●
Dermot McCabe	●	●	○	●	●	●	●
Pearse McKenna	●	●	●	●	●	●	●
Mark McKeever	●	●	●	●	●	●	●
Nicholas Walsh	●	●	●	●	●	●	●
Finbar O'Reilly	●	●	●	○	●	●	●
Jason O'Reilly	●	●	●	●	●	●	●
John Tierney	●	○					○
Larry Reilly	●	●	●	●	●	●	●
Paul Brady	○	●	●				
Paddy Brady	○			○	○	○	○
Mickey Graham	○				●		
Pauric Reilly		●	●	●	●	●	●
Paraic Cahill		○					
Ciaran Calligan		○					
Anthony Forde			●	●	●	●	●
Micheál Lyng			○	●	○	○	
Sean Johnston			○		○	●	●
Joe Jordan				○			
Cathal Collins						○	○
Cian Mackey						○	
Anthony Gaynor							○
Eoghan Elliott							
Philip Brady							
Gerald Pierson							
Eamonn Reilly							
Lorcan Mulvey							
Eoin Smith							

● Played from start ○ Substituted on

Derry Doire

Colours: Red and white
Stadium: Celtic Park, Derry
Capacity: 18,000
GAA clubs: 60

Ulster SFC: 7
1958, 1970, 1975, 1976, 1987, 1993, 1998

All-Ireland SFC: 1
1993

National Football League: 5
1947, 1992, 1995, 1996, 2000

Last five years:

2001: Beat Antrim, but lost to Tyrone at semi-final stage. Had to defeat Antrim again, this time in Qualifiers, and then Cavan, Laois and Tyrone to qualify for All-Ireland semi-final. Opponents Galway, though, were in no mood to lose.

2002: Lost to Donegal in provincial semi-final, after first accounting for Antrim. Beat Longford in Qualifiers, then lost to Tyrone.

2003: Lost to eventual All-Ireland champions Tyrone after a replay. Beat Wexford in Qualifiers before shipping too many goals against Dublin.

2004: Went on a fantastic Qualifier run after losing to Tyrone in Ulster championship, beating Wicklow, Cavan, Wexford, Limerick and Westmeath. Kerry, however, stopped them in the All-Ireland semi-final.

2005: Expectations were high in Derry after the surprise run to the All-Ireland semi-finals in 2004. A respectable loss to Armagh early in the summer didn't dampen hopes of another strong qualifier and All-Ireland championship campaign, but a wounded Laois were lying in wait.

Outlook

The county's management team must be wondering what they did to deserve such a difficult provincial draw. Still, Derry are starting a tradition of saving their best displays for later in the summer, and the latter stages of the All-Ireland championship may best be reached through the back door.

Top player: Paddy Bradley

Appreciated by Derry supporters as crucially important to their cause and an outstanding talent, even if his ability isn't always appreciated by some outside the county.

Penguin Ireland Guide ranking: **8**

Derry squad 2006

	v Monaghan won 1–17 2–8	v Armagh lost 0–10 1–11	v Down won 3–8 2–9	v Limerick won 0–13 0–9	v Laois lost 0–11 1–11
Barry Gillis	●	●	●	●	●
Kevin McGuckin	●	●	●	●	●
Kevin McCloy	●	●	●	●	●
Gerard O'Kane	●	●	○	○	●
Paul Wilson	●	●		○	○
Sean Marty Lockhart	●	●	●	●	●
Padraig Kelly	●	●			●
Fergal Doherty	●	●	●		●
Patsy Bradley	●	●	●	●	●
Johnny McBride	●	○	●	●	●
Mark Lynch	●	●	●	●	●
Paul Murphy	●	●	●	●	●
Paul Bradley	●				
Paddy Bradley	●	●	●	●	●
Enda Muldoon	●	●	●		●
Eoin Bradley	○	●	●	●	●
Colin Devlin	○	●		●	○
Michael Kelly	○	○	●	●	
Paul McFlynn		○	●	●	
Francis McEldowney		○	●	●	●
Fergal McEldowney			○		
Gavin Donaghy			○	●	
Padraig Murphy				○	○
Conleth Gilligan				○	○
Michael Conlan					
Niall McCusker					
Conleth Moran					
Conor McWilliams					
Eamon Burke					
Shane Kelly					

● Played from start ○ Substituted on

Donegal Dún na nGall

Colours: Green and gold
Stadium: Mac Cumhaill Park, Ballybofey
Capacity: 17,500
GAA clubs: 63

Ulster SFC: 5
1972, 1974, 1983, 1990, 1992

All-Ireland SFC: 1
1992

National Football League: 0

Last five years:

2001: Fermanagh got the better of the county after a replay. Revenge was immediate, though, with Fermanagh defeated at the start of the Qualifier series, before Kildare won the second-round tie.

2002: Defeated Cavan, Down and Derry to reach provincial final, where they lost to Armagh. Beat Meath in Qualifier round four before surrendering to Dublin in All-Ireland quarter-final, though only after a replay.

2003: Lost to Fermanagh in quarter-final, before going on a run through the back door – defeating Longford, Sligo, Down, Tipperary and, after a second attempt, Galway. Armagh proved a hurdle too high, however, in the All-Ireland semi-final.

2004: Wins over Antrim and Tyrone in Ulster promised much. However, a crushing defeat to Armagh in the provincial final (held in Croke Park) was followed by a surprising Qualifier loss to Fermanagh on more familiar ground – back in Clones.

2005: The season started so brightly and ended so abruptly. The draw with Armagh was more than many in Donegal had dared to hope for. Even the subsequent defeat in the replay wasn't viewed as a big setback – but the indifferent display against Wicklow and the loss to Cavan certainly were.

Outlook

Nothing short of an Ulster semi-final appearance would be acceptable this season, and after that – with the likelihood of things not going Donegal's way – a better Qualifier campaign than supporters of the county have been used to of late.

Top player: Barry Monaghan

Donegal's most consistent defender in recent seasons, the Four Masters man has made a habit of keeping forwards in his pocket while often being the central figure in setting up attacks at the other end.

Penguin Ireland Guide ranking: **10**

Donegal squad 2006

	v **Armagh** drew 0–12 0–12	v **Armagh** lost 1–10 3–11	v **Wicklow** won 0–16 0–12	v **Cavan** lost 1–10 1–11
Michael Boyle	●	●	●	●
Karl Lacy	●	●	●	●
Raymond Sweeney	●		●	●
Eamonn McGee	●	●	●	●
Damien Diver	●	●	●	●
Barry Monaghan	●	●	●	●
Shane Carr	●	●	●	●
Neil Gallagher	●	●	●	●
Kevin Cassidy	●			
Christy Toye	●	●	●	●
Brian Roper	●	●	●	●
Michael Hegarty	●	●	●	●
Colm McFadden	●	●	●	●
Adrian Sweeney	●	●	●	●
Brendan Devenney	●	●	●	●
Rory Kavanagh	○	○	○	
Niall McCready		●		
Brendan Boyle		●	○	
Stephen McDermott		○	●	●
Barry Dunnion		○		○
Ryan Bradley		○	○	
Connell Molloy			○	
Conal Dunne				○
Gavin Maguire				○
Paul Durcan				
Eamonn Reddin				
Niall McGee				
Paddy McNulty				
Michael Maguire				
Martin Caulfield				
Paul McGonigle				
John Gildea				
Sean Boylan				

● Played from start ○ Substituted on

Down An Dún

Colours: **Red and black**
Stadium: **Pairc Esler, Newry**
Capacity: **19,000**
GAA clubs: **70**

Ulster SFC: **12**
1959, 1960, 1961, 1963, 1965, 1966, 1968, 1971, 1978, 1981, 1991, 1994
All-Ireland SFC: **5**
1960, 1961, 1968, 1991, 1994
National Football League: **4**
1960, 1962, 1968, 1983

Last five years:

2001: The introduction of the Qualifier series only meant there were to be two losses, instead of one. After falling narrowly to Cavan, they had the misfortune to meet Armagh in the first round of the Qualifiers.

2002: Easily defeated by Donegal in the Ulster quarter-final. They had no better luck in the Qualifier series, losing to Longford.

2003: Beat Monaghan and Fermanagh en route to Ulster final, where they fell to Tyrone in a replay. A strong Donegal team was waiting in the Qualifiers.

2004: Finished on losing side after two games with Cavan in provincial championship. Had more luck against Carlow, before running into a determined Tyrone.

2005: Down never got the opportunity to enjoy any sort of momentum last season, with a first-round stuffing by soon-to-be All-Ireland champions Tyrone relegating the wounded side to the Qualifiers. A narrow defeat by Derry left fans, players and management frustrated that a side of such obvious potential has delivered little.

Outlook

After meeting and being beaten by heavyweights Tyrone in each of the last three seasons, Down deserved a little luck in this season's provincial draw. And they got it, drawing Cavan. Still, there's nothing easy in Ulster competition and even reaching the final would be a big ask.

Top player: Brendan Coulter

Down's most lethal presence on the football pitch – and not just for points. In the last two championship seasons, Coulter has hit the back of the net in six of eight matches.

Penguin Ireland Guide ranking: **11**

Down squad 2006

Down squad 2006	v **Tyrone** lost 1–6 1–13	v **Fermanagh** won 1–11 0–7	v **Derry** lost 2–9 3–8
Brendan McVeigh	●		
Martin Cole	●	●	●
Adrian Scullion	●	●	●
Gavin Barry	●		
Brendan Grant	●		○
Aidan O'Prey	●	●	●
Damian Rafferty	●	●	●
Alan Molloy	●	●	●
Dan Gordon	●	●	
Liam Doyle	●	●	
Ambrose Rogers	●	●	●
John Clarke	●		○
Conor Laverty	●	●	●
Brendan Coulter	●	●	●
Ronan Murtagh	●	○	●
Ronan Sexton	○	○	○
Shane Ward	○	●	●
Aidan Rice	○	○	●
Daniel Hughes	○	●	●
Joe Doran	○	○	
Michael McVeigh		●	●
Dan McCartan		●	
Paul Murphy		●	●
Colin McCrickard			●
Michael Walsh			○
Declan Alder			
Aidan Brannigan			
Sean Farrell			
Sean Ward			
Stephen Kearney			
Fintan McGreevy			

● Played from start ○ Substituted on

Fermanagh Fear Manach

Colours: **Green and white**
Stadium: **Brewster Park, Enniskillen**
Capacity: **18,000**
GAA clubs: **50**

Ulster SFC: **0**
All-Ireland SFC: **0**
National Football League: **0**
Last five years:

2001: Two games against Donegal finally resulted in victory. However, subsequent quarter-final loss to Monaghan was followed by cruel Qualifier exit at hands of Donegal.

2002: Lost to Armagh in provincial semi-final after first beating Monaghan. Impressive win over Westmeath in Qualifier series followed by heavy loss to Kerry.

2003: Defeated Donegal, but stopped by Down at semi-final stage. Embarked on Qualifier run that included victories over Cavan, Mayo and Meath. Heavy All-Ireland quarter-final loss to Tyrone.

2004: Season started with defeat to Tyrone in the provincial championship. However, an incredible Qualifier run ensued – started by a walk-over from Tipperary – with victories over Meath, Cork, Donegal and Armagh. After two hours of football, Mayo edged them to reach the All-Ireland final.

2005: An All-Ireland quarter-final date in 2003; All-Ireland semi-final appearance in 2004; two games in 2005. It's not the kind of progress that supporters in the county had hoped for. Losing to Armagh in the provincial championship last season may have been acceptable, but a rather tame exit to the hands of Down in the Qualifiers certainly wasn't.

Outlook

Antrim are always the side that each of the other eight counties in Ulster hopes to be paired with in the early stages of the provincial championship, and Fermanagh drew the traditional whipping boys this season; but a probable semi-final meeting with Armagh will be tougher. Still, Fermanagh supporters, players and officials will be hoping to write off last season as an aberration.

Top player: **Tom Brewster**
Misfired to an extent last season, but then so did the rest of the county's footballers. Still the most talented player in the panel, and the one capable of changing the course of a game in an instant.

Penguin Ireland Guide ranking: **13**

Fermanagh squad 2006

Player	v Armagh lost 1–7 2–12	v Down lost 0–7 1–11
Niall Tinney	●	
Shane Goan	●	
Barry Owens	●	●
Ryan McCluskey	●	●
Raymond Johnston	●	●
Shane McDermott	●	●
Declan O'Reilly	●	
Liam McBarron	●	
James Sherry	●	●
Eamon Maguire	●	●
Tom Brewster	●	●
Mark Little	●	●
Aidan Little	●	
Steven Maguire	●	○
Colm Bradley	●	●
Niall Bogue	○	○
Rory Gallagher	○	●
Marty McGrath	○	●
Ryan Keenan	○	
Michael Lilley	○	●
Christopher Breen		●
Shane McCabe		●
Mark Murphy		●
Damien Kelly		○
Jonathan McGurn		○
Raymond Gallagher		○
Sean Burns		
Peter Sherry		
Sean Doherty		
Kieran Donnelly		

● Played from start ○ Substituted on

Monaghan Muineachán

Colours: **White and blue**
Stadium: **St Tiernach's Park, Clones**
Capacity: **36,000**
GAA clubs: **50**

Ulster SFC: **13**
1888, 1906, 1914, 1916, 1917, 1921, 1927, 1929, 1930, 1938, 1979, 1985, 1988

All-Ireland SFC: **0**

National Football League: **1**
1985

Last five years:

2001: Gained revenge by dumping Fermanagh out of provincial championship, but couldn't build up any momentum, losing to Cavan in Ulster semi-final and Armagh in Qualifier series.

2002: Came out on the wrong side of a clash with Fermanagh in Ulster, then had an equally poor result against Louth in first-round Qualifier.

2003: Shocked All-Ireland champions Armagh, but then fell to Down in Ulster quarter-final. Recovered to defeat Westmeath, but couldn't repeat the feat against Meath in second-round Qualifier.

2004: Heavily defeated by an Armagh side still smarting from the previous year, and luck didn't change in first-round Qualifier against Longford.

2005: A double-scores defeat to Tyrone took only some of the gloss off an excellent season. Deserving Division Two champions in the league – even if the circumstances at the end of the decider were fortuitous to say the least – a decent Ulster championship performance against Derry was followed by Qualifier triumphs over London, Wexford and Louth before they ran into the All-Ireland champions in waiting.

Outlook

Division One football in the NFL was always going to be a difficult step up, but Monaghan could definitely have done without drawing Armagh in the provincial championship. Still, with top-level football in the league now under their belt, another decent campaign in the Qualifiers is within Monaghan's capabilities.

Top player: **Tomas Freeman**

He is the forward mentioned in the opponents' dressing room before games – probably the biggest compliment a player can receive.

Penguin Ireland Guide ranking: **20**

Monaghan squad 2006

	v **Derry** lost 2–8 1–17	v **London** won 2–18 1–9	v **Wexford** won 0–17 0–12	v **Louth** won 1–12 0–14	v **Tyrone** lost 1–7 2–14
Shane Duffy	●	●	●	●	●
Gary McQuaid	●	●	●		●
Vincent Corey	●	●	●	●	●
Colm Flanagan	●	●	●	●	●
Damien Freeman	●	●	●	●	●
James Coyle	●	●	●	●	●
Dermot McArdle	●	●	●	●	●
Fergal Duffy	●		○	●	○
Edmund Lennon	●	●	●	●	●
Stephen Gollogly	●	●	●	●	●
Paul Finlay	●	●	●	●	●
Nicholas Corrigan	●	○	○	○	○
Tomas Freeman	●	●	●	●	●
Raymond Ronaghan	●	○	●		
Dick Clerkin	●	●	●	●	●
Hugh McElroy	○	●	●	●	●
Shane McManus	○	●		○	
Fergal Smith	○				
Declan McKernan	○		○	○	○
James McElroy	○	●	●	●	●
Francie Doogan		○			
Bernard O'Brien		○			
James Conlon				●	
Rory Woods					●
Paul McElroy					
Mark Daly					
James Ward					

● Played from start ○ Substituted on

Tyrone Tír Eoghain

Colours: White and red
Stadium: Healy Park, Omagh
Capacity: 18,000
GAA clubs: 68

Ulster SFC: 10
1956, 1957, 1973, 1984, 1986, 1989, 1995, 1996, 2001, 2003

All-Ireland SFC: 2
2003, 2005

National Football League: 2
2002, 2003

Last five years:

2001: Gained revenge against Armagh before beating Derry and Cavan to claim provincial title. Derry gained revenge of their own in All-Ireland quarter-final.

2002: Lost to Armagh in Ulster quarter-final replay. More success in Qualifiers, beating Wexford, Leitrim and Derry before falling to Sligo in round four.

2003: Needed five matches – two against Derry, one with Antrim and two against Down – to claim Ulster title. No such problems in All-Ireland championship, with straightforward victories over Fermanagh, Kerry and Armagh to claim the biggest prize in football.

2004: Claimed scalps of Derry and Fermanagh before losing to Donegal in Ulster semi-final. Got back on track with wins over Down, Galway and Laois before Mayo stoped them in the All-Ireland semi-final.

2005: The two-point defeat to Armagh in the provincial final only served to reinforce the county's determination to capture the Sam Maguire Cup. An incredible season, involving replays against Cavan and Armagh in Ulster, another against Dublin in the All-Ireland quarter-final, a thrilling one-point win over Armagh in the semi-final, and finally the victory against favourites Kerry in the final. Six of Tyrone's ten matches were either drawn or decided by a single score.

Outlook

Tyrone have a new theme song: 'Two out of three ain't bad'. Gaelic football supporters in the county can't afford to go on foreign holidays any more, though saving up for the countless weekend trips to Dublin each year is something many other counties' supporters can only dream of. A tricky Ulster campaign will be the early focus for Tyrone players and supporters again this season, of course – but, as ever, there will be a bigger prize at the back of their minds.

Top player: Stephen O'Neill

Claimed almost every individual award on offer last season. O'Neill is the complete forward – and a nightmare to mark. To shine on a team bulging with star players, you have to be extra special.

Penguin Ireland Guide ranking: **2**

Tyrone squad 2006

	v Down won 1–13 1–6	**v Cavan** drew 0–10 1–7	**v Cavan** won 3–19 0–7	**v Armagh** drew 0–14 2–8	**v Armagh** lost 0–11 0–13	**v Monaghan** won 2–14 1–7	**v Dublin** drew 1–14 1–14	**v Dublin** won 2–18 1–14	**v Armagh** won 1–13 1–12	**v Kerry** won 1–16 2–10
Pascal McConnell	●	●			●	●	●	●	●	●
Ryan McMenamin	●	●	●	●	●		●	●	●	●
Chris Lawn	●	●	●	●	●	●	●	●	○	○
Shane Sweeney	●	●	●	●	●	●	●	○	○	
Conor Gormley	●	●	●	●	●	●	●	●	●	●
Gavin Devlin	●	●	●	●	●	●	●			
Philip Jordan	●	●	●	●	●	●	●	●	●	●
Colin Holmes	●								○	○
Sean Cavanagh	●	●	●	●	●	●	●	●	●	●
Peter Donnelly	●							○		
Martin Penrose	●	●	●	●	●	○				
Ryan Mellon	●	○			●	●	●	●	●	●
Owen Mulligan	●	●	○	○	○	●	●	●	●	●
Stephen O'Neill	●	●	●	●	●	●	●	●	●	●
Enda McGinley	●	●	●	●	●	●	●	●	●	●
Peter Canavan	○	●	●	●	○	○	○		○	●
Joe McMahon	○		○	○		●	○	●	●	●
Michael Murphy	○									
David Harte		●	●	●	●	●	●	●	●	●
Brendan Donnelly		●								
Brian Dooher		○	●	●	●	●	●	●	●	●
Brian McGuigan		○	●	●	●	●	●	●	●	●
John Devine		○	●	●						
Mickey McGee			○			○	○	●	●	●
Eoin Bradley			○					○		
Colm McCullagh			○							
Mark Harte				○						
Brian Meenan						○		○	●	
Michael Coleman										
Leo Meenan										

● Played from start ○ Substituted on

Connacht

Galway Gaillimh

Colours: **Maroon and white**
Stadium: **Pearse Stadium, Galway** **Capacity:** **35,000**
Stadium: **Tuam Stadium, Tuam** **Capacity:** **30,000**
GAA clubs: **86**

Connacht SFC: **43**
1900, 1903, 1911, 1913, 1917, 1919, 1922, 1925, 1926, 1933, 1934, 1938, 1940, 1941, 1942, 1945, 1954, 1956, 1957, 1958, 1959, 1960, 1963, 1964, 1965, 1966, 1968, 1970, 1971, 1973, 1974, 1976, 1982, 1983, 1984, 1986, 1987, 1995, 1998, 2000, 2002, 2003, 2005

All-Ireland SFC: **9**
1925, 1934, 1938, 1956, 1964, 1965, 1966, 1998, 2001

National Football League: **4**
1940, 1957, 1965, 1981

Last five years:

2001: Shocked by Roscommon in the provincial first round. Went on a successful Qualifier campaign, beating Wicklow, Cork, Armagh, Roscommon and Derry, before claiming the Sam Maguire Cup with victory over Meath.

2002: Defeated Roscommon, Mayo and Sligo to win provincial crown. Caught at All-Ireland quarter-final stage by Kerry steamroller.

2003: Claimed a second Connacht title in a row, beating Roscommon, Leitrim and Mayo en route. Lost to Donegal in replayed All-Ireland quarter-final.

2004: Lost to Mayo after easy preliminary tie with London. A Qualifier victory over Louth was followed by defeat in round three to Tyrone.

2005: The four championship ties in 2005 got progressively harder – a leisurely stroll past New York, a three-point win over Leitrim, a two-point win over Mayo in the Connacht final, and finally a three-point defeat to resurgent Cork in the All-Ireland quarter-final at headquarters. Galway's successes in 1998 and 2001 mean winning in Connacht is no longer considered an end, but just a beginning.

Outlook

Despite claiming the provincial crown, Galway players and supporters will not look back on last season as a successful one. Connacht seems nicely set up for another Galway v Mayo final this summer. Complacency, however, has been the undoing of several teams – and the other sides in the province are capable of rising to a big occasion. Despite their ambitions, retaining the provincial title will be a massive task for Galway.

Top player: Padraic Joyce

Still the lynchpin for the Connacht side, as well as for Killererin and the Irish International Rules squad. Defenders in possession almost invariably try to pick out the gifted forward.

Penguin Ireland Guide ranking: **9**

Galway squad 2006

	v New York won 3–14 0–6	**v Leitrim** won 1–11 1–8	**v Mayo** won 0–10 0–8	**v Cork** lost 2–11 2–14
Alan Keane	●			
Richie Fahey	●			
Kieran Fitzgerald	●	●	●	●
Val Feeney	●	●		
Declan Meehan	●	●	●	●
Damien Burke	●	●	●	●
Michael Comer	●	●		
Joe Bergin	●	○		●
Niall Coleman	●	●	●	●
John Devane	●			
Paul Clancy	●	●	●	●
Michael Donnellan	●	●	●	●
Michael Meehan	●	●	●	●
Padraic Joyce	●	○	●	●
Matthew Clancy	●	●	●	●
Barry Cullinane	○	●	●	●
Tomas Giblin	○	○	○	
Seán Óg de Paor	○			
Shay Walsh	○			
Clive Monaghan	○			
Brian O'Donoghue		●	●	●
Alan Burke		●	●	●
Derek Savage		●	●	
Sean Armstrong		●	○	●
Niall Coyne		○		
Tomas Meehan		○		
Finian Hanley			●	●
Kieran Comer			●	○
Paul Geraghty			○	
Noel Meehan				○
Darren Mullahy				

● Played from start ○ Substituted on

Leitrim Liatroim

Colours: Green and gold
Stadium: Seán Mac Diarmada, Carrick-on-Shannon
Capacity: 13,500
GAA clubs: 33

Connacht SFC: 2
1927, 1994
All-Ireland SFC: 0
National Football League: 0
Last five years:

2001: Beaten by Galway in provincial first round and Antrim in Qualifier first round.
2002: Beat London, but lost to Sligo in Connacht semi-final. Unfortunately, Tyrone were lying in wait in the Qualifiers.
2003: Defeated New York, then bowed out to Galway in provincial semi-final. Desperately unlucky to fall to Roscommon in round two of Qualifier series.
2004: Took Roscommon to a second game in the Connacht championship before eventually surrendering. Dublin were in no mood to entertain an upset in their Qualifier clash.
2005: The defeat of neighbours Sligo at Carrick-on-Shannon in the first round last summer will live long in the memories of locals, but the following two games were even more significant. They ran Galway extremely close down in Pearse Stadium, before drawing with Meath back at home. Unfortunately, Qualifier games go straight to extra-time, and Leitrim soon succumbed.

Outlook

No matter how many times Leitrim give supposedly stronger counties a serious fright, they continue to be treated each year with some complacency. Leitrim are not afraid of any team – and will welcome the chance to lower Mayo's flag. Even though the chances of them succeeding may not be very good, the Qualifiers were created to cater for sides such as Leitrim. A favourable draw, or even two, in the back-door system and Leitrim could go one better than last season.

Top player: Michael Foley

Not for the first time, Foley led Leitrim's season from the front, bagging a sizeable haul of scores in each championship game. Only Leitrim's relatively short campaigns prevent the talented forward from becoming a household name outside the county.

Penguin Ireland Guide ranking: **28**

Leitrim squad 2006

	v Sligo won 1–11 0–9	v Galway lost 1–8 1–11	v Meath lost 1–8 1–12
Cathal McCrann	●	●	
Michael McGuinness	●	●	●
John McKeon	●	●	●
Dermot Reynolds	●	●	●
Niall Gilbane	●	●	○
Barry McWeeney	●	●	●
Shane Foley	●	●	●
Christy Carroll	●	●	●
Gary McCluskey	●	●	●
Johnny Goldrick	●	●	●
Barry Prior	●	●	●
Michael Foley	●	●	●
James Glancy	●	●	●
Colin Regan	●	●	●
Declan Maxwell	●	●	●
Darren Duignan	○	○	●
Donal Brennan		○	○
Gareth Phelan		○	●
Daniel Beck			○
James McGovern			○

● Played from start ○ Substituted on

Mayo Maigh Eo

Colours: **Green and red**
Stadium: **McHale Park, Castlebar**
Capacity: **35,000**
GAA clubs: **52**

Connacht SFC: **40**
1901, 1902, 1904, 1906, 1907, 1908, 1909, 1910, 1914, 1916, 1918, 1920, 1921, 1923, 1924, 1929, 1930, 1931, 1932, 1935, 1936, 1937, 1939, 1948, 1949, 1950, 1951, 1955, 1967, 1969, 1981, 1985, 1988, 1989, 1992, 1993, 1996, 1997, 1999, 2004

All-Ireland SFC: **3**
1936, 1950, 1951

National Football League: **11**
1934, 1935, 1936, 1937, 1938, 1939, 1941, 1949, 1954, 1970, 2001

Last five years:

2001: Better result against Sligo this time, but narrowly lost to Roscommon in the provincial final. Also beaten by Westmeath in Qualifier round four.

2002: Galway won Connacht semi-final clash. Better news in Qualifiers, beating Roscommon, Limerick and Tipperary before falling to Cork.

2003: Defeated Sligo, but again lost to Galway, this time in the provincial final. Worse news in Qualifiers, losing to Fermanagh in round four.

2004: Accounted for New York, Galway and Roscommon to claim provincial title. An impressive win over Tyrone was followed by a more laboured victory over Fermanagh, in a replay, to reach the All-Ireland final. Surrendered rather meekly to Kerry.

2005: After a bright start against Roscommon in Connacht, Galway put a stop to their march in the decider. Dumped into the latter stages of the Qualifiers, they struggled to quell the challenge of Cavan. They probably needed at least one more game before meeting Kerry.

Outlook

Mayo never quite looked a finished product last season – despite the fact that they were within one score of defeating All-Ireland champions Kerry when the final whistle went in the All-Ireland quarter-final. Nothing less than a provincial title will do for the new management team. Certainly Mayo should reach the final, where they will probably meet last season's conquerors – but the days of their season ending there are long past. Win or lose in Connacht, supporters in the county demand the baton be carried past another few opponents.

Top player: Ciarán McDonald

One of Ireland's most talented footballers, McDonald was instrumental in Mayo's long march to the 2004 All-Ireland final, but like the county never really got going last season. Mayo needs the Crossmolina man on top form to have any chance of success.

Penguin Ireland Guide ranking: **6**

Mayo squad 2006

	v Roscommon won 1–16 0–11	v Galway lost 0–8 0–10	v Cavan won 0–11 0–8	v Kerry lost 0–18 2–15
David Clarke	●	●	●	●
Keith Higgins	●			○
David Heaney	●	●	●	●
Gary Ruane	●	●	●	●
Conor Moran	●	●		
James Nallen	●	●	●	●
Gary Mullins	●			
Ronan McGarrity	●	●	●	●
Shane Fitzmaurice	●	●	●	●
Andy Moran	●	●		○
Ciarán McDonald	●	●	●	●
Alan Dillon	●	●	●	●
Conor Mortimer	●	●	●	○
Billy Joe Padden	●	●	●	●
Stephen Carolan	●			
James Gill	○	○	○	○
Trevor Mortimer	○	●		
Barry Moran	○		○	●
Dermot Geraghty		●	●	●
Peadar Gardiner		●	●	●
Pat Kelly		○	●	●
Brian Maloney		○		
Liam O'Malley		○		
Michael Moyles			●	●
Austin O'Malley			●	●
Marty McNicholas			○	
Aidan Kilcoyne				○
Alan Costello				
James Kilcullen				
Pat Navin				
Alan Roche				
Fintan Ruddy				

● Played from start ○ Substituted on

Roscommon Ros Comáin

Colours: **Blue and yellow**
Stadium: **Hyde Park, Roscommon**
Capacity: **25,000**
GAA clubs: **51**

Connacht SFC: **19**
1905, 1912, 1915, 1943, 1944, 1946, 1947, 1952, 1953, 1961, 1962, 1972, 1977, 1978, 1979, 1980, 1990, 1991, 2001

All-Ireland SFC: **2**
1943, 1944

National Football League: **1**
1979

Last five years:

2001: Defeated Galway, New York and Mayo to claim provincial title. Came unstuck in All-Ireland quarter-final in second meeting with Galway.

2002: Lost to Galway in Connacht, then beat Waterford in Qualifiers before succumbing to Mayo.

2003: Again defeated by Galway, before a successful Qualifier run with victories over Cork, Leitrim, Kildare and Offaly. All-Ireland quarter-final meeting with Kerry proved a finishing note, however.

2004: Needed four matches – two with Sligo and two with Leitrim – to reach provincial decider. Loss to Mayo there, quickly followed by round-four Qualifier defeat to Dublin.

2005: Last season was, quite simply, a disaster for Roscommon football. Amazingly, a one-point victory over London was as good as the season got. Mayo were in no mood to indulge the high hopes of Roscommon supporters. But the defeat to Louth in the Qualifiers was a killer blow – one that eclipsed even the dreadful financial crisis that was unfolding in the county at the same time. Losing to Tipperary in the Tommy Murphy Cup was just the tin hat.

Outlook

This appears to be the beginning of a new era for football in Roscommon – new officials, new management and several new players. Success, though, will be as difficult to achieve as ever. Assuming New York can't trip the county up, a semi-final meeting with Galway or Sligo could be the defining moment of their season.

Top player: Ger Heneghan

The Castlerea man usually keeps the scoreboard operators busy, both from play and frees: he kicked 16 points in three championship games last season.

Penguin Ireland Guide ranking: **18**

Roscommon squad 2006

	v London won 0–12 1–8	v Mayo lost 0–11 1–16	v Louth lost 0–10 0–11
Shane Curran	●	●	●
Brian McNeela	●	●	
Conor Beirne	●		
John Rogers	●	●	●
Michael Ryan	●	●	●
David Casey	●	●	●
Francie Grehan	●	●	●
Seamus O'Neill	●	●	●
Michael Finneran	●	○	
Enda Kenny	●	●	●
Stephen Lohan	●	●	○
Karol Mannion	●	●	●
Gary Cox	●	●	●
Nigel Dineen	●		
Ger Heneghan	●	●	●
Sean McDermott	○	●	●
Jonathon Dunning	○	○	●
John Whyte	○	●	●
Jarlath Egan	○		●
Brian Higgins		●	●
Morgan Beirne		○	
Frankie Dolan		○	
Aidan Dooney			○
Paul Noone			
Darren Lennon			
Derek Connellan			
Ian Kilbride			
Senan Kilbride			
Martin Connolly			
Daire Donnelly			
Stuart Daly			
Geoffrey Claffey			

● Played from start ○ Substituted on

Sligo Sligeach

Colours: **Black and white**
Stadium: **Markievicz Park, Sligo**
Capacity: **13,000**
GAA clubs: **51**

Connacht SFC: **2**
1928, 1975

All-Ireland SFC: **0**

National Football League: **0**

Last five years:

2001: Mayo gained revenge in provincial semi-final. Qualifier victories were gained over Carlow and Kildare before Dublin proved a bridge too far.

2002: Defeated Sligo and Leitrim before falling to Galway in provincial decider. Bounced back with impressive victory over Tyrone and draw with soon-to-be All-Ireland champions Armagh, before bowing out in replay.

2003: Lost to Mayo in provincial semi-final, after beating London. Lost in first-round Qualifier to Donegal.

2004: Made Roscommon play two hours of football before allowing them to pass. Clare didn't find it quite so difficult in round-one Qualifier meeting.

2005: After a poor start, losing to neighbours Leitrim in their first outing in Connacht, Sligo recovered with Qualifier victories over a determined Longford, a highly rated Kildare and a Clare team that ended Sligo's season in 2004. As with all the other teams to emerge from the third round of the Qualifiers, though, meeting a losing provincial finalist – in their case Cork – was a game too far.

Outlook

Hard to know what to make of Sligo's performance in 2005. They started poorly and ended just as poorly, but recorded significant successes in between. A first-round tie against reigning provincial champions Galway is not the way Sligo would have hoped to start 2006, though there's probably no better time to face the Tribesmen. Still, assuming Sligo go for an early dip in the Qualifier pool, there's no reason why they can't put together a similar run to last summer's, though they are still short of their form of a few summers ago.

Top player: **Mark Breheny**

Responsible for some crucial scores last season for Sligo, Breheny is the player that officials, supporters and other players look to when things aren't going their way.

Penguin Ireland Guide ranking: **22**

Sligo squad 2006

	v **Leitrim** lost 0–9 1–11	v **Longford** won 0–18 0–16	v **Kildare** won 1–11 1–10	v **Clare** won 1–13 0–11	v **Cork** lost 0–11 3–13
Philip Greene	●	●	●	●	●
Patrick Naughton	●	●	●	●	●
Noel McGuire	●	●	●	●	●
Brendan Phillips	●	●	●	●	●
David Durkin	●				
Jonathan Martyn	●	●	○	●	●
Jonathan Davey	●	●	●	●	●
Sean Davey	●	●	●	●	●
Eamonn O'Hara	●	●	●		
Brendan Egan	●	●	●	●	●
John McPartland	●	●	○	●	●
Brian Curran	●	○	●	○	●
Adrian Marren	●				
Mark Breheny	●	●	●	●	●
Gerry McGowan	●	○	○	●	○
Padraig Doohan	○	●	●	●	●
Karol O'Neill	○		○	○	
Dermot McTiernan	○	●	●	●	●
Dara McGarty	○	●	●	●	○
Dessie Sloyan		●	●	●	●
Kenneth Sweeney		○	●		○
Michael Munds		○			
Tony Taylor			○	○	●
Charles Harrison					○
Paul McGovern					○
Nigel Clancy					
David Morrissey					
Ross Donovan					
Conor McGowan					
Barry Kirrane					
Fergus Roche					
Colin Neary					
Fergus Horan					
Kevin Carden					

● Played from start ○ Substituted on

London Londain

Colours: Green and white
Stadium: Emerald Grounds, Ruislip
Capacity: 5,000
GAA clubs: 38

Provincial SFC: 0
All-Ireland SFC: 0
National Football League: 0

Last five years

2001: The Foot and Mouth outbreak in England meant their game with Mayo, due to be played in Ruislip at the end of May, was called off.

2002: Lost Connacht quarter-final to Leitrim and then Qualifier series tie with Wicklow.

2003: Beaten by Sligo and Offaly in Connacht championship and Qualifier competition respectively.

2004: Galway registered eight goals at Ruislip. In the Qualifier series it was target practice for Dublin at Parnell Park.

2005: Roscommon took London lightly last summer and barely escaped. Monaghan soon put London back in their place.

Outlook

Playing for London is a vocation, rather than simply a privilege. Meeting Mayo in the first round of the Connacht championship allows less room for optimism than perhaps last season's performance does. London have not been lucky in the Qualifiers, though there are few enough pairings available that they would actually fancy.

Top player: Johnny Niblock

The former Derry footballer has been a rock in the defence and was a big reason why London were only a single point shy of Roscommon's total in last season's championship opener.

Penguin Ireland Guide ranking: **32**

London squad 2006

	v Roscommon lost 1–8 0–12	**v Monaghan** lost 1–9 2–18
Paul O'Dowd	●	●
Paddy Callaghan	●	●
Damien McKenna	●	●
James Rafter	●	●
Johnny Niblock	●	●
John McKevitt	●	●
Paddy McConigley	●	●
Senan Hehir	●	●
Eamonn Brennan	●	●
Paddy Quinn	●	●
Paul Hehir	●	●
Pat Quirke	●	●
Scott Doran	●	
Shane McInerney	●	●
Barry Solan	●	●
Jamie Coffey	○	
Vinny O'Sullivan	○	○
Colm Foody		●
Fergal Cunningham		○
Danny O'Connor		○
Gavin McEvoy		
Karl Scanlon		
Ronan Walsh		
Aidan McLernon		
Gary Scanlon		
James Quinn		

● Played from start ○ Substituted on

New York

Colours: White and blue
Stadium: Gaelic Park
Capacity: 6,500
GAA clubs: 50

Provincial SFC: 0
All-Ireland SFC: 0
National Football League: 0
Last five years:

2001: Fell to Roscommon in provincial quarter-final. Didn't enter Qualifier series.
2002: Another Connacht quarter-final meeting didn't go to plan, this time against Sligo.
2003: Desperately unlucky to maintain losing streak in Connacht championship, as Leitrim scraped through.
2004: Unfortunate to come up against a Mayo side intent on a long campaign.
2005: Last season Galway left the USA having played nothing more than a leisurely practice game.

Outlook

Uniquely, New York get just one chance to impress in championship football each season – and it shows. Every other county (Kilkenny apart) is benefiting from the increased number of championship ties each season. It is Roscommon's turn to cross the Atlantic this year, and they should return with a win under their belts. New York may have to be satisfied with the increased number of counties being sent over by the GAA for non-championship ties.

Top player: PJ Ward

The former Westmeath county footballer has been New York's most potent attacker. He kicked four of their six points against Galway last year.

Penguin Ireland Guide ranking: **33**

New York squad 2006

	v **Galway** lost 0–6 3–14
Evan Byrne	●
Pa Murphy	●
James Mitchell	●
Niall Corbett	●
Nobby Smith	●
Paul O'Connor	●
Shaun Campbell	●
Cathal Loughane	●
Sean Lordan	●
Ronan Garvey	●
Robbie Moran	●
Mark Dobbin	●
PJ Ward	●
Brian Newman	●
Paddy Smith	●
Michael Keaveney	○
Matthew Mitchell	○
Tadhg Healy	○
Martin Donaghy	○
Stephen Flynn	○

● Played from start ○ Substituted on

Football Championship Results Table

Munster

First Round			
Kerry			Waterford
Replay:			
Clare			Limerick
Replay:			

Semi-finals			
Kerry /Waterford			Tipperary
Replay:			
Clare/Limerick			Cork
Replay:			

Final			
Replay:			

Connacht

First Round			
New York			Roscommon
Replay:			
Galway			Sligo
Replay:			
London			Mayo
Replay:			

Semi-finals			
New York/Roscommon			Sligo/Galway
Replay:			
London/Mayo			Leitrim
Replay:			

Final			
Replay:			

Ulster

First Round			
Down			Cavan
Replay:			

Quarter-finals			
Armagh			Monaghan
Replay:			
Fermanagh			Antrim
Replay:			
Tyrone			Derry
Replay:			
Down/Cavan			Donegal
Replay:			

Semi-finals			
Armagh/Monaghan			Fermanagh/Antrim
Replay:			
Donegal/Down/Cavan			Tyrone/Derry
Replay:			

Final			
Replay:			

Leinster

First Round			
Westmeath			Offaly
Replay:			
Meath			Louth
Replay:			
Wicklow			Carlow
Replay:			

Quarter-finals			
Westmeath/Offaly			Kildare
Replay:			
Meath/Louth			Wexford
Replay:			
Wicklow/Carlow			Laois
Replay:			
Longford			Dublin
Replay:			

Semi-finals			
Kildare/Westmeath/ Offaly			Wexford/Meath/ Louth
Replay:			
Laois/Wicklow/ Carlow			Longford/Dublin
Replay:			

Final			
Replay:			

All-Ireland Qualifiers

Round One			

Round Two			

Round Three			

Round Four			

All-Ireland Quarter-finals			
Replay:			
Replay:			

Replay:

Replay:

All-Ireland Semi-finals

Replay:

Replay:

All-Ireland Final

Replay:

3 Women's Senior Camogie and Football Championships 2006

3
Women's Senior Camogie and Football Championships 2006

Camogie

It is now ten years since a county other than Tipperary or Cork claimed the O'Duffy Cup. While camogie has made huge strides in terms of numbers (now approaching 100,000 registered players) and profile, the championship continues to be a two-horse race. For all supporters, and especially those working tirelessly for the sport's development, camogie requires another realistic senior contender to step forward.

This summer sees several changes to the structure of intercounty camogie, all for one important objective: to stimulate and encourage the development of the game in non-traditional counties – which, at the moment, means the vast majority of the island.

The main alteration this season is that counties that field a senior side will not be able to compete in the junior championship: the organization has finally woken up to the realization that seeing a county's first team being beaten by another county's reserves doesn't do much for promoting the code beyond the traditional seats of power. The junior competition – which will now have a shield and cup grade – will be run on a league basis, with a minimum of three games for each entrant. This change also requires the restructuring of the intermediate championship, to cater for B sides from senior counties.

The changes to the minor grade may end up being one of the most important steps Cumann Camógaíochta na nGael has ever taken, perhaps even on a par with the decision to move to 15-a-side for all competitions some years ago. While 'minor' grade refers to under-18s in hurling and football, up to now it has been the term for under-16 competition in camogie. The move that brings camogie into line with the other codes this season is an important step for a code that hopes all the new changes in 2006 will bring positive results that seep upwards, as well as downwards, and encourage greater competition in senior intercounty ties.

Antrim's last-minute withdrawal from last season's senior championship was a major blow to camogie – though the annual drubbings traditionally handed out to the Ulster county were only slightly better than not participating at all. But it is from somewhere in the middle ranks that, in the short term, camogie might receive a boost. Can Wexford, Galway, Limerick or Kilkenny cause a shock this season and signal a new and more competitive future for camogie? Only time will tell, but the old guard won't be easily moved.

Championship Format

This season the revamped junior championship will be run on the same basis as the current senior championship, which is relatively straightforward. Camogie is unique in that the senior provincial and All-Ireland championships run completely separately.

All-Ireland Championship

Run on a league and knock-out basis. Teams are split into two groups with each team playing the other sides in the group once. The winner of each group plays the runner-up of the other group in the All-Ireland semi-finals.

Rules

There are five main rule differences between camogie and hurling:

1. It is not a foul to drop your hurley in camogie.
2. The camogie sliotar is slightly lighter than a hurling sliotar.
3. Hand-passed goals are allowed in camogie.
4. When the sliotar crosses the end-line off a defending player, the attacking team is awarded a 45 in camogie, rather than a 65.
5. Shouldering is not allowed in camogie. (This only seems to apply in theory.)

2005 Senior Championship Results

Opening Rounds

June 2	Group A	Gaelic Grounds, Limerick	Limerick **3–5** Kilkenny **1–7**
	Group B	Páirc Tailteann, Navan	Cork **2–8** Galway **0–13**
June 16	Group A	Nowlan Park, Kilkenny	Tipperary **0–13** Kilkenny **1–6**
	Group B	Wexford Park, Wexford	Cork **2–16** Wexford **2–7**
July 30	Group A	Semple Stadium, Thurles	Tipperary **5–17** Limerick **0–8**
	Group B	Duggan Park, Ballinasloe	Wexford **3–6** Galway **0–7**

All-Ireland Semi-finals

August 20	Nowlan Park, Kilkenny	Cork **5–17** Limerick **0–5**
	Nowlan Park, Kilkenny	Tipperary **1–13** Wexford **1–8**

All-Ireland Final

September 18	Croke Park, Dublin	Cork **1–17** Tipperary **1–13**

2005 Champions

	Champions	Runners-up
Senior	Cork	Tipperary
Junior	Clare	Dublin
Minor A	Kilkenny	Tipperary
Minor B	Offaly	Antrim
NL Division 1	Galway	Cork
NL Division 2	Cork	Galway

Camogie Roll of Honour

County	No of Titles	Years won
Dublin	26	1932, 1933, 1937, 1938, 1942, 1943, 1944, 1948, 1949, 1950, 1951, 1952, 1953, 1954, 1955, 1957, 1958, 1959, 1960, 1961, 1962, 1963, 1964, 1965, 1966, 1984
Cork	21	1934, 1935, 1936, 1939, 1940, 1941, 1970, 1971, 1972, 1973, 1978, 1980, 1982, 1983, 1992, 1993, 1995, 1997, 1998, 2002, 2005
Kilkenny	12	1974, 1976, 1977, 1981, 1985, 1986, 1987, 1988, 1989, 1990, 1991, 1994
Antrim	6	1945, 1946, 1947, 1956, 1967, 1979
Tipperary	5	1999, 2000, 2001, 2003, 2004
Wexford	3	1968, 1969, 1975
Galway	1	1996

Women's Football

Over the past decade, five counties have claimed the All-Ireland senior football title for the very first time – Monaghan, Mayo, Laois, Galway and, most recently, Cork. All four senior provincial championships have become more competitive, making the All-Ireland less predictable in turn. This increased competitiveness has surely been the single biggest factor in the recent relentless growth of the game.

Cork's arrival to the biggest stage in women's football last season was another welcome boost. The Rebel county has been slowly building towards such an assault for a number of years – with underage success at almost every level complemented by a number of the strongest women's football clubs in the country. It's a daunting lesson for other aspiring counties: winning a senior All-Ireland may bring a significant boost at underage level domestically, but top-level success simply won't arrive unless significant groundwork has already been completed.

Last season finished on a high note for the Ladies Gaelic Football Association of Ireland. The attendance at headquarters for the All-Ireland final between Cork and Galway was up 3,000 on the previous year – nothing to get carried away about, but certainly encouraging nonetheless. And, just as importantly, viewing figures on TG4 were up 50,000 on the 2004 final. In fact, over one in four of all television viewers in Ireland on the first Sunday in October 2005 were watching the women's final. And All-Ireland final week was finished off in style by the hundreds of players who had travelled from places as far away as Canada, USA and Australia for the inaugural International Ladies Football tournament in Dublin.

However, even though playing numbers and attendances at games are still on the up, there's much work still to be done. The gap between the competitive counties and the rest continues to increase. Louth's fine season in 2004 was followed by disaster last season, which culminated in withdrawal from the Leinster championship, and Clare's Munster senior championship campaign in 2005 is, well, perhaps best forgotten. The round robin system that each province operates is all well and good – so long as the guaranteed minimum number of games each offers isn't also a guaranteed minimum number of heavy losses. Finding yourself in the company of the big names in women's football, such as Galway and Mayo, should be seen as a challenge, not a death sentence. Armagh – who claimed last season's Junior All-Ireland, as well as the Division Two league crown – seem better equipped to handle the step up than most.

For the neutral, as well as the women's football organization itself, another first-time winner this season would be welcome, though that is probably asking too much. Certainly the big guns of the past few years are lining up for another tilt at the title – especially in the west, with Galway and Mayo preparing for another titantic struggle. If there is to be another first-time champion, the smart money would be on Dublin, who have earned the right to be considered a serious title contender, reaching the decider in 2003 and 2004, and the All-Ireland semi-final last season. But after every season without a trophy it becomes a little bit harder to give the time and commitment necessary to launch another major offensive on the championship. It can be much easier, in many ways, when an All-Ireland senior medal has already been pocketed – as Cork fans will hope.

At least ten county panels have realistic ambitions of playing in the 2006 All-Ireland women's football final. The dials have been reset, and history will count for little during this season's matches. Determination will count for much more.

Championship Format

The format of the women's senior football championship is relatively uncomplicated with the eight teams that reach their respective provincial finals qualifying for entry to the All-Ireland knock-out stages.

As a result, with several traditionally strong counties in each of the provinces, 'developing' counties have found it extremely difficult to make a breakthrough – though Cork, Dublin and Galway have all managed it in recent years.

Provincial Championships

Played on a round-robin basis, with each team playing the other senior county sides in their respective provincial championship (between two and five games, depending on the province). The top two teams meet in the provincial final.

All-Ireland Championship

Played on a knock-out basis – eight teams compete in All-Ireland quarter-finals, with provincial champions meeting a runner-up from another province.

Rules

There are five main rule differences between men's and women's football:

1 The ball used is slightly smaller in women's football.
2 A player holding the ball into her body cannot be legally dispossessed.
3 Shouldering is not supposed to be permitted in women's football.
4 If the referee stops play to deal with an injured player, the team in possession retains possession on the restart (though they cannot score direct from the first kick).
5 For a kick-out in women's football, the ball may be kicked from the hand (or the ground).

2005 All-Ireland Women's Senior Football Championship Results

Leinster

Opening rounds

May 14	Kilskyre, Meath	Longford **3–10** Louth **2–9**
May 15	Moynalty, Meath	Dublin **5–14** Meath **1–9**
	Stradbally, Laois	Laois **4–10** Kildare **1–10**
May 22	Navan, Meath	Meath **6–23** Longford **0–3**
	Sarsfields, Kildare	Dublin **5–14** Kildare **3–11**
June 26	Sarsfields, Kildare	Kildare **9–26** Longford **0–4**
	Stradbally, Laois	Dublin **1–10** Laois **1–10**
July 3	Naomh Mearnog, Dublin	Dublin **7–24** Longford **1–2**
	Navan, Meath	Meath **1–12** Laois **0–9**
July 10	Newbridge, Kildare	Meath **4–10** Kildare **1–16**

Semi-finals

July 16	Stradbally, Laois	Meath **0–14** Laois **0–13**
July 17	Clonsilla, Dublin	Dublin **2–18** Kildare **2–9**

Final

July 31	Dr Cullen Park, Carlow	Dublin **2–13** Meath **1–13**

Ulster

Opening rounds

June 25	Irvinestown, Fermanagh	Donegal **3–8** Monaghan **3–7**
June 26	Edendork, Tyrone	Tyrone **2–10** Down **0–12**
July 3	Irvinestown, Fermanagh	Monaghan **1–12** Tyrone **3–5**
July 3	Newry	Donegal **0–14** Down **2–6**
July 9	Clones	Monaghan **5–12** Down **0–8**
July 17	Irvinestown, Fermanagh	Tyrone **0–13** Donegal **1–7**
July 26	Irvinestown, Fermanagh	Tyrone **1–7** Donegal **0–9**

Final

July 31	Clones	Monaghan **2–8** Tyrone **1–6**

Connacht

Opening rounds

May 8	McHale Park, Castlebar	Mayo **2–12** Galway **0–10**
July 3	Dr Hyde Park, Roscommon	Mayo **0–11** Roscommon **1–7**
July 17	Tuam	Galway **5–17** Roscommon **0–8**

Final

August 6	Tuam, Galway	Galway **3–10** Mayo **1–9**

Munster

Opening rounds

June 27	Killorglin, Kerry	Cork **2–14** Kerry **2–7**
July 3	Cappamore, Limerick	Waterford **4–24** Clare **0–3**
July 9	Cooraclare, Clare	Kerry **11–31** Clare **0–4**
July 11	Páirc Uí Rinn, Cork	Cork **0–15** Waterford **1–8**
July 23	Dungarvan, Waterford	Kerry **5–8** Waterford **3–9**
August 1	Donoughmore, Cork	Cork **0–18** Clare **1–3**

Final

August 7	Fitzgerald Stadium, Killarney	Cork **2–15** Kerry **1–8**

All-Ireland Quarter-finals

August 27	O'Moore Park, Portlaoise	Cork **2–19** Meath **3–10**
	Gaelic Grounds, Limerick	Galway **4–13** Kerry **2–10**
	Croke Park, Dublin	Dublin **1–15** Tyrone **0–5**
August 28	St Loman's, Mullingar	Mayo **0–6** Monaghan **0–1**

All-Ireland Semi-finals

September 10	O'Moore Park, Portlaoise	Galway **2–10** Dublin **0–7**
	O'Moore Park, Portlaoise	Cork **0–13** Mayo **1–9**

All-Ireland Final

October 2	Croke Park, Dublin	Cork **1–11** Galway **0–8**

2005 Champions

	Champions	Runners-up
Senior	Cork	Galway
Junior	Armagh	Sligo
Intermediate	Roscommon	Down
Minor	Galway	Donegal
International	Australasia	London
NL Division One	Cork	Galway
NL Division Two	Armagh	Donegal
NL Division Three	Tipperary	Dublin
NL Division Four	Wicklow	Westmeath

Roll of Honour

County	No of Titles	Years won
Kerry	11	1976, 1982, 1983, 1984, 1985, 1986, 1987, 1988, 1989, 1990, 1993
Waterford	5	1991, 1992, 1994, 1995, 1998
Mayo	4	1999, 2000, 2002, 2003
Tipperary	3	1974, 1975, 1980
Offaly	2	1979, 1981
Monaghan	2	1996, 1997
Cavan	1	1977
Roscommon	1	1978
Laois	1	2001
Galway	1	2004
Cork	1	2005

All-Ireland Senior Championship Decade of Champions

	Senior Winners	Runner-up
2005	Cork	Galway
2004	Galway	Dublin
2003	Mayo	Dublin
2002	Mayo	Monaghan
2001	Laois	Mayo
2000	Mayo	Waterford
1999	Mayo	Waterford
1998	Waterford	Monaghan
1997	Monaghan	Waterford
1996	Monaghan	Laois

4
Results 2005

4
Results 2005

Leinster Senior Hurling Championship

First Round

May 22 Nowlan Park, Kilkenny

Laois **4–14** Dublin **0–14**

Laois P Mullaney | B Campion, P Cuddy, M McEvoy | J Fitzpatrick, D Rooney, S Dwyer (0–1) | J Young (1–9, six frees, one penalty), J Walsh | J Phelan, J Rowney, L Tynan (1–1) | T Fitzgerald, M Rooney, D Culleton (2–1)

Subs: E Meagher (0–1) for Rowney (24 mins), P Russell (0–1) for M Rooney (46 mins), C Healy for Walsh (58 mins), C Brophy for Culleton (62 mins), C Coonan for Tynan (70 mins)

Dublin G Maguire | G Bennett, S O'Shea, G O'Meara | D Sweeney (0–2), R Fallon (0–1, a 65), S Hiney | T Moore (0–1), S McDonald | M Carton, D Curtin (0–4, two frees, two 65s), D O'Reilly | E Carroll (0–3), M Breathnach, S Mullen (0–1)

Subs: S Perkins for O'Shea (33 mins), C Meehan (0–1) for M Carton (45 mins), P Carton for Mullen (50 mins), S Daly for McDonald (55 mins), A de Paor (0–1) for Fallon (70 mins)

Referee T McIntyre (Antrim)

Semi-finals

June 12 Croke Park, Dublin

Kilkenny **6–28** Offaly **0–15**

Kilkenny J McGarry | J Ryall, N Hickey, J Tyrell | R Mullally (0–1), P Barry (capt), JJ Delaney | B Barry (0–1, 65) | D Lyng (0–2) | M Comerford (1–3), E Larkin, T Walsh (0–5) | R Power (1–1), DJ Carey (1–2), H Shefflin (2–11, 0–1 pen, 0–4 frees)

Subs: C Phelan (0–1) for Lyng (55 mins), J Hoyne for DJ Carey (60 mins), M Kavanagh for Mullally, E McCormack (1–1) for Power (both 61 mins), J Tennyson for Hickey (67 mins)

Offaly B Mullins | B Teehan (capt), G Oakley, D Franks | D Hoctor, K Brady, C Cassidy | M Cordial, B Murphy | G Hannify (0–2), R Hannify (0–1), D Hayden (0–1), B Carroll (0–3, one free), J Brady, D Murray (0–7, frees)

Subs: P Cleary for Teehan (19 mins), S Browne for Franks (half-time), A Hanrahan for Murray (58 mins), P Molloy for Cordial (60 mins), C Parlon (0–1) for Hayden (64 (mins)

Referee M Haverty (Galway)

June 12 Croke Park, Dublin

Wexford **0–24** Laois **1–10**

Wexford D Fitzhenry | D O'Connor, D Ryan, K Rossiter | M Travers, D Ruth (0–4, three frees, one 65), D Lyng | R Barry (0–1), A Fenlon (0–1) | R McCarthy (0–2), E Quigley (0–2), M Jacob | D Mythen (0–3), M Jordan (0–1), R Jacob (0–7, five frees)

Subs: N Higgins (0–2) for Jordan (48 mins), P Carley (0–1) for Barry (62 mins), T Mahon for McCarthy (66 mins), D Stamp for Travers (68 mins), B Lambert for Mythen (69 mins)

Laois P Mullaney | B Campion, P Cuddy, M McEvoy | J Fitzpatrick, D Rooney, S Dwyer | J Phelan (0–1), E Meagher | J Walsh, J Young (0–7, three frees, two 65s), C Healy (0–1) | T Fitzgerald (0–1), L Tynan, D Culleton (1–0)

Subs: M Rooney for Meagher (43 mins), R Jones for Phelan (48 mins), C Coonan for Healy (61 mins), C Brophy for Walsh (69 mins)

Referee J Sexton (Limerick)

Final

July 3 Croke Park, Dublin

Kilkenny **0–22** Wexford **1–16**

Kilkenny J McGarry | J Tyrell, N Hickey, J Ryall | R Mullally (0–1), P Barry, JJ Delaney | B Barry, D Lyng | M Comerford, E Larkin (0–3), T Walsh (0–4) | R Power (0–3), C Phelan (0–1), H Shefflin (0–8, seven frees, one 65)

Subs: E McCormack for Phelan (40 mins), E Brennan (0–2) for B Barry (45 mins), M Kavanagh for Ryall (47 mins), J Hoyne for Larkin (69 mins)

Wexford D Fitzhenry | D O'Connor, D Ryan, K Rossiter | M Travers, D Ruth (0–1), D Lyng | A Fenlon, R McCarthy (0–2) | P Carley (0–1), E Quigley (0–2), D Mythen (1–1) | M Jacob (0–1), M Jordan (0–2), R Jacob (0–5, all frees)

Subs: R Barry (0–1) for Fenlon (half-time), T Mahon for Carley (60 mins), B Lambert for M Jacob (71 mins)

Referee S Roche (Tipperary)

Munster Senior Hurling Championship

First Round

May 15 Semple Stadium, Thurles

Tipperary **2–14** Limerick **2–14**

Tipperary B Cummins | M Maher, P Maher, P Curran | D Fanning, D Kennedy, E Corcoran | C Morrissey (0–1), P Kelly (0–5, four frees) | J Devane (1–0), F Devanney, B Dunne (capt) | P O'Brien, E Kelly (0–6, four frees), L Corbett (0–1)

Subs: G O'Grady (1–0) for Devanney (half-time), T Dunne (0–1) for B Dunne (44 mins), D Fitzgerald for Corcoran (63 mins), M Webster for Morrissey (66 mins), D Egan for O'Brien (71 mins)

Limerick T Houlihan | S Lucey, D Reale, M Foley | O Moran (capt), B Geary, P Lawlor | P O'Grady (0–1), D O'Grady | C Fitzgerald (0–1), N Moran (0–3), A O'Shaughnessy | D Sheehan (1–0), TJ Ryan (1–7, 1–5 frees), D Ryan

Subs: P Tobin (0–2) for Sheehan (61 mins), M Cahill for Fitzgerald (72 mins)

Referee D Kirwan (Cork)

May 21 Replay Gaelic Grounds, Limerick

Tipperary **2–13** Limerick **0–18** (AET)

Tipperary B Cummins | E Corcoran, P Maher, P Curran | D Fanning, D Kennedy, D Fitzgerald | B Dunne (capt), P Kelly (0–1) | C Morrissey, T Dunne (0–4), J Devane | E Kelly (0–7, five frees), M Webster, L Corbett (0–1)

Subs: G O'Grady (1–0) for Devane (25 mins), M O'Leary for Corbett (44 mins), J Carroll for Webster (58 mins), C O'Mahoney for B Dunne (65 mins), E Sweeney (1–0) for O'Grady (70 mins), F Devanney for O'Leary (80 mins), P O'Brien for Carroll (86 mins), P Morrissey for O'Mahoney (91 mins)

Limerick T Houlihan | M Foley, S Lucey, D Reale | O Moran (capt), B Geary, P Lawlor (0–1, free) | P O'Grady (0–1), D O'Grady (0–2) | C Fitzgerald (0–1), N Moran (0–1), A O'Shaughnessy (0–1) | D Ryan (0–1), TJ Ryan (0–8, frees), D Sheehan (0–1)

Subs: P Tobin for Fitzgerald (40 mins), S O'Connor for O'Shaughnessy (49 mins), K Tobin (0–1) for N Moran (61 mins), N Moran for O'Connor (78 mins), A O'Shaughnessy for K Tobin (79 mins)

Referee A Mac Suibhne (Dublin)

Semi-finals

May 22 Semple Stadium, Thurles

Cork **2–17** Waterford **2–15**

Cork D Cusack | P Mulcahy, D O'Sullivan (0–1, a penalty), B Murphy | J Gardiner, R Curran, S Óg Ó hAilpin, T Kenny, J O'Connor (0–2) | B O'Connor (0–4, two frees, one 65), N McCarthy (0–4), N Ronan | K Murphy (Sarsfields | 0–1), B Corcoran (1–2), J Deane (1–3, 0–1 from free)

Subs: K Murphy (Erin's Own) for N Ronan (half-time)

Waterford S Brenner | T Feeney, F Hartley, E Murphy | T Browne (0–1), K McGrath, J Murray | D Bennett, M Walsh | E Kelly (0–6), D Shanahan (1–0), P Flynn (1–6, 0–6 from frees) | J Mullane, S Prendergast (0–2), E McGrath

Subs: P O'Brien for Bennett (25 mins), B Phelan for Shanahan (65 mins)

Referee S Roche (Tipperary)

June 5 Gaelic Grounds, Limerick

Tipperary **2–14** Clare **0–14**

Tipperary B Cummins | E Corcoran, J Devane, P Curran | D Fanning, D Kennedy, D Fitzgerald | B Dunne (0–1), P Kelly (0–1) | C Morrissey, F Devanney (0–2), T Dunne (0–1) | E Kelly (0–7, four frees), M Webster (1–0), L Corbett (1–0)

Subs: E Sweeney (0–2) for L Corbett (15 mins, inj), H Maloney for D Kennedy (43 mins), C O'Mahoney for E Sweeney (68 mins), P O'Brien for T Dunne (71 mins)

Clare D Fitzgerald | F Lohan, B Lohan, G O'Grady | A Markham, S McMahon (0–2, frees), G Quinn | B O'Connell, C Lynch | D McMahon (0–2), T Griffin (0–2), B Nugent (0–2) | T Carmody (0–1), N Gilligan (0–5, 3 frees), A Quinn

Subs: D Forde for B Nugent (46 mins), D O'Connell for A Quinn (48 mins), C Plunkett for D McMahon (55 mins), C Forde for A Markham (60 mins)

Referee P O'Connor (Limerick)

Final

June 26 Páirc Uí Chaoimh, Cork

Cork **1–21** Tipperary **1–16**

Cork D Cusack | P Mulcahy, D O'Sullivan, B Murphy | J Gardiner, R Curran, S Óg Ó hAilpín (capt) | T Kenny, J O'Connor (0–2) | B O'Connor (0–6, all frees), N McCarthy (0–1), T McCarthy | K Murphy (Sarsfields | 1–2), B Corcoran (0–1), J Deane (0–5, three frees)

Subs: N Ronan (0–3) for Corcoran (13 mins), W Sherlock for B Murphy (58 mins), J O'Callaghan for Kenny (66 mins), K Murphy (Erin's Own | 0–1) for T McCarthy (69 mins)

Tipperary B Cummins | E Corcoran, P Maher, P Curran | D Fanning, D Kennedy, D Fitzgerald | B Dunne (capt), P Kelly (0–7, two frees, one 65) | C Morrissey, T Dunne (1–0), F Devanney | E Kelly (0–6, two frees), M Webster, E Sweeney

Subs: H Moloney for Kennedy (32 mins), G O'Grady for Devanney (33 mins), J Devane (0–2) for Sweeney (half-time), J Carroll (0–1) for B Dunne (48 mins)

Referee B Kelly (Westmeath)

Ulster Senior Hurling Championship

First Round

May 15 Casement Park, Belfast

Down **4–25** London **1–17**

Down Graham Clarke | L Clarke, S Murray, P Hughes | Gabriel Clarke, G Savage, S Wilson (0–5, four frees, one 65) | A Savage, P Monan (0–2) | E Clarke (0–2), P Braniff (0–2), B McGourty (0–6) | M Coulter (2–3, 1–1 from frees), G Johnston (1–2), S Clarke (0–2)

Subs: E Trainor (1–1) for Braniff (half-time), G Adair for Coulter (61 mins), C Coulter for Hughes, D Flynn for E Clarke (both 67 mins)

London JJ Burke | D Murphy, T Simms, E Phelan | B Forde, B Foley, J Dillon | M O'Meara (0–3), M Harding (0–5, all frees) | J McGaughan (0–1), J Ryan (0–2), D Bourke (0–2) | M Gordon (0–1), F McMahon (0–1), G Fenton

Subs: P Doyle for Simms (33 mins), E Kindlon (0–2) for Fenton (50 mins), K McMullen (1–0) for McGaughan (55 mins), M Murphy for D Murphy (66 mins)

Referee A Stapleton (Laois)

Semi-finals

May 22 — Casement Park, Belfast

Derry **2–9** Down **1–12**

Derry K Stevenson | B McGoldrick, L Hinphey, G Brunton | C Brunton, M Conway, P O'Kane | Gary Biggs, Gregory Biggs (0–2, free) | R Convery, R Kennedy (0–2), P Hearty | S McBride (1–0), G McGonigle (1–4, 0–4 from frees), F McGuigan

Subs: C Quinn for Hearty (30 mins), J O'Dwyer (0–1) for McGuigan (48 mins), Aaron McCloskey for Cathal Brunton (58 mins)

Down Graham Clarke | L Clarke, S Murray, C Coulter, Gabriel Clarke, G Savage, S Wilson (0–1, free) | G Adair (0–2), P Monan | E Clarke (0–1), G Johnson (0–1), B McGourty | M Coulter (1–3, one free), E Trainor (0–2), S Clarke (0–1)

Subs: A Savage (0–1) for Monan (48 mins), J McCusker for S Clarke (61 mins)

Referee G Devlin (Armagh)

May 29 Replay — Casement Park, Belfast

Down **3–21** Derry **4–9**

Down Graham Clarke | L Clarke, S Murray, C Coulter | Gabriel Clarke, G Savage, S Wilson (0–5) | A Savage (0–2), G Adair (0–1) | E Clarke, P Monan (0–1), B McGourty (0–2) | M Coulter (3–3), G Johnston (0–7), S Clarke

Sub: D Flynn for S Clarke

Derry K Stevenson | B McGoldrick, L Hinphey, G Brunton | C Brunton, M Conway, P O'Kane | P Doherty, Gregory Biggs (0–1) | R Convery (0–1), R Kennedy (0–1), C Quinn | S McBride (2–3), G McGonigle (2–3), J O'Dwyer

Subs: P Hardy for Quinn, A McCloskey for Doherty, P Sweeney for Convery

Referee B Kerry (Westmeath)

May 22 Gaelic Park, New York

Antrim **2–20** New York **2–14** (AET)

Antrim Damien Quinn | M Kettle, M McCambridge, P Hamill | G Cunningham, S Campbell, C Herron (0–1) | M Scullion, M Herron (0–3) | B McFall (1–2), C McGuckian (0–3), K Stewart (0–3) | J McIntosh (0–1), J Connolly (0–1), B Quinn (0–3)

Subs: K McKeegan (1–2) for McIntosh, P Richmond (0–2) for McGuckian, Darren Quinn for B Quinn

New York T Cullen | P Wickham, P Dalton, C Casserly | T Healy, J Madden, A Guinan | L Dunican, P Murray | M Kennedy (1–7), T Moylan, T Fletcher (0–4) | D McCarthy (0–1), K Kennedy, R Henley (0–2)

Subs: M Maher (1–0) for R Henley, T O'Meara for D McCarthy

Referee S McMahon (Clare)

Final

Sunday June 5 Casement Park, Belfast

Antrim **2–22** Down **1–18**

Antrim Damien Quinn | M Kettle, G Bell, C Hamill | G Cunningham, J Campbell (0–3), M McCambridge | P Richmond (0–2), M Scullion (0–1) | K McKeegan (0–4), K Kelly, M Herron (0–1) | J McIntosh (0–7), J Connolly (1–1), J Scullion (0–2)

Subs: K Stewart (1–1) for Kelly, C Herron for M Herron, B McFall for J Scullion, C McGuckian for Cunningham

Down Graham Clarke | L Clarke, S Murray, P Hughes | Gabriel Clarke, G Savage, S Wilson (0–1) | G Adair, A Savage | B McGourty (0–1), P Monan, E Clarke (0–2) | M Coulter (0–11), G Johnston (1–1), J McCusker (0–1)

Subs: C Coulter for Hughes, J Convery (0–1) for Monan, E Trainor for McCusker

Referee B Gavin (Offaly)

All-Ireland Hurling Qualifiers
Round One

Group A

June 18 O'Moore Park, Portlaoise

Galway 2–22 Laois 2–11

Galway L Donoghue | D Joyce, S Kavanagh, C Coen | G Mahon, D Hardiman, O Canning | T Og Regan (0–5, three frees), D Collins | R Murray (0–3), D Forde, D Tierney (0–1) | D Hayes, K Hayes (1–1), G Farragher (1–11, 1–10 from frees)

Subs: F Healy for Collins (48 mins), N Healy (0–1) for Forde (52 mins), F Moore for Mahon (58 mins), D Donoghue for D Hayes (69 mins)

Laois P Mullaney | B Campion, P Cuddy, M McEvoy | J Fitzpatrick, P Mahon, S Dwyer | J Young (0–6, four frees, one 65), J Walsh (0–1) | C Coonan, J Rowney, C Healy (0–1) | T Fitzgerald (0–2), L Tynan (1–1), D Culleton (1–0)

Subs: P Russell for Campion (20 mins), E Meagher for Rowney (52 mins), R Jones for Coonan (58 mins), C Brophy for Russell (62 mins), J Walsh for Mahon (65 mins)

Referee M Wadding (Waterford)

Group B

June 18 Parnell Park, Dublin

Clare 1–23 Dublin 0–9

Clare D Fitzgerald | F Lohan, B Lohan, B Quinn | C Forde, S McMahon (0–1, a 65), G Quinn | B O'Connell (0–1), D Forde (0–2) | D McMahon (0–4), T Griffin (0–2), A Markham | T Carmody (0–5), N Gilligan (0–6, three frees), D O'Connell (1–0)

Subs: C Plunkett for A Markham (36 mins), D Hoey for G Quinn, A Quinn for T Griffin (both 56 mins), D Clancy (0–1) for B O'Connell (58 mins), D O'Rourke (0–1) for D O'Connell (62 mins)

Dublin G Maguire | G O'Meara, S Hiney, J Cullen | D O'Reilly, R Fallon (0–1, one free), D Sweeney | T Moore, M Carton | S McDonald, D Curtin (0–5, five frees), D Russell | E Carroll, L Ryan, K Flynn (0–2, one free)

Subs: T Sweeney for S McDonald (31 mins), E Moran for D Curtin (42 mins), P Carton (0–1) for L Ryan (45 mins), S Mullen for M Carton (62 mins)

Referee D Murphy (Wexford)

Group B

June 18 Dr Cullen Park, Carlow

Waterford **1–26** Offaly **1–15**

Waterford S Brenner | T Feeney, F Hartley, J Murray | T Browne, K McGrath (0–5, two frees, one 65), E Murphy | B Phelan, E Kelly | D Shanahan, M Walsh (0–3), P Flynn (1–8, 1–6 frees) | J Mullane (0–8), S Prendergast (0–1), E McGrath (0–1)

Offaly B Mullins | P Molloy, G Oakley, D Franks | Brian Whelehan, K Brady, Barry Whelehan | M Cordial (0–2, one line ball), B Murphy (0–2) | G Hannify (0–2), R Hannify, D Hayden (0–1) | B Carroll (0–5, one free), J Brady, D Murray (0–3, frees)

Subs: A Hanrahan (1–0) for J Brady, M O'Hara for Barry Whelehan, C Parlon for Hayden

Referee D Richardson (Limerick)

Group A

June 25 Casement Park, Belfast

Limerick **4–25** Antrim **1–9**

Limerick T Houlihan | D Reale, S Lucey, P O'Dwyer | O Moran, B Geary, P Lawlor (0–3) | P O'Grady (0–1), D O'Grady | P Tobin (0–1), N Moran (0–6), A O'Shaughnessy (1–1) | D Ryan (2–1), TJ Ryan (1–5), D Sheehan (0–2)

Subs: K Tobin for Geary (half-time), S O'Connor for TJ Ryan (41 mins), C Fitzgerald (0–1) for D Ryan (43 mins) | P Kirby (0–2) for Sheahan (48 mins), A O'Connor (0–2) for O'Shaughnessy (55 mins)

Antrim Damien Quinn | M Kettle, G Bell, C Hamill | G Cunningham, J Campbell, M McCambridge (0–1) | P Richmond (0–1), M Scullion | K McKeegan (0–3), K Kelly, K Stewart (0–1), J McIntosh (0–1), J Connolly (1–0), B McFall (0–2)

Subs: C Herron for Kettle (18 mins), A Ó Cairealláin for McCambridge (inj, 30 mins) | M Herron for Stewart (47 mins) | C McGuckian for Kelly (51 mins)

Referee S McGrath (Westmeath)

Round Two

Group A

July 1 O'Moore Park, Portlaoise

Limerick **2–15** Laois **1–9**

Limerick T Houlihan | D Reale, S Lucey, P O'Dwyer | O Moran (1–0), B Geary, K Tobin | D O'Grady (0–1), P O'Grady | C Fitzgerald, N Moran (0–3), A O'Shaughnessy (0–2) | D Ryan (0–1), TJ Ryan (0–8), D Sheehan

Subs: P Kirby (1–0) for D Sheehan, P Tobin for C Fitzgerald, J O'Brien for D O'Grady, M Clifford for D Reale

Laois P Mullaney | J Walsh, P Cuddy, M McEvoy | J Fitzpatrick, D Rooney, S Dwyer | J Walsh, J Phelan (0–1) | J Rowney (0–1), L Tynan, J Young (1–5), T Fitzgerald (0–1) | M Rooney (0–1), D Culleton

Subs: P Mahon for L Tynan, A Delaney for J Walsh, C Brophy for J Rowney, C Clear for S Dwyer

Referee E Morris (Dublin)

Group A

July 2 Pearse Stadium, Galway

Galway **3–29** Antrim **0–10**

Galway L Donoghue | D Joyce, S Kavanagh, C Coen | G Mahon, D Hardiman, O Canning | T Regan, D Collins | R Murray (0–3), K Hayes (0–2), D Tierney (2–2) | G Farragher (0–12, seven frees, one 65), N Healy (1–1), Damien Hayes (0–6)

Subs: A Kerins for Tierney (50 mins), F Moore for Mahon (50 mins), F Healy (0–2) for Regan (55 mins), David Hayes for Joyce (55 mins), A Smyth (0–1) for N Healy (63 mins)

Antrim Damien Quinn | M Kettle, K Kelly, A Ó Caireallàin | J Campbell (0–1, free), G Bell, G Cunningham | M Scullion, C Herron (0–2) | C McGuckian (0–2), B Herron, P Richmond (0–1) | A Delargy (0–1), J Connolly (0–2), J Scullion

Subs: K McKeegan for J Scullion (27 mins), J McIntosh (0–1, free) for Delargy (half-time), K Stewart for Richmond (37 mins), M Herron for Kelly (48 mins, inj)

Referee J Guinan (Kilkenny)

Group B

July 2 O'Moore Park, Portlaoise

Clare **1–12** Offaly **1–11**

Clare D Fitzgerald | F Lohan, B Lohan, G O'Grady | C Forde, S McMahon (capt, 0–2, a 65 and free), G Quinn | B O'Connell, C Lynch (0–1) | D McMahon, B Nugent, A Markham (0–1) | T Carmody, N Gilligan (0–7, five frees), T Griffin (1–0)

Subs: D Forde for Nugent (24 mins), D Hoey (0–1) for G Quinn (50 mins), A Quinn for D McMahon (61 mins), D O'Connell for D Forde (65 mins), 26 D O'Rourke for T Griffin (71 mins)

Offaly B Mullins (0–1, a free) | K Brady, G Oakley, P Cleary | B Whelahan, R Hannify, B Teehan (capt) | M Cordial, G Hannify (0–1) | B Murphy (0–1), M O'Hara, S Browne (0–1) | B Carroll (0–5, four frees), A Hanrahan (0–2), D Hayden (1–0)

Subs: D Murray for D Hayden (52 mins), J Brady for M O'Hara (59 mins)

Referee G Harrington (Cork)

Group B

July 2 Walsh Park, Waterford

Waterford **4–17** Dublin **1–3**

Waterford S Brenner | T Feeney, F Hartley, J Murray | T Browne (0–1), K McGrath (0–2), E Murphy | B Phelan, E Kelly (0–4) | D Shanahan, M Walsh, P Flynn (1–3, 0–3 from frees) | J Mullane (1–2), S Prendergast (1–2), E McGrath (0–2)

Subs: D Coffey for Murphy, J Kennedy (0–1) for Walsh, B Wall for Browne, P O'Brien (1–0) for E McGrath, G Power for Prendergast

Dublin G Maguire | G O'Meara, S Hiney, J Cullen | D O'Reilly, R Fallon, S O'Shea | D Russell, T Moore | S McDonald, M Breathnach, D Curtin (0–2, frees) | T McGrane (0–1), M Carton, E Carroll

Subs: G Bennett for O'Shea, E Moran for McDonald, P Carton for McGrane, J Kingston (1–0) for Breathnach, S Mullen for Curtin

Referee B White (Tipperary)

Round Three

Group A

July 9 Casement Park, Belfast

Laois **0–21** Antrim **1–16**

Laois P Mullaney | J Walsh, P Cuddy, M McEvoy | J Fitzpatrick, P Mahon, S Dwyer | J Walsh (0–2), J Phelan (0–1) | J Rowney (0–2), L Tynan (0–3), J Young (0–8, six frees, one from 65) | T Fitzgerald (0–1), M Rooney (0–2), D Culleton

Subs: C Healy for Mahon (43 mins), E Meagher (0–1) for Phelan (43 mins), C Brophy (0–1) for Walsh (58 mins), P Russell for Rowney (67 mins)

Antrim Damien Quinn | M Kettle, K Kelly, A Ó Caireallàin | G Cunningham, J Campbell, C Herron | M Scullion, J Connolly (0–1) | K McKeegan (0–3, all from 65s), M Herron (0–1), K Stewart | J McIntosh (1–7, three frees), P Richmond (0–1), A Delargy (0–1)

Subs: C Cunning for Kelly (1 min), J Scullion (0–1) for Ó Caireallàin (10 mins) | B Quinn (0–1) for Delargy (53 mins)

Referee P Greene (Galway)

Group A

July 9 Gaelic Grounds, Limerick

Galway **1–18** Limerick **2–14**

Galway L Donoghue | D Joyce, S Kavanagh, C Coen | D Collins, D Hardiman, O Canning (0–1) | T Ó Regan (0–1, a free), F Healy (0–1) | R Murray (0–1), D Forde, D Tierney (0–1) | G Farragher (0–8, six frees), K Hayes, D Hayes (1–4)

Subs: A Kerins (0–1) for Hayes (48 mins), N Healy for Tierney (65 mins)

Limerick T Houlihan | M Clifford, S Lucey, M Foley | P O'Dwyer, B Geary, P Lawlor | P O'Grady (0–2), D O'Grady | A O'Shaughnessy, O Moran (0–1), N Moran (0–2) | D Ryan (1–0), TJ Ryan (1–2, 0–1 from free), P Kirby (0–6, five frees)

Subs: K Tobin for Clifford (23 mins), P Tobin (0–1) for O'Shaughnessy (43 mins), C Fitzgerald for N Moran (47 mins), J O'Brien for Tobin (53 mins)

Referee B Gavin (Offaly)

Group B

July 9 Parnell Park, Dublin

Offaly **2–15** Dublin **2–14**

Offaly B Mullins | K Brady, G Oakley, P Cleary | Brian Whelahan (0–1, free), R Hannify, B Teehan | M Cordial (1–0), G Hannify | B Murphy (0–1), M O'Hara (0–1), S Browne (0–1) | B Carroll (0–8, four frees), A Hanrahan (0–2), D Hayden (1–0)

Subs: N Coughlan for O'Hara (56 mins), D Murray (0–1) for Browne (58 mins), J Brady for Oakley (65 mins)

Dublin G Maquire | G O'Meara, S Hiney, J Cullen | D O'Reilly, R Fallon (0–1, a 65), G Bennett | D Sweeney (0–2, one sideline cut), D Russell (0–1) | E Moran, J Kingston, T Moore | E Carroll (0–5), M Carton (0–1), K Flynn (0–2)

Subs: C Meehan (0–1) for Cullen (31 mins), L Ryan for Russell (40 mins), S McDonald (1–1) for Kingston (42 mins), P Carton (1–0) for M Carton (48 mins)

Referee J McDonnell (Tipperary)

Group B

July 9 Cusack Park, Ennis

Clare **4–14** Waterford **0–21**

Clare D Fitzgerald | F Lohan (0–1), B Lohan, G O'Grady | D Hoey, S McMahon (0–2, one 65), G Quinn | B O'Connell (0–1), C Lynch | D McMahon (1–1), A Quinn, A Markham (2–0) | T Carmody, N Gilligan (0–6, five frees), T Griffin (1–2)

Subs: D Forde for Quinn (half-time), D O'Rourke (0–1) for Forde (57 mins), C Plunkett for Hoey (65 mins), D O'Connell for Carmody (68 mins), B Lynch for O'Connell (71 mins)

Waterford S Brenner | T Feeney, F Hartley, E Murphy | T Browne (0–1), J Murray, B Phelan | K McGrath (0–4, two frees, one 65), M Walsh (0–1) | D Shanahan (0–3), E Kelly (0–3, one free), E McGrath (0–1) | J Mullane (0–4), S Prendergast, P Flynn (0–4, all frees)

Subs: P O'Brien for Prendergast (58 mins)

Referee M Haverty (Galway)

All-Ireland Hurling Championship Finals

Quarter-finals

July 24 Croke Park, Dublin

Cork **1–18** Waterford **1–13**

Cork D Cusack | P Mulcahy, D O'Sullivan, B Murphy | J Gardiner (0–3, all frees), R Curran, S Óg Ó hAilpín (capt | 0–1) | T Kenny (0–1), J O'Connor (0–1) | B O'Connor (0–4, two frees, one 65), N McCarthy, T McCarthy | K Murphy (Sarsfields | 0–1), B Corcoran (1–1), J Deane (0–5, four frees)

Subs: N Ronan (0–1) for T McCarthy (54 mins), K Murphy (Erin's Own) for N McCarthy (56 mins), C O'Connor for Curran (73 mins)

Waterford C Hennessy | T Feeney, F Hartley, E Murphy | T Browne (0–1), K McGrath (0–1, free), J Murray | D Bennett (0–1), M Walsh | E Kelly, S Prendergast (0–4), D Shanahan (1–0) | J Mullane (0–1), P Flynn (0–5, frees), J Kennedy

Subs: P O'Brien for Kennedy (54 mins), P Foley for Flynn (61 mins)

Referee B Kelly (Westmeath)

July 24 Croke Park, Dublin

Clare **1–20** Wexford **0–12**

Clare D Fitzgerald | F Lohan, B Lohan, G O'Grady | D Hoey, S McMahon (0–2, one 65), G Quinn | B O'Connell (0–1), C Lynch (0–1) | D McMahon (0–4), T Carmody (0–3), A Markham (1–1) | B Nugent, N Gilligan (0–5, four frees), T Griffin (0–3)

Subs: D O'Rourke for B Nugent (41 mins), C Plunkett for D Hoey (41 mins), D O'Connell for T Griffin (66 mins), J Clancy for A Markham (68 mins), A Quinn for N Gilligan (70 mins)

Wexford D Fitzhenry | D O'Connor, D Ryan, K Rossiter | M Travers, D Ruth (0–1, free), D Lyng (0–1, 65) | A Fenlon (0–1), R McCarthy | M Jacob (0–2), E Quigley, P Carley | D Mythen (0–3), M Jordan, R Jacob (0–3 frees)

Subs: R Barry (0–1) for D Ruth (24 mins), T Mahon for P Carley (42 mins), W Doran for R Jacob (61 mins)

Referee B Gavin (Offaly)

July 31 Croke Park, Dublin

Galway **2–20** Tipperary **2–18**

Galway L Donoghue | D Joyce, S Kavanagh (0–1), O Canning | D Hardiman, T Óg Regan, D Collins | F Healy (0–2), D Tierney (0–2) | A Kerins (0–2), D Forde (1–0), N Healy (0–1) | G Farragher (0–9, seven frees, one 65), R Murray (0–3), D Hayes (1–0)

Subs: C Coen for D Collins (43 mins), K Hayes for N Healy 60 (mins)

Tipperary B Cummins | H Maloney, P Maher, P Curran | D Fanning, E Corcoran, D Fitzgerald (0–1) | E Enright, P Kelly (0–4, one free) | C Morrissey, J Devane, B Dunne (capt, 0–1) | E Kelly (1–9, 0–4 frees, 1–0 penalty), M Webster (0–1), T Dunne (1–1)

Subs: C O'Mahoney for Maher (half-time), G O'Grady (0–1) for Devane (42 mins), J Carroll for E Enright (60 mins), P Morrissey for C Morrissey (65 mins), D Egan for O'Grady (69 mins)

Referee A Mac Suibhne (Dublin)

July 3 Croke Park, Dublin

Kilkenny **0–18** Limerick **0–13**

Kilkenny J McGarry | M Kavanagh, J Tennyson, J Ryall | R Mullally, P Barry, JJ Delaney | B Barry (0–1, free), D Lyng (0–1) | M Comerford (0–2), E Larkin, T Walsh (0–2) | R Power, DJ Carey (0–3, one penalty), H Shefflin (0–9, seven frees)

Subs: E Brennan for Power (47 mins), E McCormack for Barry (56), J Hoyne for Larkin (61 mins)

Limerick T Houlihan | D Reale, S Lucey, M Foley | O Moran, B Geary, P Lawlor (0–3, one free, one 65) | P O'Grady (0–1), N Moran (0–1) | D Ryan, J O'Brien (0–1), M Cahill | P Kirby, TJ Ryan (0–6, five frees), A O'Shaughnessy (0–1)

Subs: A O'Connor for Cahill (27 mins), P Tobin for O'Brien (57 mins)

Referee G Harrington (Cork)

Semi-finals

August 14 — Croke Park, Dublin

Cork **0–16** Clare **0–15**

Cork D Cusack | P Mulcahy, D O'Sullivan, B Murphy | J Gardiner (0–2, one free), R Curran, S Óg Ó hAilpín (capt, 0–1) | T Kenny, J O'Connor (0–2) | K Murphy (Sarsfields | 0–1), N McCarthy (0–1), T McCarthy (0–1) | B O'Connor (0–4, two frees, one sideline), B Corcoran, J Deane (0–3)

Subs: K Murphy (Érin's Own) for T McCarthy (half-time), N Ronan (0–1) for Corcoran (50 mins), W Sherlock for Curran (50 mins)

Clare D Fitzgerald | G O'Grady, B Lohan, F Lohan | D Hoey, S McMahon (0–1, 65), G Quinn | B O'Connell (0–1), C Lynch | D McMahon, T Carmody (0–4), A Markham | A Quinn (0–2), N Gilligan (0–4, all frees), T Griffin (0–3)

Subs: J Clancy for O'Connell (63 mins), D O'Rourke for A Quinn (70 mins)

Referee D Murphy (Wexford)

August 21 — Croke Park, Dublin

Galway **5–18** Kilkenny **4–18**

Galway L Donoghue | S Kavanagh, O Canning, D Joyce | D Hardiman, T Óg Regan, D Collins | F Healy (0–1), D Tierney (0–2) | R Murray (0–2), D Forde (0–2), A Kerins | G Farragher (2–9, 0–8 from frees), N Healy (3–0), D Hayes (0–1)

Sub: K Broderick (0–1) for N Healy (67 mins)

Kilkenny J McGarry | M Kavanagh, J Tennyson, J Ryall | R Mullally, P Barry, JJ Delaney | T Walsh (0–1), D Lyng | M Comerford (0–1), H Shefflin (1–9, 0–7 from frees, 0–1 from 65), J Hoyne (1–0) | E Brennan (2–4), DJ Carey, E Larkin (0–1)

Subs: R Power (0–2) for Hoyne (44 mins), B Hogan for Barry (52 mins), E McCormack for Lyng (53 mins), J Tyrell for Larkin (63 mins)

Referee S Roche (Tipperary)

All-Ireland Final

September 11 Croke Park, Dublin

Cork 1–21 Galway 1–16

Cork D Cusack | B Murphy, D O'Sullivan, P Mulcahy | J Gardiner (0–1, a free), R Curran, S Óg Ó hAilpín | T Kenny (0–3), J O'Connor (0–2) | T McCarthy (0–2), N McCarthy (0–1), K Murphy (Sarsfields) | B O'Connor (1–7, two points from frees), B Corcoran (0–2), J Deane (0–3, all frees)

Subs: N Ronan for K Murphy (39 mins), K Murphy (Erin's Own) for N McCarthy (63 mins)

Galway L Donoghue | D Joyce, T Og Regan, O Canning | D Hardiman (0–1), S Kavanagh, D Collins | F Healy (0–2), D Tierney (0–1) | R Murray, D Forde, A Kerins (0–3) | G Farragher (0–8, six frees), N Healy (0–1), D Hayes (1–0)

Subs: K Broderick for N Healy (57 mins), K Hayes for Forde (65 mins)

Referee S Roche (Tipperary)

Tier One Relegation Playoffs

July 23 Croke Park, Dublin

Offaly 5–17 Antrim 0–18

Offaly B Mullins | K Brady, G Oakley, D Franks | Brian Whelahan, R Hannify, B Teehan (capt) | D Hoctor, G Hannify (0–1) | B Murphy (1–3), M O'Hara (0–1), M Cordial (2–3) | B Carroll (1–8), J Brady (1–0), A Hanrahan

Subs: M Corcoran for R Hannify (40–42 mins), D Murray (0–1) for A Hanrahan (52 mins), P Cleary for G Oakley (57 mins), C Parlon for R Hannify (65 mins), P Healion for K Brady, Barry Whelahan for G Hannify (both 68 mins)

Antrim G Magee | M Kettle, G Bell, C Herron (0–1) | G Cunningham, K McKeegan (0–1, 65), J Campbell | M Scullion (0–1), J Connolly (capt, 0–1) | M Herron, C McGuckian (0–1), P Richmond | J McIntosh (0–5, four frees), B McFall (0–6, four frees), A Delargy

Subs: B Herron (0–1) for C McGuckian (31 mins), C Hamill (0–1) for A Delargy (43 mins), M McCambridge for G Cunningham (45 mins), C Cunning for K McKeegan (53 mins), J Scullion for P Richmond (62 mins)

Referee J Sexton (Limerick)

July 23 Dr Cullen Park, Carlow

Dublin **3–13** Laois **1–10**

Dublin G Maguire | G O'Meara, S Hiney, J Cullen | D O'Reilly, R Fallon, G Bennett | D Sweeney (0–2), D Russell (0–1) | E Moran, D Curtin (1–8, 1–5 frees, 0–2 65s), T Moore | E Carroll, M Carton, K Flynn (2–0)

Subs: C Meehan (0–1) for Carton | L Ryan (0–1) for Moran

Laois K Galvin | B Campion, P Cuddy, C Healy | M McEvoy (0–1), John Walsh, S Dwyer (0–1) | James Walsh, E Meagher | J Rowney, J Young (0–7, 0–4 frees, 0–2 sideline cuts), P Russell (1–0) | T Fitzgerald (0–1), M Rooney, D Culleton

Subs: C Brophy for Rooney | P Mahon for Meagher | A Delaney for James Walsh | D Walsh for Campion | C Clear for Russell?

Referee B White (Tipperary)

July 30 Páirc Tailteann, Navan

Laois **1–23** Antrim **1–15**

Laois B Campion | John Walsh, P Cuddy, C Healy | M McEvoy, D Rooney, S Dwyer | James Walsh, J Young (0–11, eight frees) | J Rowney (0–3), L Tynan (0–4), T Fitzgerald | P Russell (1–3), M Rooney, D Culleton

Subs: C Clear for James Walsh (40 mins), C Coonan (0–2) for M Rooney (53 mins), E Meagher for Russell (69 mins), C Brophy for Culleton (70 mins)

Antrim Damien Quinn | M Kettle, G Bell, B Herron | M McCambridge, K McKeegan (0–1), C Herron | C Cunning (0–1), J Connolly (0–3) | B McFall (0–5, four frees), C Hamill (0–2), M Scullion | J McIntosh, P Richmond (1–2), B Quinn

Subs: M Herron (0–1) for McIntosh (half-time), L Watson for Hamill (46 mins), J Scullion for Quinn (47 mins), J Campbell for M Scullion (60 mins)

Referee M Wadding (Waterford)

All-Ireland Hurling Championship Top Scorers

Name	Team	Games	Scored	Total	Average
1 Ger Farragher	Galway	6	3–57	66	11.0
2 James Young	Laois	7	2–53	59	8.4
3 Henry Shefflin	Kilkenny	4	3–37	46	11.5
4 TJ Ryan	Limerick	6	3–36	45	7.5
5 Martin Coulter	Down	4	6–20	38	9.5
6 Eoin Kelly	Tipperary	5	1–35	38	7.6
7 Paul Flynn	Waterford	5	3–26	35	7.0
8 Niall Gilligan	Clare	6	0–33	33	5.5
9 Ben O'Connor	Cork	5	1–25	28	5.6
10 John Deane	Cork	5	1–19	22	4.4

Christy Ring Cup (Hurling Tier Two)

Group A

June 11	Down 3–17	Derry 3–14	Lavey
June 11	Westmeath 4–19	Roscommon 0–11	Mullingar
June 18	Roscommon 1–15	Derry 1–13	Athleague
June 18	Meath 3–16	Westmeath 2–10	Navan
June 25	Derry 1–14	Meath 2–11	Ballinascreen
June 25	Down 5–25	Roscommon 2–8	Ballycran
July 2	Down 3–16	Meath 1–14	Navan
July 2	Westmeath 1–14	Derry 2–8	Mullingar
July 16	Westmeath 3–21	Down 3–14	Newry
July 16	Meath 3–26	Roscommon 1–12	Athleague

	P	W	D	L	F	A	Pts
Down	4	3	0	1	14–72	9–57	6
Westmeath	4	3	0	1	10–64	8–49	6
Meath	4	2	1	1	9–77	7–62	5
Roscommon	4	1	0	3	4–46	13–83	2
Derry	4	0	1	3	7–49	7–57	1

Group B

June 4	Kildare 4–11	Kerry 1–17	Naas
June 4	Carlow 2–13	Wicklow 1–13	Carlow
June 11	Carlow 1–12	Mayo 0–12	Galway
June 11	Kildare 2–13	Wicklow 2–12	Arklow
June 25	Kildare 4–14	Mayo 4–4	Naas
July 2	Kerry 5–16	Mayo 0–12	Galway
July 6	Carlow 0–17	Kildare 1–12	Carlow
July 6	Kerry 3–11	Wicklow 2–14	Tralee
July 16	Kerry 3–15	Carlow 2–8	Tralee
July 16	Wicklow 3–16	Mayo 3–12	Arklow

	P	W	D	L	F	A	Pts
Kildare	4	3	0	1	11–54	7–50	6
Carlow	4	3	0	1	5–50	5–52	6
Kerry	4	2	1	1	12–59	8–46	5
Wicklow	4	1	1	2	9–52	9–52	3
Mayo	4	0	0	4	7–40	13–60	0

Relegation Semi-finals

July 30	Wicklow 2–27	Derry 3–22	Navan
July 31	Roscommon 1–12	Mayo 0–14	Athleague

Relegation Final

August 13	Mayo 4–14	Derry 1–10	Sligo

Tier Two Semi-finals

July 30	Westmeath 7–14	Kildare 1–12	Navan
July 31	Down 4–23	Carlow 1–11	

Tier Two final

August 14	Westmeath 1–23	Down 2–18	Croke Park

Nicky Rackard Cup (Hurling Tier Three)

Group A

June 18	Tyrone 3–17 Fermanagh 3–7	Carrickmore
June 18	Donegal 5–13 Sligo 3–6	Sligo
June 25	Sligo 3–10 Fermanagh 1–15	Enniskillen
June 25	Donegal 3–12 Tyrone 1–11	Letterkenny
July 9	Tyrone 4–16 Sligo 4–11	Carrickmore
July 9	Donegal 6–18 Fermanagh 1–8	Letterkenny

	P	W	D	L	F	A	Pts
Donegal	3	3	0	0	14–43	5–25	6
Tyrone	3	2	0	1	8–44	10–30	4
Sligo	3	1	0	2	10–27	10–44	2
Fermanagh	3	0	0	3	5–30	12–45	0

Group B

June 18	Armagh 1–16 Cavan 1–9	Crossmaglen
June 18	Louth 3–19 Leitrim 0–15	Drogheda
June 25	Louth 4–21 Cavan 2–4	Clones
June 25	Armagh 9–17 Leitrim 3–6	Carrick-on-Shanon
July 9	Louth 2–11 Armagh 2–9	Keady
	Leitrim v Cavan not played	

	P	W	D	L	F	A	Pts
Louth	3	3	0	0	9–51	4–28	6
Armagh	3	2	0	1	12–42	6–25	4
Cavan	2	0	0	2	3–12	5–37	0
Leitrim	2	0	0	2	3–21	12–36	0

Group C

June 18	London 0–21	Longford 2–12	Longford
June 18	Monaghan 0–17	Warwickshire 1–11	Monaghan
June 25	London 1–20	Monaghan 2–11	London
June 25	Longford 1–15	Warwickshire 2–7	Birmingham
July 9	Longford 3–11	Monaghan 2–8	Longford
July 9	London 1–23	Warwickshire 1–6	London

	P	W	D	L	F	A	Pts
London	3	3	0	0	2–64	5–29	6
Longford	3	2	0	1	6–38	4–36	4
Monaghan	3	1	0	2	4–36	5–42	2
Warwickshire	3	0	0	3	4–24	2–55	0

Play-off

July 16	Longford 2–14	Armagh 1–14 (AET)	Cavan

Quarter-final

July 24	Tyrone 3–14	Longford 3–13	Cavan

Semi-finals

August 6	Louth 3–10	Tyrone 1–8	Drogheda
August 7	London 3–13	Donegal 1–10	Ballybofey

Nicky Rackard Cup final

August 21	London 5–8	Louth 1–5	Croke Park

Leinster Senior Football Championship

First Round

May 8 Páirc Tailteann, Navan

Offaly **1–15** Louth **1–6**

Offaly P Kelly | C Daly, C Evans, S Brady | B Mooney (capt), S Sullivan, K Slattery | C McManus (0–3, two frees), A McNamee | J Reynolds (1–0), D Hunt (0–1), N Coughlan | C Quinn (0–3, two frees), N McNamee (0–5), J Coughlan (0–3)

Subs: M Daly for J Reynolds (55 mins), J Kenny for J Coughlan (68 mins)

Louth S McCoy | D Mackin, S Gerrard, J Carr | C Sheridan, A Hoey (0–1), A Page | D Deveney, J Kermath | P Keenan (1–0), N McDonnell, R Carroll | M Stanfield (capt), JP Rooney (0–1), D Clarke (0–4)

Subs: T O'Brien for D Deveney (50 mins), B Reilly for J Carr (54 mins), P Matthews for N McDonnell (56 mins)

Referee M Hughes (Tyrone)

May 15 Croke Park, Dublin

Dublin **2–23** Longford **0–10**

Dublin S Cluxton | P Griffin, P Christie, S O'Shaughnessy | P Casey, B Cahill, C Goggins (0–1) | C Whelan (0–1), S Ryan (0–2) | C Moran (0–1), A Brogan (1–3), B Cullen (0–2) | J Sherlock (0–1), C Keaney (1–4), T Quinn (0–5, three frees, one sideline)

Subs: M Vaughan (0–2, both frees) for Moran (50 mins), D O'Mahony for Whelan (58 mins), D O'Callaghan (0–1) for Quinn (59 mins), D Homan for Keaney (64 mins), S Connell for Brogan (67 mins)

Longford D Sheridan | D Brady, C Conefrey, E Ledwith | D Glennon, D Reilly, A O'Connor | P O'Hara, B McElvaney | J Martin (0–1), P Barden, P Dowd | B Kavanagh (0–1), N Sheridan (0–1), P Davis (0–7, six frees)

Subs: S Lynch for Glennon (33 mins), M Connor for McElvaney (41 mins), T Glendenning for O'Hara, D Corcoran for Lynch (58 mins), M Lennon for Martin (59 mins)

Referee P Russell (Tipperary)

May 15 Croke Park, Dublin

Kildare **1–17** Wicklow **2–12**

Kildare E Murphy | A Rainbow, D Hendy, P Mullarkey | M Foley (0–1), G Ryan, D Lyons | K Brennan (0–1), W Heffernan | E Callaghan (0–3), P O'Neill, R Sweeney (0–1) | T Fennin (1–3, 0–1 from a free), S McKenzie Smith, J Doyle (0–7, three frees)

Subs: M Hogarty for P O'Neill (half-time), K Ennis (0–1) for D Hendy (40 mins), D Early for K Brennan (46 mins), R Glavin for S McKenzie Smith (51 mins)

Wicklow R Hollingsworth | C Hyland, B Daly, T Burke | K Manning, D Ó'hAnnaidh, B Ó'hAnnaidh | D Dillon (0–1), J Stafford | D Smullen, L Glynn (0–1), T Harney (1–1) | P Earls (1–6, 0–2 from frees), W O'Gorman (0–2), A Ellis (0–1)

Subs: G Duffy for K Manning (25 mins), JP Davis for T Harney (53 mins), D O'Sullivan for A Ellis (61 mins), J Daniels for JP Davis (66 mins)

Referee F Flynn (Leitrim)

Quarter–finals

May 29 Croke Park, Dublin

Kildare **0–14** Westmeath **0–11**

Kildare E Murphy | A Rainbow, P Mullarkey, J Lonergan | M Wright, G Ryan, K Ennis | K Brennan, M Foley (0–1) | E Callaghan, D Earley (0–1), R Sweeney (0–1) | T Fennin (0–4, three frees), R Glavin, J Doyle (0–6, one free)

Subs: D McCormack (0–1) for Glavin (40 mins), S McKenzie–Smith for Callaghan (57 mins), D Hendy for Mullarkey (61 mins), W Heffernan for Foley (68 mins)

Westmeath G Connaughton | J Davitt, D Healy, J Keane | M Ennis, D Heavin, D Kilmartin | R O'Connell, D O'Shaughnessy | A Mangan (0–1), F Wilson (0–1), P Mulvihill (0–1) | David Glennon, Denis Glennon, D Dolan (0–7, three frees)

Subs: J McAteer for Kilmartin (30 mins), J Fallon for Wilson (46 mins), G Dolan for David Glennon (58 mins), D Duffy for Davitt (61 mins), P Conway (0–1) for Denis Glennon (66 mins)

Referee M Daly (Mayo)

May 29 Croke Park, Dublin

Laois **1–10** Offaly **1–8**

Laois F Byron | A Fennelly, D Rooney, J Higgins | C Begley, T Kelly, P McMahon | P Clancy (0–1), N Garvan (0–1) | R Munnelly (1–4, 0–3 from frees), I Fitzgerald, G Kavanagh | D Brennan (0–1), K Fitzpatrick (0–1), C Conway (0–2, one free)

Subs: B Sheehan for Kavanagh (31 mins), S Kelly for Fitzgerald (half-time), B McDonald for Brennan (69 mins)

Offaly P Kelly | C Daly, C Evans, S Brady | B Mooney, S Sullivan, K Slattery | C McManus, A McNamee | C Quinn (0–1), M Daly (1–1), N Coughlan (0–2) | J Coughlan(0–1, free), P Kellaghan (0–1), N McNamee (0–1)

Subs: J Reynolds (0–1) for J Coughlan (42 mins), J Kenny for Kellaghan (63 mins), J Grennan for Quinn (69 mins)

Referee M Collins (Cork)

June 5 Croke Park, Dublin

Wexford **3–12** Carlow **2–10**

Wexford J Cooper | N Murphy, P Wallace, C Morris | D Breen (0–1), D Murphy, P Curtis | N Lambert, D Fogarty (1–1) | R Barry (0–1), D Foran, S Cullen (0–1) | PJ Banville (1–0), P Colfer (0–1), M Forde (1–6, 0–2 from frees)

Subs: D Kinsella for Lambert (21 mins), J Darcy for Morris (43 mins), J Hegarty for Foran (54 mins)

Carlow J Brennan | B Farrell, C McCarthy, P Cashin | J Hayden, L Murphy, R Sinnott | P Walsh, T Walsh (0–1) | B Carberry (0–1), R Walker, P Hickey (0–2, both frees) | S Rea (1–6, four frees, a penalty), M Carpenter (1–0), M Brennan

Subs: P Kelly for Farrell (half-time), J Nevin for Walker (43 mins), W Power for Hayden, J Byrne for Hickey (both 65 mins), D Kelly for Rea (68 mins)

Referee J McKee (Armagh)

June 5 Croke Park, Dublin

Dublin **1–12** Meath **1–10**

Dublin S Cluxton | P Griffin, P Christie, S O'Shaughnessy | P Casey, B Cahill (0–1), C Goggins | C Whelan, S Ryan | C Moran, A Brogan (1–3), B Cullen (0–1) | J Sherlock (0–1), C Keaney (0–3, one free), T Quinn (0–1)

Subs: S Connell for Moran (half-time), M Vaughan (0–2, both frees) for Sherlock (half-time), D Homan for Quinn (60 mins), P Andrews for Casey (66 mins)

Meath D Gallagher | M O'Reilly, K Reilly, N McKeigue | D Crimmins, D Fay, C King | N Crawford (0–1), A Moyles | N Kelly (0–1), P Byrne, G Geraghty (0–3) | J Sheridan (1–0), B Farrell (0–4), S Bray

Subs: P Reynolds for Kelly (43 mins), J Cullinane for N McKeigue (blood sub for Byrne 50 mins, Byrne back on for Crimmins 72 mins), D Regan (0–1) for Sheridan (60 mins), O Murphy for Crawford (74 mins)

Referee J Bannon (Longford)

Semi-finals

June 19 Croke Park, Dublin

Dublin **1–17** Wexford **2–10**

Dublin S Cluxton | P Griffin, P Christie, S O'Shaughnessy | C Goggins, B Cahill, P Casey | C Whelan (0–1), S Ryan | C Moran (0–2), A Brogan (0–1), B Cullen (0–2) | M Vaughan, C Keaney (0–1), T Quinn (0–10, seven frees, one 45)

Subs: P Andrews for O'Shaughnessy (32 mins), S Connell for Vaughan (half-time), J Sherlock (1–0) for Moran (50 mins), D Homan for Ryan (66 mins)

Wexford J Cooper | C Morris, P Wallace, N Murphy | P Curtis, K Kennedy (0–2), D Murphy | N Lambert, D Fogarty (0–1) | R Barry (1–1, goal from penalty), S Cullen, D Kinsella | PJ Banville (1–2), P Colfer, M Forde (0–3, two frees)

Subs: J Hudson for Colfer (half-time), D Foran for Banville (55 mins), D Breen for Curtis (57 mins), J Darcy for Lambert (62 mins)

Referee B Crowe (Cavan)

June 19 Croke Park, Dublin

Laois **0–21** Kildare **0–9**

Laois F Byron | A Fennelly, D Rooney, J Higgins | C Begley, T Kelly, P McMahon | P Clancy, N Garvan (0–1) | R Munnelly (0–7, four frees), B Brennan (0–4), B Sheehan (0–2) | C Conway (0–5, three frees), K Fitzpatrick (0–1), B McDonald (0–1)

Subs: G Kavanagh for B McDonald, S Cooke for K Fitzpatrick (both 58 mins), P McDonald for C Begley (65 mins)

Kildare E Murphy | A McLoughlin, A Rainbow, J Lonergan | M Wright, G Ryan, K Ennis | K Brennan, M Foley (0–2) | D McCormack (0–2), D Earley, R Sweeney | T Fennin (0–1, one free), R Glavin, J Doyle (0–2, one 45)

Subs: E Callaghan for M Wright (23 mins), S McKenzie Smith (0–1) for R Glavin (41 mins), W Heffernan (0–1) for K Brennan (45 mins), A Barry for D McCormack (54 mins)

Referee J Geaney (Cork)

Final

July 17 Croke Park, Dublin

Dublin **0–14** Laois **0–13**

Dublin S Cluxton | P Griffin, P Christie, S O'Shaughnessy (0–1) | C Goggins, B Cahill, P Casey | C Whelan (0–1), S Ryan | C Moran (0–1), A Brogan (0–1), B Cullen (0–3) | J Sherlock (0–2), C Keaney (0–1), T Quinn (0–4, three frees, one 45)

Subs: P Andrews for Christie (18 mins), S Connell for Goggins (half-time), D Homan for Ryan (60 mins)

Laois F Byron | A Fennelly, D Rooney, J Higgins | C Begley, T Kelly, P McMahon | P Clancy, N Garvan (0–2) | R Munnelly (0–5, two frees), B Brennan, B Sheehan | C Conway (0–4, two frees), K Fitzpatrick, B McDonald

Subs: D Brennan (0–2) for B Brennan (27 mins), M Dunne for McDonald (51 mins), D Conroy for Rooney (51 mins)

Referee J McQuillan (Cavan)

Munster Senior Football Championship

First Round

May 29 Cusack Park, Ennis

Clare **2–14** Waterford **2–10**

Clare D O'Brien | P Gallagher, K Dilleen, B Moloney | A Clohessy, D Kelly, M O'Connell | G Quinlan (capt), D Russell (0–1) | P O'Dwyer (0–1), E Coughlan (1–3), O O'Dwyer (0–2, all frees) | R Donnelly (1–6, 0–4 from frees), D Nealon, M O'Dwyer

Subs: G Tubridy for Moloney, S Hickey (0–1) for Neylon, R Slattery for Dilleen, M O'Shea for M O'Dwyer

Waterford T Wall | P Ogle, L Hurney, N Hennessy | A Heffernan, M Ahern, T Costelloe (capt) | S Briggs (0–1), A Hubbard | K O'Keeffe, W Kavanagh, G Power | N Curran (1–8, 0–7 from frees), G Hurney (1–1), L Ó Lionáin

Subs: E Walsh for L Hurney, J Wall for Kavanagh, S Cunningham for Wall, F Halpin for Ó Lionáin

Referee P McGovern (Galway)

May 29 Semple Stadium, Thurles

Kerry **2–22** Tipperary **0–13**

Kerry D Murphy | A O'Mahony, M McCarthy, T O'Sullivan | T Ó Sé, E Fitzmaurice, M Ó Sé (0–1) | D Ó Sé, W Kirby | P Galvin, E Brosnan (1–4), L Hassett (0–3) | C Cooper (1–5), D O'Sullivan, MF Russell (0–8, four frees, one 45)

Subs: P Kelly for Kirby (51 mins), B Sheehan (0–1) for Galvin (54 mins), D Ó Cinnéide for D O'Sullivan (54 mins), B Guiney for T Ó Sé (62 mins), D Quill for Cooper (63 mins)

Tipperary P Fitzgerald | D Byrne, N Curran, P King | P Morrissey (0–1), B Lacey, R Costigan | K Mulryan (0–1), F O'Callaghan (0–1) | G Burke, L English, P Cahill | B Hickey (0–1), D Browne (0–9, six frees), B Mulvihill

Subs: N Fitzgerald for Burke (57 mins), D O'Brien for Cahill (61 mins), E Hanrahan for English (67 mins)

Referee D Fahy (Longford)

Semi-finals

June 12 — Cusack Park, Ennis

Cork **0–18** Clare **0–6**

Cork K O'Dwyer | N Geary, S Levis (capt), G Murphy | E Sexton, A Lynch, Martin Cronin | G Canty, D Kavanagh | J Masters (0–5, one free, one 45), C McCarthy (0–2), N Murphy (0–1) | J Hayes (0–1), F Gould (0–1), Micheál Ó Croinín (0–6, three frees)

Subs: N O'Leary for Lynch, K O'Sullivan (0–1) for Hayes, A Cronin (0–1) for Gould, D Hurley for N Murphy, K O'Connor for G Murphy

Clare D O'Brien | P Gallagher, K Dilleen, M O'Connell | A Clohessy, D Kelly, R Slattery | G Quinlan (capt), D Russell (Kilkee) | O O'Dwyer (0–2, one free), P O'Dwyer, E Coughlan | R Donnelly (0–3, one free), S Hickey (0–1), M O'Dwyer

Subs: G Tubridy for O'Connell, M O'Shea for Kelly, D Callanan for Clohessy, D Russell (Eire Óg) for Quinlan, S O'Meara for Dilleen

Referee P Fox (Westmeath)

June 19 — Gaelic Grounds, Limerick

Kerry **2–10** Limerick **0–10**

Kerry D Murphy | M Ó Sé, M McCarthy, T O'Sullivan | A O'Mahony, E Fitzmaurice (0–1), T Ó Sé | D Ó Sé, P Kelly | P Galvin, E Brosnan, L Hassett (0–1) | MF Russell, D O'Sullivan (capt), C Cooper (2–5, 0–3 from frees)

Subs: D Ó Cinnéide (0–1, free) for Russell (half-time), S Moynihan (0–1) for T O'Sullivan (55 mins), W Kirby for Kelly (56 mins), B Sheehan (0–1) for Hassett (61 mins), D Quill for D O'Sullivan (65 mins)

Limerick S O'Donnell | T Stack, J McCarthy (0–1), C Mullane | P Browne, S Lucey, S Lavin (0–1) | J Quane, J Galvin | M Crowley, M Gavin (0–7, all frees), S Kelly | C Fitzgerald (0–1), J Stokes, S Buckley

Subs: M O'Riordan for Browne (40 mins), M O'Brien for Crowley (62 mins), J Murphy for Quane (62 mins) Red card: O'Riordan (56 mins)

Referee E Murtagh (Longford)

Final

July 10 Páirc Uí Chaoimh, Cork

Kerry **1–11** Cork **0–11**

Cork K O'Dwyer | N Geary, G Canty, G Murphy | N O'Leary (0–1), A Lynch, E Sexton (capt) | D Kavanagh, N Murphy | J Masters (0–3, three frees), C McCarthy (0–1), K McMahon | J Hayes (0–2), F Gould (0–1), M Ó Cróinín (0–2, frees)

Subs: K O' Connor for Geary (half-time), P Clifford (0–1) for Ó Cróinín, BJ O'Sullivan for Goold (both 46 mins), K O'Sullivan for Hayes (64 mins), A Cronin for K McMahon (65 mins)

Kerry D Murphy | A O'Mahony, M McCarthy, T O'Sullivan | T Ó Sé (0–2), S Moynihan, M Ó Sé (0–1) | D Ó Sé (0–1), E Brosnan (0–1) | P Galvin, D O'Sullivan (1–0, capt), L Hassett (0–1) | C Cooper (0–2), D Ó Cinnéide (0–1), MF Russell (0–2, one free)

Subs: W Kirby for Galvin (52 mins), E Fitzmaurice for D Ó Sé (57 mins), B Sheehan for D O'Sullivan (59 mins), K Donaghy for Hassett (62 mins), R O'Connor for Brosnan (67 mins)

Referee D Coldrick (Meath)

Ulster Senior Football Championship

First Round

May 15 St Tiernach's Park, Clones

Armagh **2–12** Fermanagh **1–7**

Armagh P Hearty | A Mallon, F Bellew, K McElvanna | A Kernan, K McGeeney, C McKeever | J Toal, P McGrane | M O'Rourke (0–2), J McEntee (0–1), O McConville (0–4, two frees) | S McDonnell (0–1, free), R Clarke (1–1), B Mallon (1–3)

Subs: P Loughran for J Toal (58 mins), A McCann for K McElvanna (65 mins), A O'Rourke for C McKeever (65 mins), M Mackin for S McDonnell (65 mins), P Duffy for A Mallon (65 mins)

Fermanagh N Tinney | S Goan, B Owens, R McCluskey | R Johnston, S McDermott, D O'Reilly | L McBarron (0–1), J Sherry (0–1) | E Maguire, T Brewster, M Little (0–4, three frees) | A Little, S Maguire, C Bradley

Subs: N Bogue for D Reilly (15 mins), R Gallagher (1–1, 50), for T Brewster (34 mins), M McGrath for S Maguire (52 mins), R Keenan for C Bradley (53 mins), M Lilley for L McBarron (60 mins)

Referee D Coldrick (Meath)

Quarter-finals

May 22 — Healy Park, Omagh

Down **1–6** Tyrone **1–13**

Tyrone P McConnell | R McMenamin, C Lawn, S Sweeney | C Gormley, G Devlin, P Jordan (0–1) | C Holmes, S Cavanagh (0–2) | P Donnelly (0–1), M Penrose (1–1), R Mellon | O Mulligan (0–3, all frees), S O'Neill (0–2), E McGinley (0–1)

Subs: P Canavan (0–2, one free) for Mellon (51 mins), J McMahon for Donnelly (54 mins), M Murphy for Penrose (71 mins)

Down B McVeigh | M Cole, A Scullion, G Barry | B Grant, A O'Prey, D Rafferty | A Molloy, D Gordon | L Doyle (0–2, one free), A Rogers (0–3), J Clarke | C Laverty, B Coulter (1–1), R Murtagh

Subs: R Sexton for Clarke (43 mins), S Ward for Laverty (56 mins), A Rice for Barry (61 mins), D Hughes for Murtagh (65 mins), J Doran for Molloy (71 mins)

Referee M Deegan (Laois)

May 29 — Breffni Park, Cavan

Antrim **0–11** Cavan **0–11**

Cavan J Reilly | M Hannon, D Rabbitte, K Fannin | K Crotty, P Reilly, M Cahill | D McCabe (0–1, free), P McKenna (0–1) | M McKeever, N Walsh, F O'Reilly (0–5, three 45s, two frees) | J O'Reilly, J Tierney, L Reilly (0–4)

Subs: Paul Brady for McKeever (46 mins), Paddy Brady for Tierney (56 mins) M Graham for Jason Reilly (71 mins)

Antrim P Murray | C Brady, A McClean, D Gault | T Scullion, G Adams, S Kelly | J Quinn, M McCarry | C Close (0–3, all frees), B Herron, T O'Neill | K Brady (0–2), M McCann, K Madden (0–6, all frees)

Subs: S Devlin for Adams (half-time), A Gallagher for McCann (45 mins), K Murray for Gault (63 mins)

Referee M Ryan (Limerick)

June 4 Replay Casement Park, Belfast

Cavan **1–15** Antrim **2–6**

Cavan J Reilly | M Hannon, D Rabbitte, K Fannin | P Brady, Peter Reilly, M Cahill | D McCabe (0–1, free), P McKenna (0–1) | M McKeever, N Walsh, F O'Reilly (0–4, three frees) | J O'Reilly (1–4), Pauric Reilly, L Reilly (0–4)

Subs: J Tierney for McKeever (39 mins), P Cahill for Fannin (64 mins), C Galligan (0–1) for M Cahill (68 mins)

Antrim P Murray | K Murray, A McLean, S Devlin | T Scullion, G Adams, S Kelly (0–1) | J Quinn, P Logan | C Close (0–1), P Doherty (2–0), T O'Neill | K Brady (0–2), M McCann, K Madden

Subs: B Herron for McCann (32), K McGourty (0–2) for O'Neill (half-time), T Convery for K Murray (47 mins), C McGourty for Madden (55 mins), M McCrory for Logan (65 mins)

Referee P McEnaney (Monaghan)

June 5 St Tiernach's Park, Clones

Derry **1–17** Monaghan **2–8**

Derry B Gillis | K McGuckin, K McCloy, G O'Kane | P Wilson, SM Lockhart, P Kelly | F Doherty, Patsy Bradley (0–1) | J McBride, M Lynch, P Murphy (0–1) | Paul Bradley, Paddy Bradley (1–10, 0–2 from frees), E Muldoon (0–4, three frees)

Subs: E Bradley for McBride (11 mins), C Devlin (0–1) for Paul Bradley (ht) | M Kelly for E Muldoon (70 mins)

Monaghan S Duffy | G McQuaid, V Corey, C Flanagan | D Freeman, J Coyle, D McArdle | F Duffy, E Lennon | S Gollogly (0–1), P Finlay (0–3, all frees), N Corrigan | T Freeman (0–3), R Ronaghan, D Clerkin

Subs: H McElroy for D Freeman (40 mins), S McManus (1–1) for Duffy (41 mins), F Smith for McQuaid (48 mins), D McKernan for Corrigan (51 mins), J McElroy (1–0) for Gollogly (58 mins)

Referee M Duffy (Sligo)

June 12 St Tiernach's Park, Clones

Armagh **0–12** Donegal **0–12**

Armagh P Hearty | A Mallon, F Bellew, P McCormack | A Kernan (0–2, one free), K McGeeney, C McKeever | J Toal, P McGrane (0–1) | M O'Rourke, J McEntee, O McConville (0–2, one free) | S McDonnell (0–2), R Clarke (0–3), B Mallon (0–2)

Subs: A McCann for McCormack (42 mins), A O'Rourke for McKeever (42 mins), P McKeever for O'Rourke (46 mins), P Loughran for McEntee (59 mins)

Donegal M Boyle | K Lacy, R Sweeney, E McGee | D Diver, B Monaghan, S Carr | N Gallagher, K Cassidy | C Toye (0–1), B Roper (0–1), M Hegarty | C McFadden (0–5, four frees), A Sweeney (0–4, one free), B Devenney (0–1, free)

Subs: R Kavanagh for Devenney (60 mins)

Referee J McQuillan (Cavan)

June 18 Replay St Tiernach's Park, Clones

Armagh **3–11** Donegal **1–10**

Armagh P Hearty | A Mallon, F Bellew, E McNulty | A Kernan (0–3, two frees), K McGeeney, A McCann | P Loughran, P McGrane | M O'Rourke (0–2), J McEntee, O McConville (0–1) | S McDonnell (1–3, 0–1 from free), R Clarke (1–1), B Mallon

Subs: M Mackin (1–0) for R Clarke (half-time inj), A O Rourke (0–1) for A McCann (42 mins), T McEntee for J McEntee (46 mins), J Toal for P McGrane (64 mins), K McElvanna for A Mallon (64 mins)

Donegal M Boyle | N McCready, E McGee, K Lacy | S Carr, B Monaghan, D Diver | B Boyle, N Gallagher | C Toye, M Hegarty, B Roper | C McFadden (0–6, five frees, one 45), A Sweeney, B Devenney (1–4, all frees)

Subs: R Kavanagh for N McCready (half-time), S McDermott for B Boyle (43 mins), B Dunnion for D Diver (63 mins), R Bradley for B Devenney (65 mins)

Referee M Deegan (Laois)

Semi-finals

June 19 St Tiernach's Park, Clones

Tyrone **0–10** Cavan **1–7**

Tyrone P McConnell | R McMenamin (0–2), C Lawn, S Sweeney | D Harte, G Devlin, P Jordan | C Gormley, S Cavanagh | B Donnelly, P Canavan (0–3, two frees), M Penrose | O Mulligan (0–1), S O'Neill (0–4, two frees), E McGinley

Subs: B Dooher for Penrose, B McGuigan for Donnelly (both 35 mins), R Mellon for Dooher (65 mins), J Devine for McConnell (75 mins)

Cavan J Reilly | M Hannon, D Rabbitte, K Fannin | P Brady, Peter Reilly, Pádraig Reilly | N Walsh, P McKenna | M Cahill (0–1), M McKeever, F O'Reilly | J O'Reilly (1–2, 0–1 from free), A Forde, L Reilly (0–3, one free)

Subs: M Lyng (0–1, one free) for A Forde (44 mins), D McCabe for F Reilly (54 mins), S Johnston for Peter Reilly (60 mins)

Referee G Ó Conamha (Galway)

June 25 Replay St Tiernach's Park, Clones

Tyrone **3–19** Cavan **0–7**

Tyrone J Devine | R McMenamin, C Lawn, S Sweeney | D Harte, G Devlin, P Jordan (1–1) | C Gormley (0–2), S Cavanagh (0–1) | B Dooher, B McGuigan, M Penrose (0–1) | P Canavan (1–7, three frees, one 45), S O'Neill (1–5, 0–1 from free), E McGinley (0–1)

Subs: M McGee for McMenamin (50 mins), J McMahon for Lawn (60 mins), O Mulligan (0–1) for Dooher (63 mins), E Bradley for Sweeney (69 mins), C McCullagh for Canavan (69 mins)

Cavan J Reilly | M Hannon, D Rabbitte, K Fannin | A Forde, Peter Reilly, Pauric Reilly | N Walsh, P McKenna | M Cahill, M McKeever (0–2, two frees) | M Lyng (0–1, 45) | J O'Reilly (0–3), D McCabe, L Reilly

Subs: J Jordan for Fannin (14 mins), F O'Reilly (0–1, free) for McCabe (half-time), Paddy Brady for Lyng (56 mins)

Referee P Russell (Tipperary)

June 26 Casement Park, Belfast

Armagh **1–11** Derry **0–10**

Armagh P Hearty | A Mallon, F Bellew, E McNulty | A Kernan (0–4, three frees), K McGeeney (capt), A O'Rourke | P Loughran, P McGrane | M O'Rourke (0–1), J McEntee, O McConville (0–1) | S McDonnell (0–2, one free), R Clarke (0–1), B Mallon (0–2)

Subs: T McEntee for P Loughran, J Toal (1–0) for J McEntee (both 48 mins), S Kernan for B Mallon (64), M Mackin for R Clarke (65 mins), C McKeever for A Kernan (69 mins)

Derry B Gillis | K McGuckin, K McCloy, G O'Kane | P Wilson, SM Lockhart, P Kelly | F Doherty, Patsy Bradley | P Murphy (0–1), M Lynch (0–1), E Bradley (0–2) | C Devlin, Paddy Bradley (capt) (0–5, two frees), E Muldoon (0–1, free)

Subs: P McFlynn for P Kelly (50 mins), J McBride for C Devlin (55 mins), F McEldowney for P Wilson (59 mins), M Kelly for G O'Kane (68 mins)

Referee M Monahan (Kildare)

Final

July 10 Croke Park, Dublin

Armagh **2–8** Tyrone **0–14**

Armagh P Hearty | A Mallon, F Bellew, E McNulty | A Kernan (0–1, free), K McGeeney, A O'Rourke | J Toal, P McGrane (0–1) | M O'Rourke, T McEntee, O McConville (1–1) | S McDonnell (1–2, 0–1 from free, 0–1 from 45), R Clarke (0–1), B Mallon (0–1)

Subs: P McKeever for M O'Rourke (25 mins), P Loughran for Toal (33 mins), J McEntee (0–1) for McEntee (45 mins), M Mackin for B Mallon (68 mins), C McKeever for Kernan (68 mins)

Tyrone J Devine | R McMenamin, C Lawn, S Sweeney | D Harte, G Devlin, P Jordan | C Gormley (0–1), S Cavanagh (0–1) | B Dooher (0–2), B McGuigan, M Penrose | P Canavan, S O'Neill (0–10, four frees), E McGinley

Subs: M Harte for Canavan (half-time), O Mulligan for Penrose (half-time), J McMahon for D Harte (51 mins)

Referee J Bannon (Longford)

July 23 Replay Croke Park, Dublin

Armagh **0–13** Tyrone **0–11**

Armagh P Hearty | A Mallon, F Bellew, E McNulty | A Kernan (0–2, one free), K McGeeney, A O'Rourke | P Loughran, P McGrane | C McKeever, J McEntee, O McConville (0–3, two frees) | S McDonnell (0–3, two frees, one 45), R Clarke (0–3), B Mallon (0–1)

Subs: P McKeever (0–1) for B Mallon (57 mins), A McCann for A O'Rourke (57 mins) | Red card: K McKeever (53 mins)

Tyrone P McConnell | R McMenamin (0–1), C Lawn, S Sweeney | D Harte (0–1), G Devlin, P Jordan | C Gormley, S Cavanagh | B Dooher (0–1), B McGuigan (0–1), M Penrose (0–1) | R Mellon (0–1), S O'Neill (0–5, two frees), E McGinley

Subs: P Canavan for M Penrose (53 mins), O Mulligan for B McGuigan (53 mins) | Red cards: P Canavan (53 mins), S O'Neill (62)

Referee M Collins (Cork)

Connacht Senior Football Championship

First Round

May 15 Gaelic Park, New York

Galway **3–14** New York **0–6**

Galway A Keane | R Fahey, K Fitzgerald, V Feeney | D Meehan, D Burke, M Comer | J Bergin (0–2), N Coleman | J Devane, P Clancy (1–2), M Donnellan (0–2) | M Meehan (2–2), P Joyce (0–2), M Clancy (0–3)

Subs: B Cullinane for Coleman, T Giblin for Feeney, S Óg de Paor for Burke, S Walsh (0–1) for Clancy, C Monaghan for Fitzgerald

New York E Byrne | P Murphy, J Mitchell, N Corbett | M Smith, P O'Connor, S Campbell | C Loughane, S Lordan | R Garvey, R Moran, M Dobbin | PJ Ward (0–4), B Newman, P Smith

Subs: M Keaveney (0–1) for Ward, M Mitchell (0–1) for Smith, T Healy for Loughane, M Donaghy for Garvey, S Flynn for Newman

Referee J White (Donegal)

May 22 — Carrick-on-Shannon

Leitrim **1–11** Sligo **0–9**

Leitrim C McCrann | M McGuinness, J McKeon, D Reynolds | N Gilbane, B McWeeney, S Foley | C Carroll, G McCluskey | J Goldrick (1–0), B Prior, M Foley (0–3, two frees) | J Glancy (0–3), C Regan, D Maxwell (0–3)

Subs: D Duignan (0–2) for Gilbane (51 mins)

Sligo P Greene | P Naughton, N McGuire, B Phillips | D Durkin, J Martyn, J Davey (0–2, one 45) | S Davey (0–2, frees), E O'Hara | B Egan, J McPartland (0–1), B Curran (0–1) | A Marren, M Brehony (0–3, two frees), G McGowan *Subs*: P Doohan for Naughton (29 mins), K O'Neill for Durkin (41 mins), D McTiernan for McGowan (42 mins), D McGarty for Curran (48 mins)

Referee S McGonigle (Donegal)

May 29 — Ruislip, London

Roscommon **0–12** London **1–8**

Roscommon S Curran | B McNeela, C Beirne, J Rogers | M Ryan D Casey, F Grehan | S O'Neill (0–1), M Finneran (0–1) | E Kenny (0–2), S Lohan (0–3), K Mannion | G Cox, N Dineen, G Heneghan (0–5, four frees)

Subs: S McDermott for C Byrne, J Dunning for E Kenny, J Whyte for F Grehan, J Egan for N Dineen

London P O'Dowd | P Callaghan, D McKenna, J Rafter | J Niblock, J McKevitt, P McConigley | S Hehir, E Brennan (0–1) | P Quinn (0–1), P Hehir, P Quirke | S Doran, J McInerney (1–0), B Solan (0–5, four frees)

Subs: J Coffey (0–1) for P Quirke, V O'Sullivan for P Callaghan

Referee S McCormack (Meath)

Semi-finals

June 12 — Pearse Stadium, Galway

Galway **1–11** Leitrim **1–8**

Galway B O'Donoghue | A Burke, K Fitzgerald, V Feeney | D Meehan, D Burke, M Comer | N Coleman, B Cullinane (0–1) | P Clancy (1–1), M Donnellan (0–4, three frees), M Clancy (0–1) | M Meehan (0–2, both frees), D Savage (0–1), S Armstrong (0–1)

Subs: T Giblin for Feeney (30 mins), N Coyne for Comer (half-time), J Bergin for Armstrong, (56 mins), P Joyce for Savage (66 mins), T Meehan for A Burke (68 mins)

Leitrim C McCrann | D Reynolds, J McKeon, M McGuinness | N Gilbane, B McWeeney, S Foley | C Carroll, G McCloskey | J Goldrick, B Prior (0–1), C Regan | M Foley (0–3, one free), D Maxwell (0–3), J Glancy (0–1)

Subs: D Duignan for Gilbane (23 mins), D Brennan (1–0) for Goldrick (half-time), G Phelan for McCrann (49 mins)

Referee M Monagh (Kildare)

June 19 — Hyde Park, Roscommon

Mayo **1–16** Roscommon **0–11**

Mayo D Clarke | K Higgins, D Heaney, G Ruane | C Moran, J Nallen, G Mullins | R McGarrity, S Fitzmaurice | A Moran (0–2), C McDonald (0–2, one free), A Dillon (0–1, free) | C Mortimer (1–4, three frees), BJ Padden (0–2), S Carolan (0–2)

Subs: J Gill (0–1) for A Dillon (half-time), T Mortimer (0–2) for S Carolan (55 mins), B Moran for S Fitzmaurice (67 mins)

Roscommon S Curran | B McNeela, J Whyte, S McDermott | M Ryan, D Casey, J Rogers (0–1) | S O'Neill, B Higgins | K Mannion, F Grehan (0–1), E Kenny | G Cox (0–2 frees), S Lohan, G Heneghan (0–6, 3 frees)

Subs: M Beirne for S McDermott (half-time), J Dunning (0–1) for G Cox (42 mins), M Finneran for E Kenny (46 mins), F Dolan for M Beirne (60 mins)

Referee M Collins (Cork)

Final

July 10 Pearse Stadium, Galway

Galway 0–10 Mayo 0–8

Galway B O'Donoghue | A Burke, F Hanley, K Fitzgerald | D Meehan, P Clancy, D Burke | B Cullinane, N Coleman | D Savage (0–1), M Donnellan (0–4, three frees), M Clancy | M Meehan (0–2, one 45), P Joyce, (0–2, one free), K Comer (0–1)

Subs: S Armstrong for K Comer, T Giblin for D Burke (both 59 mins), P Geraghty for N Coleman (65 mins)

Mayo D Clarke | D Geraghty, D Heaney, G Ruane (0–1) | C Moran, J Nallen, P Gardiner | R McGarrity, S Fitzmaurice | A Moran, C McDonald (0–1, free), A Dillon (0–1, free) | C Mortimer (0–4, two frees), BJ Padden (0–1, free), T Mortimer

Subs: J Gill for A Moran (half-time), P Kelly for C Moran (half-time), B Maloney for A Dillon (53 mins), L O'Malley for P Gardiner (inj, 56 mins) inj

Referee J Geaney (Cork)

All-Ireland Football Championship Qualifiers

Round One

June 18 Markievicz Park, Sligo

Sligo 0–18 Longford 0–16

Sligo P Greene | P Naughton, N McGuire, B Phillips (0–1) | P Doohan, J Martyn, J Davey | S Davey (0–4), E O'Hara (0–4) | B Egan, J McPartland, D McGarty (0–1) | D Sloyan (0–1), M Breheny (0–5, two frees), D McTiernan (0–1)

Subs: K Sweeney for McPartland (43 mins), B Curran for Egan, G McGowan (0–1) for McTernan (both 51 mins), M Munds for Sloyan (71 mins)

Longford D Sheridan | D Brady, D Corcoran, E Ledwith | A O'Connor, C Conefrey, D Reilly | P Barden (0–5, two frees), L Keenan | T Smullen (0–1), K Mulligan (0–1), P Dowd (0–1) | J Martin (0–2, one free), B Kavanagh (0–5, four frees), P Davis (0–1)

Subs: N Sheridan for Davis (47 mins), K Smith for Mulligan (55 mins), B McElvaney for Martin (58 mins), S Mulligan for Dowd (62 mins)

Referee R O'Donnell (Donegal)

June 18 — Casement Park, Belfast

Meath **5–12** Antrim **0–13**

Meath D Gallagher | N McKeigue, K Reilly, C King | T O'Connor, D Fay, P Reynolds | N Crawford, A Moyles | N Kelly, D Crimmins (0–1), P Byrne (1–2) | G Geraghty (1–4), B Farrell (0–2), S Bray (2–0)

Subs: J Sheridan (1–2) for Bray (25 mins), R Magee (0–1) for Farrell (50 mins), M Burke for Byrne (57 mins), N McLaughlin for O'Connor (63 mins), M Ward for Geraghty (67 mins)

Antrim P Murray | C Brady, A McClean, D Gault | T Scullion, G Adams, S Kelly (0–3) | J Quinn, M McCrory | C Close (0–3, two frees), K McGourty, T O'Neill (0–1) | K Brady (0–1), C McGourty (0–4), K Madden (0–1)

Subs: N Enright for Brady (31), C Lynch for O'Neill (half-time), P McCann for Close (47), T Convery for Gault (51), M McCann for McCrory (53)

Referee P Carney (Roscommon)

June 18 — Dr Cullen Park, Carlow

Carlow **0–14** Offaly **1–10**

Carlow J Brennan | C McCarthy (0–1), L Murphy, P Cashin | J Hayden, W Power, R Sinnott | P Walsh, T Walsh | B Carbery (0–1), J Byrne, P Hickey | S Rea (0–8, six frees), M Carpenter (0–2), B Kelly (0–2)

Subs: J Kehoe for Power (inj), P Kelly for Sinnott, R Walker for Hickey

Offaly P Kelly | C Daly, C Evans, S Brady | J Keane, S Sullivan, K Slattery | C McManus, A McNamee | C Quinn, M Daly (0–1), N Coughlan (0–1) | N McNamee (1–6, one penalty, four frees), P Kellaghan, J Reynolds (0–1)

Subs: J Coughlan (0–1) for M Daly, T Deehan for Kellaghan

Referee A Mangan (Kerry)

June 18 O'Rahilly's, Drogheda

Louth **1–12** Waterford **1–8**

Louth S McCoy | A Page, B Reilly, J Carr | C Sheridan, B Keenan, S Gerard | D Deveney (0–1), J Kermath | P Matthews, (0–2), S Lennon (0–2), R Carroll (0–1) | D Clarke (0–5, two frees, one 45), JP Rooney (1–0), T O'Brien

Subs: D Martin for T O'Brien (49 mins), N McDonnell (0–1) for S Lennon (51 mins)

Waterford T Wall | P Ogle, E Walsh, R Hennessy | A Heffernan, M Ahern, T Costelloe | A Hubbard (0–1), K O'Keefe | S Cunningham, S Briggs, L Ó Lionain (1–1) | N Curran (0–4, three frees), Gary Hurney (0–1), Shane Walsh (0–1, free)

Subs: S Dempsey for P Ogle (half-time), J Wall for S Dempsey (64 mins), P Hurney for Ó Lionain (69 mins)

Referee T Quigley (Wexford)

June 18 Páirc Esler, Newry

Down **1–11** Fermanagh **0–7**

Down M McVeigh | M Cole (0–1), A Scullion, D McCartan | P Murphy (0–1), A O'Prey (0–1), D Rafferty | A Molloy, D Gordan (0–1) | C Laverty, A Rodgers, D Hughes | L Doyle (0–2), B Coulter (0–4), S Ward (0–1)

Subs: A Rice for McCartan, R Murtagh for Laverty, R Sexton (1–0) for Ward, J Doran for Scullion

Fermanagh C Breen | M Lily, B Owens, R McCluskey | R Johnston, S McDermott, S McCabe | M McGrath, M Murphy | T Brewster (0–2), J Sherry, M Little | E Maguire (0–1), R Gallagher (0–1), C Bradley (0–2)

Subs: D Kelly (0–1) for Lily, J McGurn for Murphy, S Maguire for Gallagher, R Gallagher for Brewster, N Bogue for McGrath

Referee M McGrath (Donegal)

June 18 Semple Stadium, Thurles

Westmeath **0–12** Tipperary **1–8**

Westmeath G Connaughton | J McAteer, D O'Donoghue, J Keane | M Ennis, D Healy, P Mulvihill (0–2) | R O'Connell, D O'Shaughnessy (0–1) | D Heavin (0–1), P Conway, F Wilson (0–3) | A Mangan, Denis Glennon, D Dolan (0–5)

Subs: G Dolan for Glennon | David Glennon for Conway | D Kilmartin for McAteer | Denis Glennon for D Dolan | J Fallon for Mangan

Tipperary P Fitzgerald | D Byrne, N Curran, P King | P Morrissey, B Lacey, R Costigan | K Mulryan (0–1), F O'Callaghan | G Burke (0–1), L English, C Maher | B Mulvihill (0–1), D Browne (1–2), B Hickey (0–2)

Subs: D O'Brien for England | N Fitzgerald (0–1) for Mulryan

Referee H Beirne (Roscommon)

June 18 St Tiernach's Park, Clones

Monaghan **2–18** London **1–9**

Monaghan S Duffy | D McArdle, J Coyle, C Flanagan | D Freeman, V Corey, G McQuaid | D Clerkin (0–1), E Lennon | J McElroy, P Finlay (0–6), S McManus | T Freeman (0–3), H McElroy (1–8), S Gollogly (1–0)

Subs: R Ronaghan for J McElroy, F Doogan for E Lennon, N Corrigan for S McManus, B O'Brien for H McElroy

London P O'Dowd | P Callaghan, D McKenna, J Rafter (0–1) | J Niblock (capt), J McKevitt, P McConigley | S Hehir 0–1, E Brennan 0–1 | B Solen 0–2, P Hehir 0–2, P Quinn 0–2 | C Foody, S McInerney, P Quirke 1–0

Subs: V O'Sullivan for P Callaghan, F Cunningham for P Quirke, D O'Connor for B Solan

Referee C Reilly (Meath)

June 26 Croke Park, Dublin

Donegal **0–16** Wicklow **0–12**

Donegal M Boyle, E McGee, R Sweeney, S McDermott (0–2), D Diver (0–1, free), S Carr, K Lacey, B Monaghan, N Gallagher, C Toye (0–2), M Hegarty, B Roper (0–1), C McFadden (0–5, four frees), A Sweeney (0–1), B Devenney (0–4, two frees)

Subs: R Kavanagh for Roper (53 mins) | B Boyle for McDermott (57 mins) | R Bradley for Toye (63 mins) | C Molloy for A Sweeney (68 mins)

Wicklow R Hollingsworth, C Hyland (0–1), B Daly, T Burke, K Manning, W Callaghan, B Ó'hAnnaidh (0–1), D Dillon, J Stafford, D Smullen, L Glynn (0–1), T Harney (0–4), P Earls, W O'Gorman (0–4, one free), A Ellis

Subs: G Duffy for Dillon (25 mins) | J Daniels (0–1) for Earls (40 mins) | D O'Sullivan for Ellis (45 mins) | C Davis for O'hAnnaidh (63 mins) | G Doran for Smullen (68 mins)

Referee G Ó Conámha (Galway)

Round Two

July 2 O'Rahilly's, Drogheda

Louth **0–11** Roscommon **0–10**

Louth S McCoy | A Page, B Reilly, J Carr | C Sheridan, A Hoey, S Gerrard | D Deveney, J Kermath | M Stanfield, P Keenan (0–1), D Clarke (0–4, two frees) | P Matthews (0–3), S Lennon (0–1), J P Rooney (0–1)

Subs: N McDonnell for Stanfield (half-time), C Grimes (0–1, one free) for Devaney (51 mins), O McDonnell for Clarke (62 mins), R Kelly for Matthews (68 mins)

Roscommon S Curran | J Egan, J Whyte, S McDermott | M Ryan (0–1), D Casey, J Rogers (0–1) | S O'Neill, B Higgins | K Mannion (0–2), F Grehan, E Kenny | G Cox, J Dunning (0–1), G Heneghan (0–5, three frees)

Subs: Stephen Lohan for Kenny (half-time), A Dooney for Cox (46 mins)

Referee M McGrath (Donegal)

July 2 Markievicz Park, Sligo

Sligo **1–11** Kildare **1–10**

Sligo P Greene | P Naughton, N McGuire, B Philips | P Doohan, B Egan, J Davey | S Davey (0–2, both frees), E O'Hara | B Curran, M Breheny (0–4, two frees), D McGarty | D McTiernan (0–1), D Sloyan (0–3), K Sweeney

Subs: T Taylor for E O'Hara (1 min), J McPartland (1–1) for B Curran (1 min), G McGowan for D McTiernan (48 mins), J Martyn for T Taylor (56 mins), K O'Neill for K Sweeney (66 mins)

Kildare E Murphy | A Rainbow, P Mullarkey, A McLoughlin | D Lyons (0–1), D Hendy, K Ennis | K Brennan, M Foley | R Glavin, D Earley, J Kavanagh | T Fennin (0–8, five frees), R Sweeney, J Doyle (1–1, 0–1 from free)

Subs: T O'Connor for B Hendy (half-time), T O'Neill for R Glavin (42 mins), W Heffernan for W Brenan (61 mins), M Hagarty for P Mullarkey (65 mins), M Wright for M Foley (69 mins)

Referee M Hughes (Tyrone)

July 2 Dr Cullen Park, Carlow

Limerick **2–15** Carlow **0–7**

Limerick S O'Donnell | T Stack, C Mullane, J McCarthy | P Browne, S Lucey, S Lavin (0–1) | J Quane, J Galvin (0–1) | S Kelly (0–1), M Gavin (0–6, four frees), S Buckley | C Fitzgerald (0–3), M Reidy (2–2), M Crowley (0–1)

Subs: M O'Riordan for Stack (half-time), M O'Brien for Buckley (47 mins), D Reidy for Lucey, J Stokes for Fitzgerald, J Murphy for Gavin (all 62 mins)

Carlow J Brennan | C McCarthy, L Murphy, P Cashin | J Hayden, J Kehoe, R Sinnott | P Walsh, M Brennan | B Carbery (0–2), J Byrne, R Walker (0–1) | S Rea (0–3, 0–2 frees), M Carpenter, B Kelly (0–1, free)

Subs: P Kelly for Cashin (26 mins), D Byrne for J Byrne, P Hickey for Kelly (both 45 mins), J Nevin for Rea (53 mins), W Minchin for Walsh (65 mins)

Referee C Broderick (Down)

July 3 Páirc Seán Mac Diarmada, Carrick-on-Shannon

Meath **1–12** Leitrim **1–8**

Meath D Gallagher | N McKeigue, K Reilly, C King | T O'Connor | D Fay, M O'Reilly | N Crawford, A Moyles (0–1) | N Kelly, D Crimmins, P Byrne (0–2) | G Geraghty (1–2), B Farrell (0–1, free), S Bray (0–2)

Subs: J Sheridan (0–2, one free) for N Kelly (23 mins), M Burke (0–1) for B Farrell (44 mins), O Murphy (0–1) for P Byrne (70 mins), R Magee for J Sheridan (80 mins), N McLaughlin for C King (80 mins), S Kenny for M O'Reilly (85 mins)

Leitrim G Phelan | M McGuinness, J McKeon, D Reynolds | C Regan, B McWeeney, S Foley | C Carroll, G McCloskey | J Goldrick, B Prior, M Foley (0–4, three frees) | J Glancy (1–1), D Duignan, D Maxwell (0–1)

Subs: D Beck (0–1) for J Goldrick (63 mins), D Brennan (0–1) for G McCloskey, N Gilbane for C Regan (64 mins), J McGovern for S Foley (77 mins)

Referee J White (Donegal)

July 3 Cusack Park, Ennis

Clare **0–12** Westmeath **0–9**

Clare D O'Brien | P Gallagher, D Kelly, G Tubridy | A Clohessy (0–1), K Dilleen, D Callanan | G Quinlan (0–1), David Russell (Kilkee, 0–1) | E Coughlan (0–2), S Daniels, P O'Dwyer (0–1) | O O'Dwyer (0–3, two frees), S Hickey, R Donnelly (0–3, two frees)

Subs: M O'Shea for Daniels (15 mins), M O'Connell for Callinan (38 mins)

Westmeath G Connaughton | J McAteer, D O'Donoghue, J Keane | M Ennis, D Healy, P Mulvihill (0–1) | C Galligan, D O'Shaughnessy | F Wilson (0–1), D Heavin, J Fallon | David Glennon (0–2), Denis Glennon (0–3, frees), A Mangan (0–2)

Subs: D Duffy for McAteer (27 mins), R O'Connell for Fallon, D Kilmartin for Duffy (both 49 mins), D Gavin for Galligan (56 mins), D Martin for Heavin (69 mins)

Referee F Flynn (Leitrim)

July 3 Páirc Esler, Newry

Derry **3–8** Down **2–9**

Derry B Gillis | K McGuckin, K McCloy, M Kelly | Francis McEldowney, SM Lockhart, P McFlynn | F Doherty, Patsy Bradley | P Murphy, E Bradley (1–0), J McBride (0–1) | M Lynch (0–2), P Bradley (1–4), E Muldoon (1–1)

Subs: G O'Kane for P McFlynn (46–48 mins), Fergal McEldowney for P Murphy (52 mins), G Donaghy for F Doherty (60 mins)

Down M McVeigh | M Cole, A Scullion, A Rice | P Murphy (0–1), A O'Pey, D Rafferty | A Molloy, C McCrickard | C Laverty, A Rogers (0–2, one 45), D Hughes (0–2) | R Murtagh (0–1), B Coulter (1–2, 0–2 from frees), S Ward

Subs: B Grant for A Rice (33 mins), R Sexton (1–0) for C Laverty (half-time), M Walsh for C McCrickard (43 mins), J Clarke (0–1) for S Ward (51 mins)

Referee S McCormack (Meath)

July 3 Breffni Park, Cavan

Cavan **1–11** Donegal **1–10**

Cavan J Reilly | M Hannon, D Rabbitte, P O'Reilly | M Cahill, A Forde (0–1), P Reilly | D McCabe, P McKenna | M McKeever (0–1 free), N Walsh, F O'Reilly (0–6, three frees, one 45) | L Reilly (1–2) J O'Reilly (0–1), M Graham

Subs: M Lyng for Graham (45 mins), P Brady for McCabe (72 mins), S Johnston for L Reilly (74 mins)

Donegal M Boyle | E McGee, R Sweeney, K Lacey | D Diver, B Monaghan, S Carr | S McDermott, N Gallagher | C Toye, M Hegarty, B Roper (0–1) | C McFadden (0–3, all frees), A Sweeney (0–1), B Devenney (1–5, 0–2 from frees)

Subs: C Dunne for Sweeney (45 mins), B Dunnion for Monaghan (55 mins), G Maguire for Roper (65 mins)

Referee E Murtagh (Longford)

July 9 St Tiernach's Park, Clones

Monaghan 0–17 Wexford 0–12

Monaghan S Duffy | D McArdle, J Coyle, C Flanagan | D Freeman (0–2), V Corey, G McQuaid (0–1) | D Clerkin, E Lennon | J McElroy, P Finlay (0–4, all frees), R Ronaghan (0–1) | T Freeman (0–4), H McElroy (0–3, two frees), S Gollogly

Subs: N Corrigan (0–1) for S Gollogly, D McKernan (0–1) for S McManus, F Duffy for E Lennon

Wexford J Cooper | C Morris, N Murphy, D Breen | K Kennedy, D Murphy, P Curtis (0–1) | N Lambert (0–1), D Fogarty | R Barry, S Cullen, J Hudson | PJ Banville, D Kinsella (0–3), M Forde (0–7, six frees, one 45)

Subs: J Hegarty for PJ Banville, P Colfer for J Hudson, J Lawlor for D Murphy, D Browne for S Cullen

Referee P McGovern (Galway)

Round Three

July 16 Breffni Park, Cavan

Monaghan 1–12 Louth 0–14

Monaghan S Duffy | D McArdle, J Coyle, C Flanagan | D Freeman, V Corey, J Conlon | F Duffy, E Lennon | J McElroy, P Finlay (0–5), D Clerkin (0–2) | T Freeman (0–2), H McElroy (1–3), S Gollogly

Subs: N Corrigan for F Duffy (52 mins), D McKernan for S Gollogly (65 mins), S McManus for J McElroy (70 mins)

Louth S McCoy | A Page, B Reilly, J Carr | C Sheridan, A Hoey, S Gerrard | J Kermath, P Keenan | D Clarke (0–10, nine frees) C Grimes (0–1), P Matthews (0–1) | L McDonnell (0–1), S Lennon (0–1), J P Rooney

Subs: R Carroll for C Sheridan (15 mins), M Stanfield for J Kermath (30), O McDonnell for S Lennon (58), D Deveney for C Grimes (inj, 63 mins) Red card: N McDonnell (46)

Referee M Duffy (Sligo)

July 17 St Tiernach's Park, Clones

Cavan **1–8** Meath **1–6**

Cavan J Reilly | M Hannon, D Rabbitte, P O'Reilly | M Cahill, A Forde, P Reilly | D McCabe (0–1), P McKenna | M McKeever, N Walsh, F O'Reilly (0–2, two frees) | S Johnston (0–2), J O'Reilly (1–1), L Reilly (0–2)

Subs: M Lyng for Walsh (50 mins), C Collins for Rabbitte (53 mins), P Brady for P McKenna (61), C Mackey for Johnston (62 mins)

Meath D Gallagher | N McKeigue, K Reilly, C King | T O'Connor, D Fay, M O'Reilly | N Crawford, A Moyles | J Sheridan (0–3), D Crimmins, P Byrne (0–1) | G Geraghty (1–1, goal from penalty), R Magee (0–1), S Bray

Subs: M Burke for Crimmins (45 mins), N Kelly for Byrne (52 mins), O Murphy for Bray (53 mins), P Reynolds for O'Connor (55 mins)

Referee G O'Conamha (Galway)

July 17 McHale Park, Castlebar

Sligo **1–13** Clare **0–11**

Sligo P Greene | P Naughton (0–1), J Martyn, B Phillips | P Doohan, B Egan, J Davey | S Davey (0–2), N McGuire | J McPartland (0–4), M Breheny (1–6, 0–5 from frees), D McGarty | D McTiernan, D Sloyan, G McGowan

Subs: K O'Neill for McGowan (33 mins), B Curran for McTiernan (49 mins), T Taylor for McGarty (51 mins)

Clare D O'Brien | P Gallagher, D Kelly, G Tubridy | A Clohessy, R Slattery, M O'Connell | G Quinlan, P O'Dwyer (0–1) | M O'Shea, E Coughlan (0–1), D Russell | R Donnelly (0–7, all frees), S Hickey, O O'Dwyer (0–1)

Subs: M O'Dwyer (0–1) for Hickey (20 mins), C Whelan for Tubridy (21 mins), J Moody for Ó Sé (60 mins)

Referee M Deegan (Laois)

July 17 McHale Park, Castlebar

Derry **0–13** Limerick **0–9**

Derry B Gillis | K McGuckin, K McCloy, M Kelly | F McEldowney, SM Lockhart, P McFlynn (0–1) | J McBride, P Bradley | Paul Murphy, E Bradley (0–3, one 45), G Donaghy (0–1) | M Lynch (0–2, one free), P Bradley (0–6, three frees), C Devlin

Subs: G O'Kane for M Kelly (half-time), Padraig Murphy for C Devlin (46 mins), C Gilligan for F McEldowney (56 mins), P Wilson for P McFlynn (73 mins inj)

Limerick S O'Donnell | M O'Riordan, T Stack, J McCarthy | P Browne, S Lucey, C Mullane | J Quane, J Galvin | S Kelly (0–1), M Gavin (0–8, seven frees), S Buckley | C Fitzgerald, M Reidy, M Crowley

Subs: J Stokes for J Quane (half-time), J Donovan for M Reidy (half-time), M O'Brien for S Buckley (57 mins)

Referees J Bannon (Longford, inj half-time), M Daly (Mayo, second half)

Round Four

July 30 O'Moore Park, Portlaoise

Cork **3–13** Sligo **0–11**

Cork K O'Dwyer | N Geary, G Canty, G Murphy | E Sexton, A Lynch, N O'Leary (0–3) | D Kavanagh (0–1), N Murphy (1–0) | J Masters (1–1), C McCarthy (0–1), K MacMahon (1–0) | BJ O'Sullivan (0–2), J Hayes (0–4, two frees), F Gould

Subs: K O'Sullivan for Hayes (25–30 minutes), M Cronin (0–1) for Sexton (39 mins), P Clifford for Gould (51 mins), D Hurley for N Murphy (62 mins), A Cronin for Masters, S Levis for Lynch (both 66 mins)

Sligo P Greene | P Naughton, J Martyn, B Philips | P Doohan, B Egan, J Davey | S Davey (0–4, three frees), N McGuire | J McPartland (0–1), M Brehony (0–3, two frees), T Taylor | D McTiernan, D Sloyan (0–1), B Curran (0–1)

Subs: D McGarty for Taylor (31 mins), G McGowan (0–1) for McTiernan (half-time), K Sweeney for Sloyan (59 mins), C Harrison for Martyn (67 mins), P McGovern for Egan (70 mins)

Referee M Hughes (Tyrone)

July 30 Hyde Park, Roscommon

Mayo **0–11** Cavan **0–8**

Mayo D Clarke | D Geraghty, D Heaney, G Ruane | P Kelly, J Nallen, P Gardiner | R McGarrity (0–1), S Fitzmauice | M Moyles (0–3), C McDonald (0–1), A Dillon (0–3 one free) | C Mortimer, BJ Padden, A O'Malley (0–3)

Subs: M McNicholas for Mortimer (51 mins), J Gill for Moyles (56 mins), B Moran for Fitzmaurice (70 mins)

Cavan J Reilly | M Hannon, D Rabbitte, P O'Reilly | M Cahill, A Forde, P Reilly | D McCabe (0–3 two frees), P McKenna | M McKeever, N Walsh, F O'Reilly (0–1) | S Johnston, J O'Reilly, L Reilly (0–4, two frees)

Subs: C Collins for Rabbitte (8 mins), P Brady for P Reilly, J Tierney for Johnston, A Gaynor for McKenna (all at half-time)

Referee T Quigley (Wexford)

August 6 Croke Park, Dublin

Laois **1–11** Derry **0–11**

Laois F Byron | A Fennelly, D Rooney, J Higgins | C Begley, T Kelly (0–1), P McMahon | P Clancy (0–1), N Garvan (0–1) | R Munnelly (0–4, one free), K Fitzpatrick, B Sheehan (1–1) | D Brennan (0–1), S Cooke, C Conway

Subs: G Kavanagh (0–1) for S Cooke (25 mins), S Kelly (0–1) for K Fitzpatrick, B McDonald for C Conway (both half-time), M Dunne for D Brennan (72 mins)

Derry B Gillis | K McGuckin, K McCloy, G O'Kane | Francis McEldowney, SM Lockhart, P Kelly (0–1) | Patsy Bradley, Fergal Doherty | Paul Murphy (0–2), E Bradley (0–1), J McBride (0–1) | M Lynch (0–1), Paddy Bradley (0–4, one free), E Muldoon (0–1, one free)

Subs: C Gilligan for P Murphy (51 mins), Padraig Murphy for E Muldoon (59 mins), C Devlin for E Bradley, P Wilson for P Kelly (both 68 mins)

Referee P Russell (Tipperary)

August 6 Croke Park, Dublin

Tyrone **2–14** Monaghan **1–7**

Tyrone P McConnell | J McMahon, C Lawn, S Sweeney | D Harte (0–1), G Devlin, P Jordan | C Gormley (0–1), S Cavanagh (0–1) | B Dooher, B McGuigan, S O'Neill (2–6, 0–4 from frees) | R Mellon (0–1), O Mulligan (0–1), E McGinley

Subs: M McGee for Lawn (25 mins), P Canavan (0–2, one free) for Sweeney (half-time), M Penrose (0–1) for Mulligan (54 mins), B Meenan for Mellon (71 mins)

Monaghan S Duffy | D McArdle, J Coyle, C Flanagan | D Freeman, V Corey, G McQuaid | D Clerkin, E Lennon (0–1, free) | J McElroy, P Finlay (0–2), R Woods (0–1) | T Freeman (1–0), H McElroy (0–3, frees), S Gollogly

Subs: F Duffy for Gollogly (54 mins), N Corrigan for J McElroy (54 mins), D McKernan for Woods (58 mins)

Referee M Monahan (Kildare)

All-Ireland Football Championship Finals

Quarter-finals

August 7 Croke Park, Dublin

Kerry **2–15** Mayo **0–18**

Kerry D Murphy | M Ó Sé (0–1), M McCarthy, T O'Sullivan | T Ó Sé, S Moynihan, A O'Mahony (0–1) | D Ó Sé (1–0), W Kirby (0–1) | L Hassett (0–1), D O'Sullivan (0–1, capt), E Brosnan (0–2) | C Cooper (1–1), D Ó Cinnéide (0–1, free), MF Russell (0–3)

Subs: P Galvin (0–3) for Hassett (52 mins), E Fitzmaurice for T O'Sullivan (52 mins), B Sheehan for Ó Cinnéide (57 mins), K Donaghy for D Ó Sé (61 mins), D Quill for Russell (62 mins)

Mayo D Clarke | D Geraghty, D Heaney (0–1), G Ruane | P Kelly, J Nallen, P Gardiner | R McGarrity, S Fitzmaurice | M Moyles, C McDonald (0–6, two frees, capt), A Dillon (0–4, two frees) | B Moran (0–1), BJ Padden, A O'Malley (0–5)

Subs: A Kilcoyne for Moyles (18 mins), K Higgins for Gardiner (42 mins), J Gill for Padden (48 mins), C Mortimer for Kilcoyne (56 mins), A Moran (0–1) for B Moran (62 mins)

Referee B Crowe (Cavan)

August 7 Croke Park, Dublin

Cork **2–14** Galway **2–11**

Cork K O'Dwyer | N Geary, G Canty, G Murphy | E Sexton (0–1), A Lynch (0–2), N O'Leary | D Kavanagh, N Murphy | J Masters (0–3, two frees), C McCarthy, K McMahon (0–1) | P Clifford (0–2, one free), BJ O'Sullivan (1–3), J Hayes (1–2)

Subs: K O'Connor for Geary (half-time), A Cronin for Masters (60 mins)

Galway B O'Donoghue | A Burke, F Hanley, K Fitzgerald | D Meehan, P Clancy, D Burke: B Cullinane, N Coleman | S Armstrong (0–2), M Clancy, J Bergin | M Meehan (2–2), P Joyce (0–7, four frees), M Donnellan

Subs: N Meehan for Coleman (42 mins), K Comer for Clancy (59 mins)

Referee M Deegan (Laois)

August 13 Croke Park, Dublin

Dublin **1–14** Tyrone **1–14**

Dublin S Cluxton | P Griffin, P Christie, S O'Shaughnessy | C Goggins, B Cahill, P Casey | C Whelan, S Ryan | C Moran, A Brogan (0–2), B Cullen | J Sherlock (0–2), C Keaney (0–3, one free), T Quinn (1–7, 0–5 from frees, 0–1 from 45)

Subs: P Andrews for Christie (55 mins), S Connell for Moran (62 mins), D Homan for Goggins (66 mins), D Magee for Whelan (70 mins), D Farrell for Brogan (73 mins)

Tyrone P McConnell | R McMenamin, C Lawn, S Sweeney | D Harte, G Devlin, P Jordan | C Gormley, S Cavanagh (0–3) | B Dooher (0–1), B McGuigan (0–1), O Mulligan (1–1, 0–1 from free) | R Mellon (0–1), S O'Neill (0–6, three frees), E McGinley (0–1)

Subs: J McMahon for Devlin (half-time), P Canavan for Mellon (49 mins), M McGee for Harte (73 mins)

Referee A Mangan (Kerry)

August 20 Croke Park, Dublin

Armagh **2–17** Laois **1–11**

Armagh P Hearty | C McKeever, F Bellew, E McNulty | A Kernan (0–2, both frees), A O'Rourke, A Mallon | P Loughran, P McGrane (0–1) | M O'Rourke (0–2), J McEntee (0–1), O McConville (1–3, 0–2 from frees) | S McDonnell (1–5, 0–1 from a free), R Clarke (0–3), B Mallon

Subs: T McEntee for J McEntee (53 mins), S Kernan for B Mallon, K McElvanna for A O'Rourke (both 64 mins), A McCann for A Kernan (65 mins), 26 M Mackin for M O'Rourke (68 mins)

Laois F Byron | A Fennelly, D Rooney, J Higgins | C Begley, T Kelly, P McMahon | P Clancy (0–1), N Garvan | R Munnelly (0–4, three frees), B Brennan (1–1), B Sheehan (0–3) | D Brennan, S Kelly (0–1), B McDonald

Subs: C Conway (0–1) for S Kelly, G Kavanagh for McDonald (both half-time), K Fitzpatrick for D Brennan (51 mins), M Dunne for Garvan (61 mins)

Referee J Geaney (Cork)

August 27 Replay Croke Park, Dublin

Tyrone **2–18** Dublin **1–14**

Tyrone P McConnell | R McMenamin, C Lawn, M McGee | D Harte, C Gormley, P Jordan | E McGinley, J McMahon | B Dooher (0–3), B McGuigan (0–1), S Cavanagh (0–2) | R Mellon (0–2), S O'Neill (1–3, 1–0 from a goal, 0–1 from a free), O Mulligan (1–7, 0–2 from frees)

Subs: S Sweeney for Lawn (24 mins), B Meenan for Sweeney (53 mins), E Bradley for McGee (63 mins), P Donnelly for McGinley (68 mins)

Dublin S Cluxton | P Griffin, P Andrews, S O'Shaughnessy | S Ryan (0–1), B Cahill, P Casey | C Whelan, D Magee | C Moran (0–1), C Keaney (0–5, two frees), B Cullen (0–1) | J Sherlock (0–1), A Brogan (0–2), T Quinn (0–2, one free)

Subs: S Connell (0–1) for Brogan (26 mins), D Lally for Magee (half-time), M Vaughan for Quinn (57 mins), D O'Callaghan for Lally (60 mins), D Farrell (1–0) for Keaney (67 mins)

Referee G Ó Conámha (Galway)

Semi-finals

August 28 — Croke Park, Dublin

Kerry 1–19 Cork 0–9

Kerry D Murphy | T O'Sullivan, M McCarthy (0–1), A O'Mahony (0–1) | T Ó Sé (0–1), M Ó Sé, S Moynihan | D Ó Sé, W Kirby (0–1) | P Galvin (0–3), E Brosnan (1–2), L Hassett (0–1) | C Cooper (0–5), D O'Sullivan (0–2, both frees, capt), B Sheehan

Subs: D Ó Cinnéide (0–1, free) for Sheehan (49 mins), MF Russell (0–1) for Hassett (58 mins), E Fitzmaurice for T Ó Sé, D Quill for Cooper (67 mins), K Donaghy for Kirby (68 mins)

Cork K O'Dwyer | G Murphy, G Canty, N Geary | N O'Leary, A Lynch (0–1), E Sexton (capt) | D Kavanagh, N Murphy | J Masters (0–2, both frees), C McCarthy, K McMahon (0–2) | P Clifford (0–2, one free), BJ O'Sullivan, J Hayes (0–2, both frees)

Subs: K O'Connor for Geary (19 mins), A Cronin for Masters (half-time), M Cronin for O'Leary (51 mins), K O'Sullivan for McCarthy (53 mins)

Referee J McQuillan (Cavan)

September 4 — Croke Park, Dublin

Tyrone 1–13 Armagh 1–12

Tyrone P McConnell | M McGee, J McMahon, R McMenamin (0–1) | D Harte, C Gormley, P Jordan | B Meenan, S Cavanagh (0–2) | B Dooher, B McGuigan, E McGinley | R Mellon, S O'Neill (1–4, 1–0 from, 0–3 from frees), O Mulligan (0–3, one free)

Subs: P Canavan (0–2, one free) for McGinley (half-time), C Holmes for Meenan (44 mins), C Lawn for Jordan (65 mins), S Sweeney (0–1) for Harte (67 mins)

Armagh P Hearty | F Bellew, C McKeever, A Mallon | K McGeeney (0–1), A Kernan (0–2, both frees), A O'Rourke | P Loughran, P McGrane | M O'Rourke, B Mallon (0–1), P McKeever | S McDonnell (1–3), R Clarke (0–1), O McConville (0–3, all frees)

Subs: T McEntee for Loughran (34 mins), J McEntee (0–1) for B Mallon (half-time), E McNulty for McGeeney (63 mins), A McCann for A O'Rourke (71)

Referee P Russell (Tipperary)

Final

September 25 Croke Park, Dublin

Tyrone **1–16** Kerry **2–10**

Tyrone P McConnell | M McGee, J McMahon, R McMenamin | D Harte, C Gormley, P Jordan (0–1) | E McGinley, S Cavanagh | B Dooher (capt, 0–1), B McGuigan (0–3), R Mellon (0–2) | P Canavan (1–1), S O'Neill (0–4, two frees), O Mulligan (0–4, two frees)

Subs: C Holmes for P Canavan (half-time), C Lawn for McMahon (48 mins), P Canavan for McGinley (55 mins)

Kerry D Murphy | M McCarthy, A O'Mahony, T O'Sullivan | T Ó Sé (1–0), M Ó Sé, S Moynihan | D Ó Sé (0–2), W Kirby | L Hassett, E Brosnan (0–2), P Galvin | C Cooper (0–5, two frees), D O'Sullivan (capt), D Ó Cinnéide (1–1, 0–1 from free)

Subs: MF Russell for Hassett (44 mins), Darren O'Sullivan for Ó Cinnéide (61 mins), B Sheehan for Galvin (68 mins), E Fitzmaurice for Moynihan (68 mins)

Referee M Monahan (Kildare)

All-Ireland Football Championship Top Scorers

Name	Team	Games	Scored	Total	Average
1 Stephen O'Neill	Tyrone	10	5–49	64	6.4
2 Paddy Bradley	Derry	5	2–29	35	7.0
3 Colm Cooper	Kerry	6	4–23	35	5.8
4 Stephen McDonnell	Armagh	8	4–21	33	4.1
5 Tomas Quinn	Dublin	6	1–29	32	5.3
6 Ross Munnelly	Laois	5	1–24	27	5.4
7 Owen Mulligan	Tyrone	10	2–21	27	2.7
8 Mark Breheny	Sligo	5	2–21	27	5.4
9 Oisín McConville	Armagh	8	2–18	24	3.0
10 Hugh McElroy	Monaghan	5	2–17	23	4.6

5
The GAA

5 The GAA

Structure of the GAA

The primary function of the GAA (Gaelic Athletic Association) is the promotion of the national games: Gaelic football, hurling, handball and rounders. The organizations that administer women's football and camogie are officially separate from the GAA, but the women's codes receive most of the benefits of GAA membership. Membership of the association can only be obtained through GAA clubs, and full membership is open to all over the age of 18. The association's structure has five primary layers which have not changed fundamentally since they were devised over 100 years ago.

The Club

The club is the basic unit of the GAA. At least 15 playing members are needed before a club can be accepted into the organization. The members of the club elect a chairperson, secretary and other members annually to organize and control the assets and affairs of the club. There are over 2,500 GAA clubs.

Did you know? While many clubs are named after former local heroes, a GAA club cannot be named after a living person.

The County

The 32 county boards usually have a number of divisional or juvenile boards to organize competitions at district and youth levels. The boards are, of course, also responsible for the organization and facilitation of teams at inter-county level – at all age groups from Under-10 to Senior. Some boards have a particular interest in one of the codes, which usually leads to the neglect of the other (or even to its non-existence). An annual county convention is held before the end of each calendar year – with two delegates representing each adult club in the county – at which the chairperson, secretary and other officials are elected or re-elected for the following year. Being a member of a county board is a rather thankless job in the GAA, with fans really getting interested only when the board has to make difficult decisions.

Did you know? Missing three consecutive county board meetings automatically disqualifies a representative from attending meetings for the rest of the year, unless he or she can come up with a good excuse.

The Province

The four provincial councils organize the provincial championships for clubs and counties in both hurling and football, and the interprovincial teams in hurling and football; they also control many of the financial matters of the association within the province.

By secret ballot a chairperson and other officials are elected to serve on the provincial committee. All candidates for election as a provincial officer have to be nominated from county level. (A maximum of six representatives are allowed from each county at the provincial convention.) The provincial council consists of a chairperson, vice-chairperson, treasurer, PRO, secretary and two representatives from each county.

Did you know? At the start of each year, the provincial council has to give Central Council a fee of €1 for each club in its area.

National

The GAA is run by Central Council (Árd Comhairle), with the management committee controlling day-to-day affairs. The council runs the All-Ireland series of the club and county championships. Ever since Maurice Davin became the first president of the GAA in 1884, rule changes and amendments to GAA structures have been implemented at national level. Major changes to GAA affairs have to be ratified by these bodies.

The Central Council usually consists of the president, director-general, vice-presidents, two trustees, and a representative from each county in Ireland, as well as delegates from Britain, London, New York, handball, the players' committee and each of the first-, second- and third-level schools' committees.

Between the annual congresses, the Central Council is the supreme governing body of the Gaelic Athletic Association. Its decisions are binding and final.

Did you know? The Central Council vice-presidents are always the presidents of the provincial councils.

Annual Congress

The annual congress takes place before May each year, at a venue of the Central Council's choosing. It comprises the outgoing council, past presidents, and up to ten delegates from each county. Each county or provincial committee is allowed to submit one motion.

The main functions of the annual congress are to debate and (sometimes) vote on motions – various motions relating to Rule 42, which forbids the use of GAA stadiums for 'foreign' games, being the most talked-about in recent years – and to elect a president by secret ballot (a GAA president cannot hold office for more than three consecutive years).

Did you know? The GAA is committed to holding a Youth Congress, comprising delegates under 18 years of age, every second year.

Timeline

1884 The GAA is founded in Miss Hayes's Commercial Hotel in Thurles.

1885 Rules for hurling and football are agreed.

1886 County committees introduced, with Wexford being the first formed.

Artane Boys' Band gives its first GAA public performance.

1887 First All-Ireland Championship in hurling and football, involving club champions.

1888 First All-Ireland Championship finals (of 1887 competition) played.

Members of Royal Irish Constabulary banned from playing GAA sports.

1892 Teams reduced from 21 to 17 players a side.

1894 Over 10,000 attend All-Ireland football final replay.

1895 Cork fields a county side for inter-county competition (instead of using club champions).

1896 Goal reduced from five to three points.

1900 Provincial structure introduced.

1904 First public camogie game held in Navan, Co. Meath.

1905 Foundation of Cumann Camogaiochata, with Máire Ní Chinneide as President.

1912 Junior All-Ireland Championships introduced.

1913 GAA purchases Croke Park for £3,500.

Teams reduced to 15 players a side.

1918 Dublin Castle proscribes GAA as a dangerous organization.

1920 Twelve people killed in Croke Park by Black and Tans during Tipperary–Dublin football match.

1921 Liam McCarthy Cup established as the prize for the All-Ireland hurling champions; Limerick are the first winners.

1922 GAA relinquishes control of athletics to a new national athletics body.

1926 Galway v Kilkenny hurling game broadcast on radio.

National Leagues introduced.

Tipperary hurlers tour America.

1927 Sam Maguire dies of tuberculosis in west Cork at the age of 48.

Railway Cups introduced.

Birth of minor championships.

1928 Sam Maguire Cup established as prize for the All-Ireland football champions; Kildare are the first winners.

1931 GAA adopt the name Cumann Luthcleas Gael.

1932 First All-Ireland camogie championship.

1933 Ulster finally produces an All-Ireland champion, with Cavan claiming the football title.

1937 Cusack Stand opened at Croke Park.

1938 Mícheál O'Hehir commentates on his first GAA match.

1939 'Thunder & Lightning' hurling final between Cork and Kilkenny.

1947 In an attempt to boost the profile of the game abroad, the All-Ireland football final between Cavan and Kerry is played in the Polo Grounds, New York.

1954 84,856 attend Cork–Wexford All-Ireland hurling final at Croke Park.

1956 Cork's Christy Ring appears in his tenth All-Ireland senior hurling final.

1959 New cantilevered Hogan Stand opened at Croke Park.

1961 90,556 attend Down–Offaly All-Ireland football final at Croke Park.

Intermediate hurling competition introduced.

1962 RTE broadcasts GAA match live on television for first time.

1964 Under-21 competition introduced.

All-Ireland camogie club championship introduced.

Five countries compete in first world handball championships in New York.

1967 Tipperary's John Doyle equals Christy Ring's record, appearing in his tenth All-Ireland senior hurling final.

1970 World handball championship staged in Croke Park.

1971 First All-Star awards scheme.

Ban on playing 'foreign' games is lifted.

Tipperary beat Waterford in what is believed to be the first inter-county women's football match.

1973 Junior championships discontinued.

1974 Ladies Gaelic Football Association officially founded.

First All-Ireland B Championship.

1976 Páirc Uí Chaoimh in Cork is offcially opened.

1980 National League structure revamped, with promotion and relegation between divisions.

1983 Junior championships re-introduced.

Kilkenny's Noel Skehan wins record ninth All-Ireland hurling winner's medal.

1984 All-Ireland hurling final staged at Semple Stadium in GAA's centenary year.

1989 Nicky English of Tipperary claims highest-ever individual score in senior hurling final – 2–12 against Antrim.

1997 First phase of new Croke Park development completed (Cusack Stand side).

'Back door' system introduced in senior hurling championship.

2001 Qualifier format introduced in senior football championship.

2003 Last phase of Croke Park development begins (replacement of Hill 16 and Nally Stand).

2004 Westmeath win Leinster senior football crown, leaving only two teams – Fermanagh and Wicklow – still without a senior hurling or football championship title.

Camogie celebrates 100th anniversary, with 24,500 attending All-Ireland senior and junior camogie final.

2005 Three-tier senior hurling championship introduced.

The Pitch

GAA supporters have long maintained a tradition of dual measurement – yards and metres. Simultaneous calls can be heard at hurling and football matches for a '21' (yards) or a '20' (metres). Demanding a '50' or a '45' also means exactly the same thing (in sporting if not mathematical terms), and, similarly, you can claim either a '70' or a '65' and the referee will know what you mean.

Playing pitches are officially measured in metres, and, as the government is encouraging everyone to embrace the metric system, we've mapped the field of play using that method.

While 130 metres by 80 metres is the minimum allowed playing area of a GAA field, some under-age grades are allowed to use a smaller pitch.

A modern addition – the substitution zone – is an area at the side of the playing field, five metres either side of the centre-line: all players entering and exiting the field have to pass through this zone. (That's what is supposed to happen, anyway.)

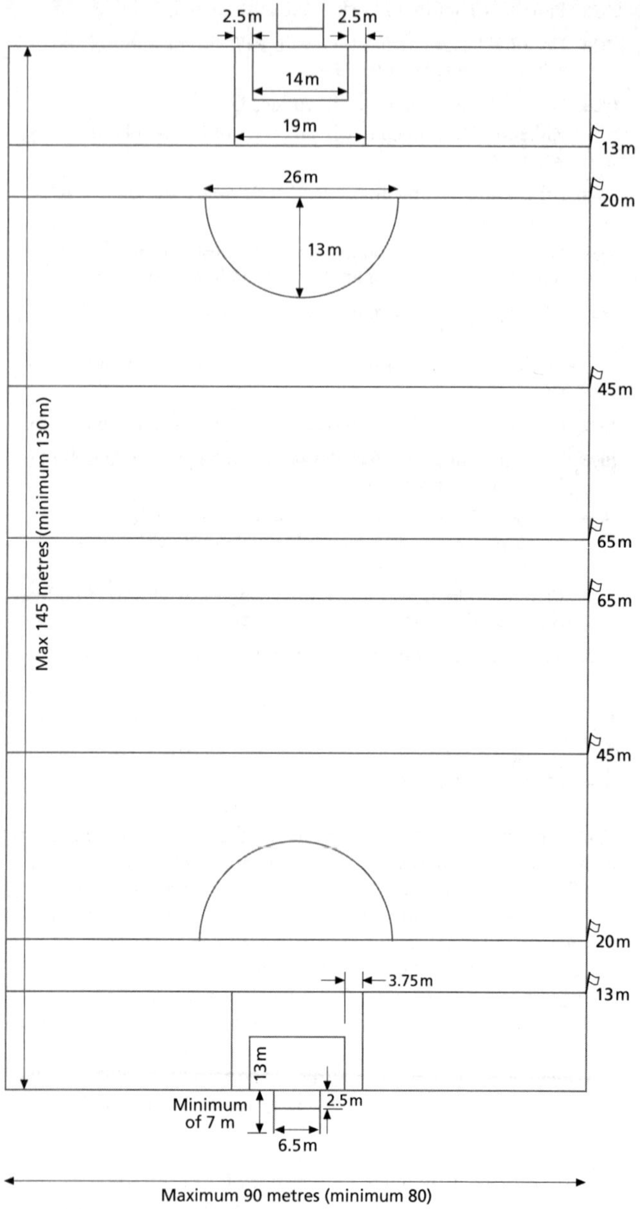
2.5m
2.5m
14m
19m
13m
26m
20m
13m
45m
65m
65m
45m
20m
3.75m
13m
13m
Minimum of 7 m
2.5m
6.5m
Max 145 metres (minimum 130m)
Maximum 90 metres (minimum 80)

The Rules

It is quite common to witness even the most seasoned campaigners arguing over the rules of hurling and football. Here we list some of the most commonly misunderstood – and some of the most fundamental – rules of the games.

Basic rules that can cause confusion

- Boundary lines are part of the field of play.
- A team may start a match with 13 players, but must have 15 players (inclusive of any players sent off or taken off) by the start of the second half.
- A maximum of five substitutions is allowed in a game. However, in extra-time, a further three substitutions are allowed and both teams can start again with 15 players, even if a player was sent off in regular time (though the player who was sent off cannot come back on).
- All club and county matches – from Under-16 to adult – are 60 minutes long, except inter-county senior championship and National League games, which are 70 minutes.
- If a ball hits a sideline flag it is out of play, even if it bounces back on to the playing field.
- A player who has caught the sliotar and placed it on his hurley may bring it back into his hand only once, and the sliotar may be carried in the hand for only four steps (or the time needed to take four steps).
- If a player taking a free fails to strike the sliotar, or fails to raise it off the ground, he must strike the ball on the ground immediately, otherwise an opposing player can approach. However, if a player taking a puck-out misses the sliotar, he can raise it off the ground and strike it (but not handle the sliotar again).
- If a player taking a sideline cut fails to strike the sliotar, he may make another attempt, but an opposing player may approach if he delays.
- A referee can order a player who is bleeding (or who has blood on him) off the field to receive medical attention. In these circumstances, a temporary substitution may be used.
- A player can score a goal by striking the sliotar or football in flight with the hand (as distinct from a hand-pass).
- It is a foul to jump up and down or wave the hands or a hurley while a player is taking a free (a player may hold the hurley upright, though).
- The football may be passed from one hand to the other, provided the original hand maintains contact with the ball until the change is completed.

- A goalkeeper may move along the goal-line before a penalty is struck.

Some unusual rules

- The referee can award a goal to the attacking team if the sliotar or football was prevented from going over the line by a spectator or official.
- A player may not lift a sliotar or football off the ground using his knees.
- If the goalposts move during play, the referee may award (or deny) a score depending on which side of the posts he believes the ball would have passed had they been in their proper position.
- If a player refuses to leave the pitch after being sent off, the referee can give a three-minute warning, and then terminate the match if the offending player is still on the pitch after the time-limit elapses.
- One of the official duties of the referee is to present the ball to the captain of the winning team at the end of a provincial or All-Ireland final.
- You may not wear a hurling helmet in a football game.

All-Ireland Finals 1887–2005

For the first few years of the All-Ireland championships, counties were represented by their champion club rather than by a county side; names of the competing clubs are given in brackets below. Another early tradition was the 'away' final, in which the All-Ireland champion would play London – and win, usually. London managed a win in the 1901 away hurling final, and so we list that result to mark the one occasion when the All-Ireland champion did not win both finals.

Hurling

1887 Tipperary (Thurles) 1–1
Galway (Meelick) 0–0

1888 Unfinished due to USA tour

1889 Dublin (Kickhams) 5–1
Clare (Tulla) 1–6

1890 Wexford (Castlebridge) 2–2
Cork (Aughabullogue) 1–6
(Unfinished: Cork awarded title)

1891 Kerry (Ballyduff) 2–3
Wexford (Crossabeg) 1–5

1892 Cork 2–4 Dublin 1–1
(Unfinished: Cork awarded title)

1893 Cork 6–8 Kilkenny 0–2

1894 Cork 5–20 Dublin 2–0

1895 Tipperary 6–8 Kilkenny 1–0

1896 Tipperary 8–14 Dublin 0–4

1897 Limerick 3–4 Kilkenny 2–4

1898 Kilkenny 3–3 Clare 2–3

1899 Tipperary 3–12 Wexford 1–4
(Unfinished: Tipperary awarded title)

1900 Tipperary 6–13 Galway 1–5
1901 Cork 2–8 Wexford 0–6
(Away final: London 1–5
Cork 0–4)
1902 Cork 1–7 Dublin 1–7
Replay
Cork 2–6 Dublin 0–1
1903 Cork 8–9 Kilkenny 0–8
1904 Kilkenny 1–9 Cork 1–8
1905 Cork 5–10 Kilkenny 3–13
Refixture (due to objections)
Kilkenny 7–7 Cork 2–9
1906 Tipperary 3–16 Dublin 3–8
1907 Kilkenny 3–12 Cork 4–8
1908 Tipperary 2–5 Dublin 1–8
Replay
Tipperary 3–15 Dublin 1–5
1909 Kilkenny 4–6 Tipperary 0–12
1910 Wexford 7–0 Limerick 6–2
1911 Kilkenny 3–3 Tipperary 1–1
1912 Kilkenny 2–1 Cork 1–3
1913 Kilkenny 2–4 Tipperary 1–2
1914 Clare 5–1 Laois 1–0
1915 Laois 6–2 Cork 4–1
1916 Tipperary 5–4 Kilkenny 3–2
1917 Dublin 5–4 Tipperary 4–2
1918 Limerick 9–5 Wexford 1–3
1919 Cork 6–4 Dublin 2–4
1920 Dublin 4–9 Cork 4–3
1921 Limerick 8–5 Dublin 3–2
1922 Kilkenny 4–2 Tipperary 2–6
1923 Galway 7–3 Limerick 4–5
1924 Dublin 5–3 Galway 2–6
1925 Tipperary 5–6 Galway 1–5
1926 Cork 4–6 Kilkenny 2–0
1927 Dublin 4–8 Cork 1–3
1928 Cork 6–12 Galway 1–0
1929 Cork 4–9 Galway 1–3
1930 Tipperary 2–7 Dublin 1–3
1931 Cork 1–6 Kilkenny 1–6
Replay
Cork 2–5 Kilkenny 2–5
2nd replay
Cork 5–8 Kilkenny 3–4
1932 Kilkenny 3–3 Clare 2–3
1933 Kilkenny 1–7 Limerick 0–6
1934 Limerick 2–7 Dublin 3–4
Replay
Limerick 5–2 Dublin 2–6
1935 Kilkenny 2–5 Limerick 2–4
1936 Limerick 5–6 Kilkenny 1–5
1937 Tipperary 3–11 Kilkenny 0–3
1938 Dublin 2–5 Waterford 1–6
1939 Kilkenny 2–7 Cork 3–3
1940 Limerick 3–7 Kilkenny 1–7
1941 Cork 5–11 Dublin 0–6
1942 Cork 2–14 Dublin 3–4
1943 Cork 5–16 Antrim 0–4
1944 Cork 2–13 Dublin 1–2
1945 Cork 7–5 Kilkenny 3–8
1946 Cork 7–5 Kilkenny 3–8
1947 Kilkenny 0–14 Cork 2–7
1948 Waterford 6–7 Dublin 4–2
1949 Tipperary 3–11 Laois 0–3
1950 Tipperary 1–9 Kilkenny 1–8
1951 Tipperary 2–14 Wexford 7–7
1952 Cork 2–14 Dublin 0–7
1953 Cork 3–3 Galway 0–8
1954 Cork 1–9 Wexford 1–6
1955 Wexford 3–13 Galway 2–8
1956 Wexford 2–14 Cork 2–8
1957 Kilkenny 4–10 Waterford 3–12
1958 Tipperary 4–9 Galway 2–5
1959 Waterford 1–17 Kilkenny 5–5
Replay
Waterford 3–12 Kilkenny 1–10
1960 Wexford 2–15 Tipperary 0–11
1961 Tipperary 0–16 Dublin 1–12
1962 Tipperary 3–10 Wexford 2–11
1963 Kilkenny 4–17 Waterford 6–8
1964 Tipperary 5–13 Kilkenny 2–8
1965 Tipperary 2–16 Wexford 0–10
1966 Cork 3–9 Kilkenny 1–10
1967 Kilkenny 3–8 Tipperary 2–7
1968 Wexford 5–8 Tipperary 3–12
1969 Kilkenny 2–15 Cork 2–9
1970 Cork 6–21 Wexford 5–10
1971 Tipperary 5–17 Kilkenny 5–14
1972 Kilkenny 3–24 Cork 5–11
1973 Limerick 1–21 Kilkenny 1–14
1974 Kilkenny 3–19 Limerick 1–13
1975 Kilkenny 2–22 Galway 2–10
1976 Cork 2–21 Wexford 4–11
1977 Cork 1–17 Wexford 3–8
1978 Cork 1–15 Kilkenny 2–8
1979 Kilkenny 2–12 Galway 1–8
1980 Galway 2–15 Limerick 3–9
1981 Offaly 2–12 Galway 0–15
1982 Kilkenny 3–18 Cork 1–13
1983 Kilkenny 2–14 Cork 2–12
1984 Cork 3–16 Offaly 1–12
1985 Offaly 2–11 Galway 1–12
1986 Cork 4–13 Galway 2–15

1987 Galway 1–12 Kilkenny 0–9
1988 Galway 1–15 Tipperary 0–14
1989 Tipperary 4–24 Antrim 3–9
1990 Cork 5–15 Galway 2–21
1991 Tipperary 1–16 Kilkenny 0–15
1992 Kilkenny 3–10 Cork 1–12
1993 Kilkenny 2–17 Galway 1–15
1994 Offaly 3–16 Limerick 2–13
1995 Clare 1–13 Offaly 2–8
1996 Wexford 1–13 Limerick 0–14
1997 Clare 0–20 Tipperary 2–13
1998 Offaly 2–16 Kilkenny 1–13
1999 Cork 0–13 Kilkenny 0–12
2000 Kilkenny 5–15 Offaly 1–14
2001 Tipperary 2–18 Galway 2–15
2002 Kilkenny 2–20 Clare 0–19
2003 Kilkenny 1–14 Cork 1–11
2004 Cork 0–17 Kilkenny 0–9
2005 Cork 1–21 Galway 1–16

Football

1887 Limerick (Commercials) 1–4 Louth (Young Irelands) 0–3
1888 Unfinished due to USA tour
1889 Tipperary (Bohercrowe) 3–6 Laois (Portlaoise) 0–0
1890 Cork (Midleton) 2–4 Wexford (Blues & Whites) 0–1
1891 Dublin (Young Irelands) 2–1 Cork (Clondrohid) 1–9
1892 Dublin 1–4 Roscommon 1–0
1893 Wexford 1–1 Cork 0–1
1894 Dublin 1–1 Cork 0–6
Replay
Dublin 0–5 Cork 1–2
1895 Tipperary 0–4 Meath 0–3
1896 Limerick 1–5 Dublin 0–7
1897 Dublin 2–6 Cork 0–2
1898 Dublin 2–8 Waterford 0–4
1899 Dublin 1–10 Cork 0–6
1900 Tipperary 2–20 Galway 0–1
1901 Dublin 1–2 Cork 0–4
1902 Dublin 0–6 Tipperary 0–5
1903 Kerry 1–4 Kildare 1–3 (Unfinished)
Refixture
Kerry 0–7 Kildare 1–4
Replay
Kerry 0–8 Kildare 0–2
1904 Kerry 0–5 Dublin 0–2
1905 Kildare 1–7 Kerry 0–5
1906 Dublin 0–5 Cork 0–4
1907 Dublin 0–6 Cork 0–2
1908 Dublin 0–10 Kerry 0–3
1909 Kerry 1–9 Louth 0–6
1910 Louth walkover from Kerry (Kerry refused to travel)
1911 Cork 6–6 Antrim 1–2
1912 Louth 1–7 Antrim 1–2
1913 Kerry 2–2 Wexford 0–3
1914 Kerry 1–3 Wexford 0–6
Replay
Kerry 2–3 Wexford 0–6
1915 Wexford 2–4 Kerry 2–1
1916 Wexford 3–4 Mayo 1–2
1917 Wexford 0–9 Clare 0–5
1918 Wexford 0–5 Tipperary 0–4
1919 Kildare 2–5 Galway 0–1
1920 Tipperary 1–6 Dublin 1–2
1921 Dublin 1–9 Mayo 0–2
1922 Dublin 0–6 Galway 0–4
1923 Dublin 1–5 Kerry 1–3
1924 Kerry 0–4 Dublin 0–3
1925 Galway 3–2 Cavan 1–2
1926 Kerry 1–3 Kildare 0–6
Replay
Kerry 1–4 Kildare 0–4
1927 Kildare 0–5 Kerry 0–3
1928 Kildare 2–6 Cavan 2–5
1929 Kerry 1–8 Kildare 1–5
1930 Kerry 3–11 Monaghan 0–2
1931 Kerry 1–11 Kildare 0–8
1932 Kerry 2–7 Mayo 2–4
1933 Cavan 2–5 Galway 1–4
1934 Galway 3–5 Dublin 1–9
1935 Cavan 3–6 Kildare 2–5
1936 Mayo 4–11 Laois 0–5
1937 Kerry 2–5 Mayo 1–8
Replay
Kerry 4–4 Cavan 1–7
1938 Galway 3–3 Kerry 2–6
Replay
Galway 2–4 Kerry 0–7
1939 Kerry 2–5 Meath 2–3
1940 Kerry 0–7 Galway 1–3
1941 Kerry 1–8 Galway 0–7
1942 Dublin 1–10 Galway 1–8
1943 Roscommon 1–6 Cavan 1–6
Replay
Roscommon 2–7 Cavan 2–2
1944 Roscommon 1–9 Kerry 2–4
1945 Cork 2–5 Cavan 0–7

1946 Kerry 2–4 Roscommon 1–7
Replay
Kerry 2–8 Roscommon 0–10
1947 Cavan 2–11 Kerry 2–7
1948 Cavan 4–5 Mayo 4–4
1949 Meath 1–10 Cavan 1–6
1950 Mayo 2–5 Louth 1–6
1951 Mayo 2–8 Meath 0–9
1952 Cavan 2–4 Meath 1–7
Replay
Cavan 0–9 Meath 0–5
1953 Kerry 0–13 Armagh 1–6
1954 Meath 1–13 Kerry 1–7
1955 Kerry 0–12 Dublin 1–6
1956 Galway 2–13 Cork 3–7
1957 Louth 1–9 Cork 1–7
1958 Dublin 2–12 Derry 1–9
1959 Kerry 3–7 Galway 1–4
1960 Down 2–10 Kerry 0–8
1961 Down 3–6 Offaly 2–8
1962 Kerry 1–12 Roscommon 1–6
1963 Dublin 1–9 Galway 0–10
1964 Galway 0–15 Kerry 0–10
1965 Galway 0–12 Kerry 0–9
1966 Galway 0–10 Meath 0–7
1967 Meath 1–9 Cork 0–9
1968 Down 2–12 Kerry 1–13
1969 Kerry 0–10 Offaly 0–7
1970 Kerry 2–19 Meath 0–18
1971 Offaly 1–14 Galway 2–8
1972 Offaly 1–13 Kerry 1–13
Replay
Offaly 1–19 Kerry 0–13
1973 Cork 3–17 Galway 2–13
1974 Dublin 0–14 Galway 1–6
1975 Kerry 2–12 Dublin 0–11
1976 Dublin 3–8 Kerry 0–10
1977 Dublin 5–12 Armagh 3–6
1978 Kerry 5–11 Dublin 0–9
1979 Kerry 3–13 Dublin 1–8
1980 Kerry 1–9 Roscommon 1–6
1981 Kerry 1–12 Offaly 0–8
1982 Offaly 1–14 Kerry 0–17
1983 Dublin 1–10 Galway 1–8
1984 Kerry 0–14 Dublin 1–6
1985 Kerry 2–12 Dublin 2–8
1986 Kerry 2–15 Tyrone 1–10
1987 Meath 1–14 Cork 0–11
1988 Meath 0–12 Cork 1–9
Replay
Meath 0–13 Cork 0–12
1989 Cork 0–17 Mayo 1–11
1990 Cork 0–11 Meath 0–9
1991 Down 1–16 Meath 1–14
1992 Donegal 0–18 Dublin 0–14
1993 Derry 1–14 Cork 2–8
1994 Down 1–12 Dublin 0–13
1995 Dublin 1–10 Tyrone 0–12
1996 Meath 0–12 Mayo 1–9
Replay
Meath 2–9 Mayo 1–11
1997 Kerry 0–13 Mayo 1–7
1998 Galway 1–14 Kildare 1–10
1999 Meath 1–11 Cork 1–8
2000 Kerry 0–14 Galway 0–14
Replay
Kerry 0–17 Galway 1–10
2001 Galway 0–17 Meath 0–8
2002 Armagh 1–12 Kerry 0–14
2003 Tyrone 0–12 Armagh 0–9
2004 Kerry 1–20 Mayo 2–9
2005 Tyrone 1–16 Kerry 2–10

Table of Honours

All-Ireland Hurling Titles

Cork	30
Kilkenny	28
Tipperary	25
Limerick	7
Dublin	6
Wexford	6
Galway	4
Offaly	4
Clare	3
Waterford	2
Kerry	1
Laois	1
London	1

All-Ireland Football Titles

Kerry	33
Dublin	22
Galway	9
Meath	7
Cork	6
Cavan	5
Down	5
Wexford	5
Kildare	4
Tipperary	4
Louth	3
Mayo	3
Offaly	3
Limerick	2
Roscommon	2
Tyrone	2
Armagh	1
Derry	1
Donegal	1

All-Ireland Titles in Both Codes

Cork	36
Kerry	34
Tipperary	29
Dublin	28
Kilkenny	28

Galway	13
Wexford	11
Limerick	9
Meath	7
Offaly	7
Cavan	5
Down	5
Kildare	4
Clare	3
Louth	3
Mayo	3
Roscommon	2
Tyrone	2
Waterford	2
Armagh	1
Derry	1
Donegal	1
Laois	1
London	1

Reigning Champions

All-Ireland

Football

Senior	Tyrone	(Final: Tyrone 1–16 Kerry 2–10)
Junior	Cork	(Final: Cork 0–10 Meath 1–4)
Under-21	Galway	(Final: Galway 6–5 Down 4–6)
Minor	Down	(Final: Down 1–15 Mayo 0–8)
Masters	Longford	(Final: Longford 1–10 Down 1–7)
Masters Shield	Tyrone	(Final: Tyrone 3–8 Roscommon 1–4)
Tommy Murphy Cup	Tipperary	(Final: Tipperary 3–10 Wexford 0–15)
Vocational Schools	Tyrone	

Hurling

Senior	Cork	(Final: Cork 1–21 Galway 1–16)
Christy Ring Cup	Westmeath	(Final: Westmeath 1–23 Down 2–18)
Nicky Rackard Cup	London	(Final: London 5–8 Louth 1–5)
Intermediate	Wexford	(Final: Wexford 1–15 Galway 0–16)
Under-21	Galway	(Final: Galway 1–15 Kilkenny 1–14)
Minor	Galway	(Final: Galway 3–12 Limerick 0–17)
Under-21 B	Meath	(Final: Meath 1–17 Kerry 0–16)

Leinster

Football

Senior	Dublin	(Final: Dublin 0–14 Laois 0–13)
Junior	Meath	(Final: Meath 1–09 Louth 0–5)
Under-21	Dublin	(Final replay: Dublin 0–12 Kildare 0–11)
Minor	Laois	(Final: Laois 1–12 Offaly 1–7)

Hurling

Senior	Kilkenny	(Final: Kilkenny 0–22 Wexford 1–16)
Intermediate	Wexford	(Final: Wexford 0–14 Kilkenny 0–13)
Junior Shield	Longford	(Final: Longford 2–14 Down 1–16)
Under-21	Kilkenny	(Final: Kilkenny 0–17 Dublin 1–10)
Minor	Dublin	(Final: Dublin 0–17 Wexford 0–12)

Munster

Football

Senior	Kerry	(Final: Kerry 1–11 Cork 0–11)
Junior	Cork	(Final: Cork 2–13 Kerry 0–8)
Under-21	Cork	(Final: Cork 1–14 Limerick 1–11)
Minor	Cork	(Final: Cork 3–8 Kerry 1–11)

Hurling

Senior	Cork	(Final: Cork 1–21 Tipperary 1–16)
Intermediate	Cork	(Final: Cork 2–17 Tipperary 2–11)
Under-21	Cork	(Final: Cork 4–8 Tipperary 0–13)
Minor	Cork	(Final: Cork 2–18 Limerick 1–12)

Connacht

Football

Senior	Galway	(Final: Galway 0–10 Mayo 0–8)
Junior	Sligo	(Final: Sligo 0–12 Mayo 0–11)
Under-21	Galway	(Final: Galway 1–13 Mayo 0–4)
Minor	Galway	(Final: Galway 0–10 Mayo 0–9)

Ulster

Football

Senior	Armagh	(Final replay: Armagh 0–13 Tyrone 0–11)
Under-21	Down	(Final: Down 2–14 Cavan 2–12)
Minor	Armagh	(Final: Armagh 0–11 Down 0–10)

Hurling

Senior	Antrim	(Final: Antrim 2–22 Down 1–18)
Under-21	Antrim	(Final: Antrim 3–12 Down 0–16)
Minor	Antrim	(Final: Antrim 3–18 Derry 2–7)

Websites

Official Gaelic Games websites

GAA	http://www.gaa.ie
Women's Football	http://www.ladiesgaelic.ie
Camogie	http://www.camogie.ie
Handball	http://www.handball.ie
Rounders	http://www.rounders.ie
Leinster	http://leinster.gaa.ie
Carlow	http://carlow.gaa.ie
Dublin	http://www.hill16.ie
Kildare	http://kildare.gaa.ie
Kilkenny	http://kilkenny.gaa.ie
Laois	http://laois.gaa.ie
Longford	http://longford.gaa.ie
Louth	http://louthgaa.ie
Meath	http://meath.gaa.ie
Offaly	http://offaly.gaa.ie
Westmeath	http://westmeath.gaa.ie
Wexford	http://wexford.gaa.ie
Wicklow	http://wicklow.gaa.ie
Munster	http://munster.gaa.ie
Clare	http://claregaa.ie
Cork	http://cork.gaa.ie
Kerry	http://kerry.gaa.ie
Limerick	http://limerick.gaa.ie
Tipperary	http://tipperary.gaa.ie
Waterford	http://waterford.gaa.ie
Connacht	http://www.connachtgaa.ie
Galway	http://galwaygaa.ie
Leitrim	http://leitrimgaa.ie
Mayo	http://www.mayogaa.com
Roscommon	http://www.gaaroscommon.ie
Sligo	http://www.sligogaa.com
Ulster	http://ulster.gaa.ie
Antrim	http://www.antrimgaa.net
Armagh	http://www.armagh-gaa.com
Cavan	http://cavan.gaa.ie
Derry	http://derry.gaa.ie
Donegal	http://www.donegal-gaa.com
Down	http://www.downgaa.net
Fermanagh	http://fermanagh.gaa.ie
Monaghan	http://monaghan.gaa.ie
Tyrone	http://tyrone.gaa.ie

Alternative county websites

Dublin	http://www.dubsforum.tk
Dublin	http://www.reservoirdubs.com
Cork	http://www.rebelgaa.com
Tipperary	http://www.premierview.pro.ie
Tyrone	http://www.teamtalkmag.com
Roscommon	http://www.sheepstealers.com
Sligo	http://friendsofsligofootball.com
Armagh	http://www.orchardcounty.com

Other sites of interest

Sigerson Cup	http://www.sigersoncup.com
Gaelic Games journalists	http://www.ulstergaawriters.com
Views & humour	http://www.anfearrua.ie
Worldwide sports	http://www.setanta.com
News site	http://www.hoganstand.com
Club management system	http://www.gaelsport.com
News & views	http://www.gaelicgazette.com
Weeshie Fogarty (Radio Kerry)	http://www.terracetalkireland.com
Discussion board	http://www.gaaboard.com
For kids	http://www.cul4kidz.com
Azzurri	http://www.azzurri.ie
O'Neill's	http://www.oneills.ie
Online shop	http://www.pride.ie
Gaelic Gear	http://www.gaelicgear.com

Websites abroad

North America	http://www.nagaa.org
New York	http://www.ny-gaa.org
London	http://www.londongaa.org
Australasia	http://www.gaelicfootball.com.au
Europe	http://europe.gaa.ie
Asia	http://www.asiangaelicgames.com

How to Contact the GAA

Gaelic Athletic Association
Croke Park
Dublin 3
Tel: +353 (0)1 836 3222
Fax: +353 (0)1 855 8436
E-mail: queries@gaa.ie
Tickets: tickets@gaa.ie

Connacht Provincial Council
Clare Road
Ballyhaunis
Co. Mayo
Tel: +353 (0)94 963 0335
Fax: +353 (0)94 963 0175
E-mail:
connachtgaa@eircom.net

Leinster Provincial Council
Leinster GAA Office
Portlaoise
Co. Laois
Tel: +353 (0)502 20871
Tel: +353 (0)502 20958
Fax: +353 (0)502 20958
E-mail: leinster@gaa.ie

Munster Provincial Council
Dublin Road
Limerick
Tel: +353 (0)61 493060
E-mail: munsterweb@gaa.ie

Ulster Provincial Council
St Tiernach's Park
Clones
Co. Monaghan
Tel: +353 (0)47 52380
Fax: +353 (0)47 52384
E-mail ulsterpro@ulstergaa.ie

Ladies Gaelic Football
Croke Park
Dublin 3
Tel: +353 (0)1 836 3156
Fax: +353 (0)1 836 3111
E-mail: info@ladiesgaelic.ie

Camogie
Croke Park
Dublin 3
Tel: +353 (0)1 836 4619
Fax: +353 (0)1 855 6063
E-mail: info@camogie.ie

Irish Handball
Croke Park
Dublin 3
Tel: +353 (0)1 836 4186
Fax: +353 (0)1 836 4454
E-mail: info@handball.ie

Gaelic Games Museums

GAA Museum, Croke Park

Officially opened in 1998 by the GAA President, Joe McDonagh, and the Taoiseach, Bertie Ahern, the GAA Museum – located at the Cusack Stand side of Croke Park – communicates the extraordinary history of the Gaelic Athletic Association, both on the field of play and off it.

Designed for both supporters of Gaelic Games and visitors to Ireland who may have no previous experience of the sport, the museum uses interactive exhibits, databanks, guides, videos, photographs and art to honour the players and officials who have made exceptional contributions to the national games.

The video archive includes footage of the 1939 'Thunder and Lightning' senior hurling final, contested by Cork and Kilkenny in appalling weather conditions, and the 1982 football final, when Offaly stopped Kerry's bid for five All-Ireland championships in a row.

And with Croke Park now one of the most modern sporting arenas in the world, the stadium tours – which commence from the reception area of the museum – are proving particularly popular. The guided tour lasts approximately one hour and takes you to the corporate levels, the media centre, the pitch and the dressing rooms.

The museum is open seven days a week. On match days the museum opens at the same time as the stiles.

GAA Museum
Croke Park
St Joseph's Avenue
Dublin 3

Tel: +353 (0)1 819 2323
Fax: +353 (0)1 819 2324
E-mail: gaamuseum@crokepark.ie
Website: http://www.gaa.ie/museum

Lar na Páirce, Thurles

Lar na Páirce is Tipperary's answer to the main GAA museum, though it was actually opened before the Dublin centre, in 1994. It is located in a 19th-century building on Slievenamon Road in Thurles – only yards from Liberty Square and Hayes' Hotel, where the GAA was founded in 1884. Its collection includes football boots, hurleys, footballs, sliotars, newspaper cuttings, trophies, photographs, and jerseys – many signed by legendary footballers and hurlers. Much of the memorabilia on display was donated by Sam Melbourne, a local GAA enthusiast.

Lar na Páirce
Slievenamon Road
Thurles
Co. Tipperary

Tel: +353 (0) 504 23579

6
Watching the Championship

6 Watching the Championship

Towns and Stadiums

During last season's senior football championship, Cavan fans were asked to journey to Roscommon, Westmeath supporters to Thurles, and Meath and Wexford supporters had to travel up to Belfast and Clones respectively. In the hurling championship, the new qualifier system brought about several unusual championship pairings and venues, such as Galway taking on Limerick at the Gaelic Grounds. With the increased number of summer games in recent years and the absence of any border for qualifier ties, loyal fans are being introduced to more and more unfamiliar venues and towns. Road maps can only point you in the right direction; here we attempt to take you the rest of the way, with advice on traffic, parking, pubs, hotels and other supporters' landmarks.

Belfast

Casement Park

Belfast, Co. Antrim
Stadium capacity: 32,500

The stadium

Roger Casement Park was once the principal GAA venue in Ulster. Two of the first games ever held at the Belfast ground – in the summer of 1953 – were the inaugural Ulster club football final (with Armagh Harps beating local side St John's) and the Ulster senior football final in which Armagh defeated reigning All-Ireland champions Cavan. The success of the Antrim football team in the 1940s helped with the substantial fundraising necessary to purchase and develop the Andersonstown Road stadium. Since the 1953 Ulster final, Casement has hosted seven other inter-county senior football championship deciders, but none since 1971, with St Tiernach's Park in Clones establishing itself as the premier venue for Ulster games. In an effort to remedy that situation, a major facelift was undertaken at the Belfast ground in the late 1990s. Almost a half-century after it was officially opened, the vast majority of the viewing area around the ground was still grass. The new concrete terracing has elevated the stadium to a new level – one capable of challenging Clones for a bigger share of the high-profile football championship ties.

Getting there

Casement Park is located off Andersonstown Road in west Belfast – not far from junction 2 of the M1, which puts it within relatively easy reach of road users from other counties. Parking isn't a huge problem, and there are plenty of supervised multi-storey car parks in the centre of Belfast, but leaving in good time is advisable on days Casement's capacity might be tested – which isn't often. Belfast's main bus station is on Glengall Street (behind the Europa Hotel and beside Great Victoria Street Rail Station) at the west side of the city centre – within walking distance, or a very short taxi ride, of Casement Park. The city bus service is called Metro, with buses marked '10' stopping at or near the stadium. Trains regularly stop at Finaghy rail station, which is five minutes from the ground. The Central Rail Station, in the city centre, connects with Derry to the north-west and Dublin to the south.

The city

Close to the famous Europa Hotel in the city centre is Jury's Inn on Great Victoria Street. Travelling GAA fans are also known to use the Holiday Inn on Ormeau Avenue. In the city centre, the Fountain Bar and Restaurant is popular for a pre-match bite, and around the corner on Winecellar Entry (off High Street) is the popular White's Tavern. The Rock Bar on the Falls Road (491) is a good pub for a pre-match drink, as is Hoppy Dobbins on Andersonstown Road. The Hatfield House on Ormeau Road is a well-known GAA pub, while a little further away on the Malone Road is the Botanic Inn. A sports fan's dream, the 'Bot' shows all sporting codes on big screens located in every corner. It also serves lunch and dinner daily and has a night-club upstairs.

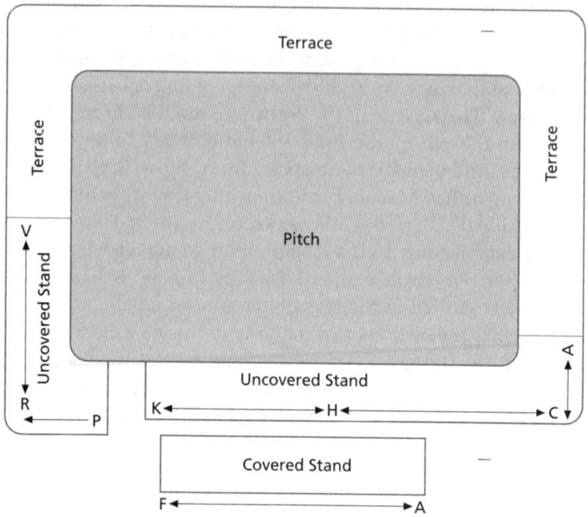

Travel distances

Cavan town	141 km (87 miles)
Cork city	421 km (261 miles)
Downpatrick	35 km (23 miles)
Dublin city	167 km (104 miles)
Dundalk	83 km (51 miles)
Dungannon	67 km (41 miles)
Enniskillen	134 km (83 miles)
Letterkenny	166 km (103 miles)
Monaghan town	93 km (58 miles)
Newry	60 km (37 miles)
Omagh	109 km (68 miles)

Clones

St Tiernach's Park

Clones, Co. Monaghan
Stadium capacity: 36,000

The stadium

Clones was once again deserted on Ulster football final day last season, as Croke Park hosted the northern decider (as well as, more strangely, the replay). Still, St Tiernach's Park has never been busier than in the past few seasons, with several annual qualifier ties adding to the regular high percentage of provincial matches. There are many reason why Clones was chosen and developed over the years as the main GAA stadium in Ulster. The area has been associated with Gaelic games from the early days of the organization: Clones contested the first-ever Monaghan club championship in the late 1880s. The £1 million development of the west stand has ensured the importance of St Tiernach's Park in the province for many years to come.

Getting there

St Tiernach's Park is located to the north of the town of Clones, on Church Hill. With the town situated near the Fermanagh border in west Monaghan, Clones is the ideal location for a major GAA stadium in Ulster – at least when you look at where it is on a map. However, it's a long, long time since the town was a major railway hub, and driving to Clones on big match days can be a gruelling experience, especially when the supporters of the competing counties are approaching from the same direction, which is often the case. Still, a big match day in Clones makes for a rather unique experience, because the town – which has fewer than 2,000 inhabitants – is

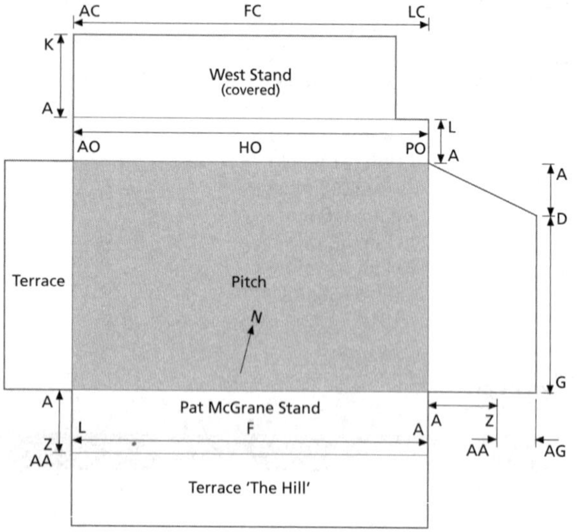

almost completely taken over by visiting supporters. Just make sure you leave in plenty of time if you hope to soak up the atmosphere before the game.

The town

For travelling supporters, there are two focal points in the town: the Diamond (the centre of Clones) and Fermanagh Street (running north-west from the centre of town) – both of which have received face-lifts in the past few years. Supporters congregate on Fermanagh Street on match days, and it is the main route taken by most to St Tiernach's Park. At the stadium end of Fermanagh Street is the Creighton Hotel, which has a large outdoor area for supporters on match days. At the other side of the road is the Tower Bar, and closer to the centre of town is the Paragon Bar, a popular spot for GAA fans to meet before and after the game. The Diamond area of the town also has a number of restaurants and bars that are well worth a visit, including Cuildarach Bar and Restaurant – which also offers accommodation.

Travel distances

Belfast city	113 km (70 miles)
Cavan town	28 km (18 miles)
Derry city	128 km (79 miles)
Donegal town	93 km (58 miles)

Dublin city	128 km (80 miles)
Enniskillen	39 km (24 miles)
Galway city	201 km (125 miles)
Mullingar	100 km (62 miles)
Newry	78 km (48 miles)
Omagh	72 km (45 miles)

Cork

Páirc Uí Chaoimh

Cork city
Stadium capacity: 43,000

The stadium

Known for decades as the Cork Athletic Grounds, Páirc Uí Chaoimh was rechristened in 1976, the same year that the Rebels defeated Limerick in the Munster senior hurling final at the venue. For locals, especially, there is nothing to compare with a full ground on a championship afternoon in the summer. Probably the most significant change of recent years was made in 1999, when the field was reseeded and the drainage system improved. Another more recent alteration did not go so smoothly. GAA supporters are slimmer in Cork than the rest of the country, or so officials hoped when they saw the new seats on the uncovered stand early last year. The problems with the seating – especially the narrow space between each row of seats – were an

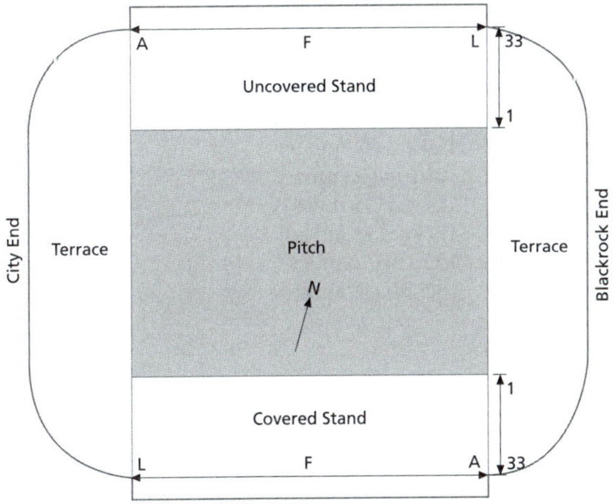

unwelcome distraction during the summer, especially in the run-up to the Munster senior hurling final.

Getting there

Páirc Uí Chaoimh is located to the east of the city centre, on the south banks of the river Lee. The opening of the Jack Lynch Tunnel in 1999 was a godsend, allowing travelling supporters to bypass the city centre on their way to the stadium. Still, even if you are travelling by car, it is advisable to leave enough time for at least a 15-minute walk to the stadium – parking in the immediate vicinity of the ground on big summer Sundays is almost impossible. It's the reason many supporters prefer to arrive at the city centre's train station or main bus station. The train station – which frustratingly is on the north side of the river and necessitates a walk towards town to cross the Lee before turning east towards the stadium – is always full of fans on the morning of a big game.

The city

Because of the route GAA fans must take to get from the train station and the city centre to the Cork ground, some of the most popular meeting places and watering holes are along by the docks. Jury's Inn on Anderson's Quay is always busy on match day, and, around the corner, public houses such as Idle Hour and the nearby Port Bar and Marina Bar usually kept very busy. One of the closest pubs to Páirc Uí Chaoimh and a popular haunt for a last-minute pre-match drink is the Venue in Ballintemple, while a little further down the road you'll find the Temple Inn (which also serves food), the Leaping Salmon and, at the end of the road, the Pier Head Inn. Back in the city centre, Washington Street has much to offer by way of bars, restaurants and accommodation, with Reardan's among the most popular.

Travel distances

Dublin city	252 km (157 miles)
Galway city	204 km (127 miles)
Kilkenny city	149 km (93 miles)
Limerick city	100 km (63 miles)
Thurles	119 km (74 miles)
Tralee	117 km (73 miles)
Waterford town	122 km (76 miles)
Wexford town	182 km (113 miles)

Dublin

Croke Park

Jones's Road, Dublin 3
Stadium capacity: 82,300

The stadium

Croke Park stands on the site formerly occupied by the City and Suburban Racecourse, a ground used regularly by the GAA before the organization purchased the 14-acre site for £3,500 in 1913 and renamed it after the association's first patron, Archbishop Croke.

The Hill 16 terrace was constructed in 1917, using rubble from the Easter 1916 rebellion. On 21 November 1920 the ground was stormed by Black and Tans, who shot dead 11 supporters and one player during a football match between Tipperary and Dublin. Four years later, the Hogan Stand was built and dedicated to the fallen player, Tipperary captain Michael Hogan. An upper deck was added to the Cusack Stand in 1936, the Canal End terrace was constructed in 1948 and the Nally Stand in 1952.

Over the past decade the GAA has replaced the old stands and

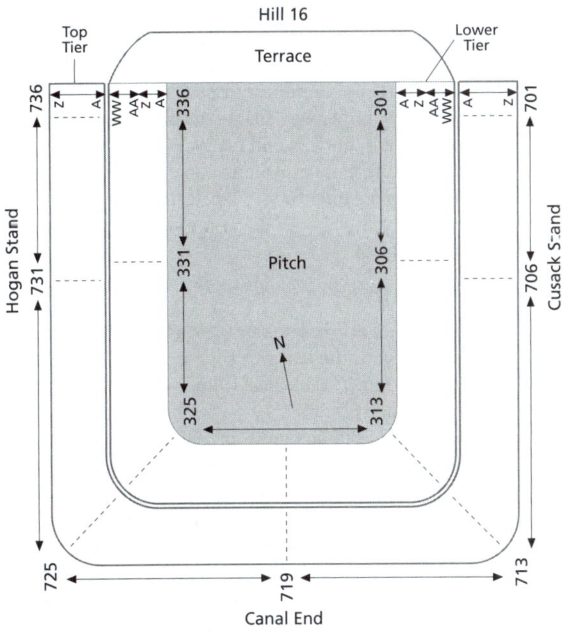

terraces with a more fitting monument to the national games. Phase One of the reconstruction involved the razing of the Cusack Stand and its replacement with a modern three-tiered stand, completed in 1997 with a seating capacity of 25,000. Phase Two extended the new stand around the canal side of the stadium and Phase Three involved the replacement of the Hogan Stand, completing the horseshoe. In 2003 the final phase began, with the replacement of the Nally Stand and the Hill 16 terrace with a new terrace at the railway end. The completion of this phase has brought the capacity of Croke Park up to a remarkable 82,300.

Getting there

Croke Park is located in the Ballybough area of the north inner city of Dublin, with the Hogan Stand backing on to Jones's Road and the Cusack Stand best approached from the side to the east. Just six counties didn't play a senior hurling or senior football game at headquarters last season – even the London hurlers had their day. It's a fact that underlines the growing importance of the stadium in the sporting lives of supporters every year, and not just ones from counties that are considered giants of the game.

Supporters travelling by train to Dublin from the south and west are able to use the Luas tram line to take them from Heuston Station to Abbey Street or Connolly Station. Fans arriving from the north and north-west of the island to Connolly have no need for the new tram service, of course, as the station is only a short walk from Croke Park, as is Busáras, Dublin's central bus station. Last season, the GAA woke up to the fact that the clamping of hundreds of cars around the north inner city every summer weekend is causing serious annoyance – not to mention cost – to hurling and football fans. There are plenty of legal and safe parking garages around the city and, last summer, the 'park & ride' areas outside town – especially the one at the Red Cow Luas stop – were hugely popular on several big-match days. They can't clamp the Luas.

The city

The new Jury's Croke Park has taken over as the closest meeting point to the stadium, with the bar area so close to the action they've named it the Sideline Bar. There's also a Jury's Inn on Parnell Street, near the top of O'Connell Street.

There are a number of public houses in Dublin that are associated with particular counties, and others that attract GAA supporters on big-match weekends no matter who is playing. James Gill on Russell Street (which becomes Jones's Road) benefits greatly from its location, being one of the closest pubs to Croke Park. Probably the most popular thoroughfare on big match days at headquarters, though, is the Drumcondra Road, with Quinn's bar a particular pre- and post-match favourite (there is a restaurant upstairs). A few doors down is McGrath's, and on the opposite side of the road, at the corner of North Circular Road, is the refurbished Big Tree, which is usually full of GAA fans on summer Sundays. At the other side of Croke Park, Smyth's in Fairview is a good place for a bite to eat before a game, as is the Clonliffe House on Ballybough Road. Closer to town, many fans coming from the city centre stop off to soak up the atmosphere, meet friends and maybe even exchange tickets in places such as the Hill 16 on Gardiner Street, Barry's Hotel on Denmark Street and the Hogan Stand on North Circular Road. At the south side of the Liffey, Chaplin's on Hawkins Street, Doyle's around the corner on D'Olier Street and the Palace Bar in Temple Bar are all well-known watering holes for hurling and football fans. For fans travelling by car, An Poitin Stil in Rathcoole and the Red Cow Hotel on the Naas Road are popular for breaking a journey.

Tips

If the weather isn't good, a double-letter Croke Park stand ticket (e.g. KK) is much more valuable than a single letter ticket, as – depending on the direction of the wind and rain – the first 30 rows can be very open to the elements.

If you are approaching the stadium from a side that your ticket is not for, please note it can take a long time to push through the crowds to the correct side of the stadium.

The Lower Cusack Stand starts at Section 301 and ends at 312, the Lower Canal End goes from Section 313 to 324 and the Lower Hogan from 325 to 336. The Upper decks are 701 to 712 (Cusack), 713 to 724 (Canal) and 725 to 736 (Hogan).

While many assume that lower-tier tickets are better than upper-tier ones, there is a considerably better view from the front row of the middle section of the Upper Cusack Stand, for example, than from the back row of the corner section of the Lower Cusack, so it's wise to be careful when buying or swapping tickets.

Travel distances

Belfast	166 km (103 miles)
Cork	256 km (159 miles)
Derry	232 km (144 miles)
Galway	216 km (134 miles)
Kilkenny	124 km (77 miles)
Killarney	306 km (190 miles)
Limerick	197 km (123 miles)
Navan	49 km (30 miles)
Sligo	209 km (130 miles)
Thurles	146 km (91 miles)
Waterford	160 km (100 miles)
Wexford	140 km (87 miles)

Galway

Pearse Stadium

Salthill, Galway
Stadium capacity: 34,000

The stadium

The recent massive redevelopment of Pearse Stadium has made it possible for Galway to bid for big provincial and qualifier games each year. It also has helped to re-establish the GAA's presence in one of the country's fastest-growing cities, where hurling and football face a constant battle with other sports for the attentions of locals. The redevelopment included an 8,000-seater stand, a newly laid pitch, dressing rooms, warm-up areas and toilets. Probably the biggest game Pearse Stadium has hosted in recent years – outside of the usual quota of provincial ties, which last year included the Connacht final between Galway and Mayo – was the 2003 All-Ireland senior hurling qualifier between Tipperary and Galway, which the visitors won by a single point.

Getting there

Pearse Stadium is located at the corner of Dr Mannix Road and Rockbarton Road, beside the Salthill GAA Grounds – the home of

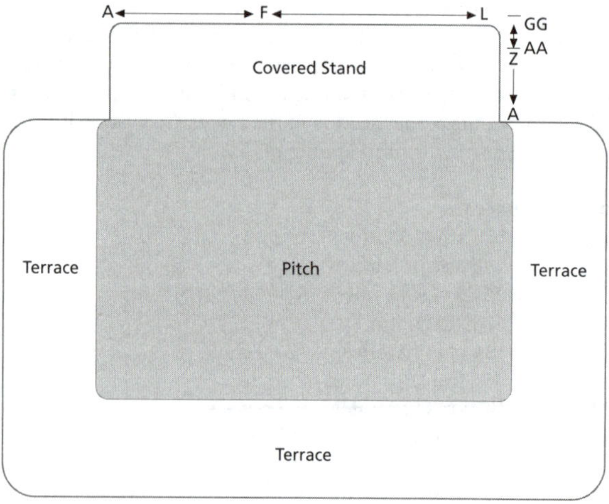

the current club champions of Galway football. Traffic and parking is a major problem in the vicinity of the ground before big games, probably more so than around any other stadium in the country. Galway's ring road is busy on any summer weekend, and even busier when a big match is on. Being located in the south-west of Galway city doesn't make the stadium especially convenient for most supporters, who would be approaching from the other side of the city. For provincial ties in particular, the N17 to the north of the city is normally overladen with jersey-clad fans in cars on the mornings of games. Deciding whether to approach the area using Salthill Road or Taylor's Hill Road can be merely a choice between one traffic jam and another. Parking and walking may be a wise choice, though it can be a very long walk to the ground if the decision to abandon the logjam is made too quickly. The city is well served by rail, with the Dublin–Galway line intersected by rail lines from the north and south.

The city

Galway city has an atmosphere its own, on any weekend, though a big entire match certainly adds to the festival flavour. Eyre Square in the centre of the city is surrounded by hotels and bars, including the Eyre Square Hotel at Forster Street, which has a large bar and nightclub, The Skeffington Arms Hotel (The Skeff), on the west side of the square, and Garvey's Inn – all of which do a very busy day-time food trade. Just off the square, William Street and Shop Street are popular meeting points, boasting many public houses and restaurants – including Taaffe's, Garavan's, the Dew Drop Inn a little further down on Mainguard Street and the lively Róisín Dubh, just across the river on Dominic Street. However, the centre of Galway city is not within walking distance of Pearse Stadium, unless you're fit and have a lot of time to spare before the throw-in. Upper Salthill Road, however, is within a few minutes' stroll of the ground, and boasts several meeting places, including Killoran's, the Cullinane Inn, O'Connor's and PJ Flaherty's.

Travel distances

Carrick-on-Shannon	121 km (75 miles)
Castlebar	87 km (54 miles)
Cork	203 km (126 miles)
Dublin	213 km (133 miles)
Limerick	104 km (65 miles)
Mullingar	149 km (93 miles)
Roscommon	79 km (49 miles)
Sligo	138 km (86 miles)
Thurles	142 km (88 miles)

Kilkenny

Nowlan Park

Kilkenny City
Stadium capacity: 30,000

The stadium

Even though Kilkenny didn't participate in last season's competition, it's still incredible that not a single senior football championship tie was played at Nowlan Park in 2005. And the venue hosted just one senior hurling championship game – a rather unglamorous opening-round provincial tie between Dublin and Laois. In fact, the biggest inter-county fixture in Kilkenny city last season was the triple-header when the Dublin and Limerick minor teams shared billing with the All-Ireland camogie semi-finals. Considering its location and standard, it is probably the most under-exploited stadium in the country – in spite of regular structural improvements over the past number of decades, including the construction of the covered New Stand, replacing the old bank. And, on the rare days when the stadium is full, the atmosphere in the stands and terraces is simply second to none.

Getting there

Nowlan Park – located in the north-east of the city, between Hebron Road and O'Loughlin Road – is within easy walking distance of the city centre. Kilkenny city is situated on the Dublin–Waterford railway line, and McDonagh Station is a 10-minute walk from the stadium. More or less equidistant from Cork and Dublin, the city is adequately served by national primary roads, and the ring road – which runs across the south side of the city – has made the stadium much more easily accessible for supporters travelling from the south. No matter from which direction you approach the city, it is possible (and preferable) to bypass the traditional city-centre traffic jam.

The city

There are no non-GAA pubs in the Marble City; there are merely some more associated with hurling than others. From a location point of view, perhaps MJ McGuinness's bar, situated right outside the stadium on O'Loughlin Road, has the advantage. However, John Street – which connects the city centre to the east side, crossing the River Nore – is probably the most popular location for supporters before and after big games. On this road lies the city's main public house, Langton's, which boosts a massive bar, restaurant and nightclub. Other tenants on the street include Lawlor's bar, Billy Byrne's and the Kilford Arms Hotel – all of which offer accommodation.

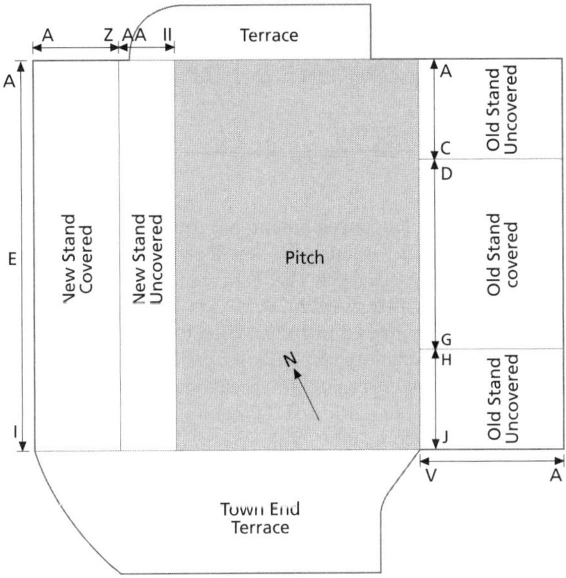

Also on the street is Matt the Miller's, at the bridge, which has large television screens whichever way you look. For those approaching Kilkenny from the north, the Newpark Hotel is situated on the Castlecomer road.

Travel distances

Carlow	38 km (24 miles)
Cork city	150 km (93 miles)
Dublin city	120 km (74 miles)
Galway city	193 km (120 miles)
Limerick city	130 km (81 miles)
Portlaoise	50 km (31 miles)
Thurles	64 km (40 miles)
Waterford Town	48 km (30 miles)
Wexford Town	107 km (67 miles)

Limerick

Gaelic Grounds

Limerick city
Stadium capacity: 49,500

The stadium

A recent €12 million development has transformed the Gaelic Grounds in Limerick – though the new-look stadium hasn't had its impressive capacity tested yet. The main stand is named in memory of legendary Limerick forward Mick Mackey, who played at the official opening of the ground in 1928. When Croke Park replaced its Hogan Stand in the late 1950s, Limerick gratefully accepted the old stand, which allowed over 60,000 spectators to watch the Munster hurling final between Cork and Tipperary in 1961. The Mackey Stand was completed in 1988, with another Munster final between Cork and Tipperary marking its official opening. With a new 12,000 uncovered stand now facing the Mackey – and modern terraces on both sides – Páirc na nGael will be a serious contender for major games in the Munster and All-Ireland qualifier competitions for the foreseeable future.

Getting there

The Gaelic Grounds is located on the Ennis Road, to the west of the Shannon, which makes it convenient for Clare supporters at least. It is simply impossible to estimate the time it will take to drive from

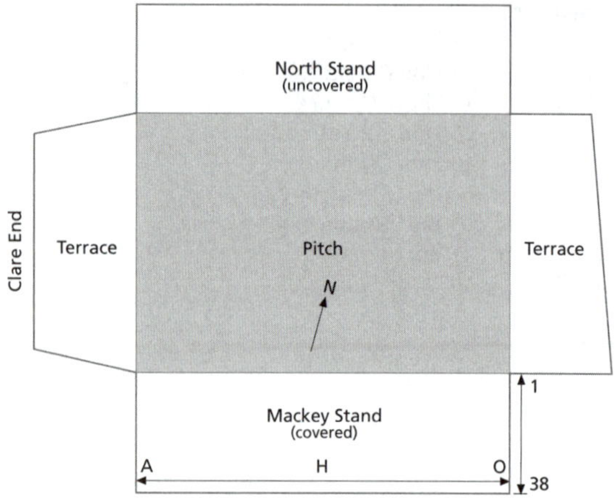

the outskirts of the city to the ground, or vice versa, on match day. As many GAA fans use Thomond Bridge and park near, or on, the northern ring road – within easy walking distance of the Gaelic Grounds to the south – it is vital to allow plenty of time if there is a rugby game at Thomond Park around the same time. Congestion on the roads is possibly the reason many supporters prefer public transport, arriving into the city by train or bus to Colbert Station in the city centre.

The city

Limerick is a compact city, with most of the restaurants, bars and hotels within walking distance of each other. Close to the Gaelic Grounds on the Ennis Road is the Woodfield House Hotel, which is particularly popular if the weather is good on big-match weekends, as there is room for fans to sit outside and soak up the atmosphere. Sarsfield Bridge connects the Ennis Road to the city centre, and the Sarsfield Bridge Hotel is also a popular haunt for GAA fans looking for a bite to eat or a drink before the game, with big plasma screens allowing fans to enjoy other games, or the highlights later on. A little further south, Jury's Inn is located on lower Mallow Street, but is still easily within walking distance of the stadium. And you won't be surprised to learn that the Railway Hotel, near the city centre, is located opposite the station and is often the first port of call for visiting fans.

Travel distances

Athlone	146 km (90 miles)
Cork city	100 km (62 miles)
Dublin city	191 km (118 miles)
Ennis	36 km (23 miles)
Galway city	104 km (64 miles)
Kilkenny city	130 km (81 miles)
Tralee	101 km (62 miles)
Waterford town	126 km (78 miles)

Roscommon

Dr Hyde Park

Roscommon town
Stadium capacity: 30,000

The stadium

Raftery's Field was long used by the GAA for various grades of competition before 1969, when the organization purchased the site and named it after the first president of Ireland, Douglas Hyde. Over the next three decades Dr Hyde Park would undergo regular and gradual improvements, with the grass banks around three sides of the pitch replaced by modern terracing in the early 1990s. More recently, a covered stand was built behind open seating, which added significantly to the stadium's attractiveness, not just for Connacht championship games, but also for the modern qualifier encounters.

Getting there

Dr Hyde Park is located on the Athlone Road, to the south-east of the town centre. Roscommon's railway station is to the south-west of the town, a relatively short distance from the stadium; the line serves Ballina and Westport to the north and joins the Dublin–Galway line to the south. The town is relatively well served by national roads, though Lough Ree has to be circumvented if you are travelling from the east or south-east. Parking is usually not a big problem on big summer GAA Saturdays or Sundays, though that's not to say you will find a spot right outside the stadium. And if you have to travel through the town to reach the ground, it may be wise to allow for some delays.

The town

The centre of Roscommon town is Market Square, where many GAA fans frequent Gleeson's Townhouse and Restaurant and Regan's Guesthouse. On the Galway side of the town you'll find the Abbey Hotel, while just off Market Square, to the north, is O'Gara's Royal Hotel on Castle Street. Closer to Dr Hyde Park to the south is Main Street and then Church Street, where you will find Church Street Station, a public house that has walls decorated with pictures of former Roscommon footballing heroes, and Down the Hatch, another pub with strong local GAA connections.

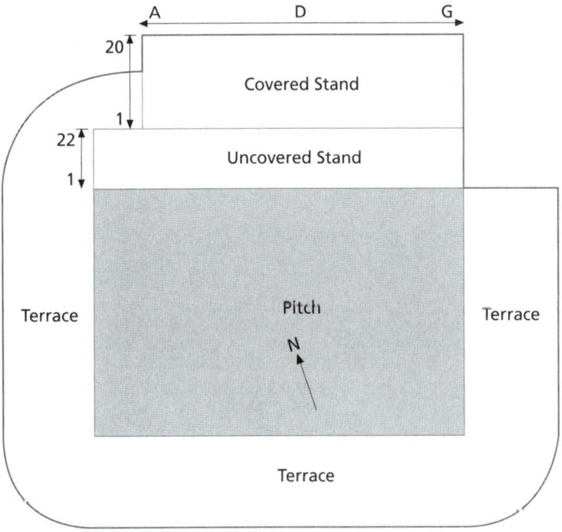

Travel distances

Castlebar	94 km (58 miles)
Carrick-on-Shannon	41 km (26 miles)
Cavan town	85 km (53 miles)
Cork city	272 km (169 miles)
Dublin city	154 km (96 miles)
Galway city	79 km (49 miles)
Mullingar	75 km (47 miles)
Sligo town	84 km (52 miles)
Tullamore	71 km (44 miles)

Thurles

Semple Stadium

Thurles, Co. Tipperary
Stadium capacity: 53,000

The stadium

The second-largest GAA stadium is named after Tom Semple, a Thurles man who claimed All-Ireland hurling championship medals in 1900, 1906 and 1908. He also captained the Tipperary team that played exhibition games against Cork in Belgium in 1910, the same

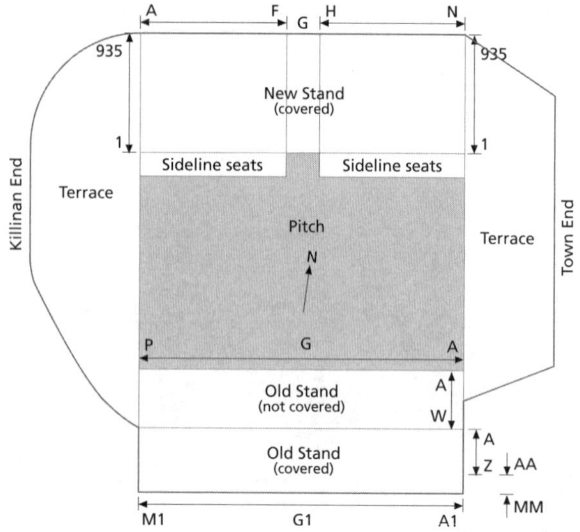

year that a local committee – of which Semple was a prominent member – purchased land from the Thurles Agricultural Show. He died in 1943; 24 year later, after the second stand was completed, the sports field was given its new official name, Semple Stadium. It has what is considered by many to be the best surface for hurling on the island. The 1984 All-Ireland final was played here, in commemoration of the founding of the GAA in the town 100 years earlier. The New Stand (Ardan Uí Riain) was completed by then; more recently, the Old Stand (Ardan Uí Chuineain) has received a major face lift.

Getting there

Semple Stadium – situated in the north-west of the town, just off the Nenagh road – benefits greatly from its location. Of the 12 teams competing in this season's All-Ireland senior hurling championship, eight share a border with Tipperary (which is, of course, also one of the 12). And with the addition of Westmeath to the Liam MacCarthy Cup competition (and the absence of Antrim), Thurles – which was always considered the sentimental centre of hurling – is undoubtedly also the geographical centre of the hurling championship. The town's railway station, which is a short walk from both Liberty Square and the stadium, lies on the line that connects Dublin with Cork, Tralee and Limerick. The town is also easily accessible by car, lying just a few miles off the main Dublin–Cork road. Supporters from the north and west of the county, and counties such as Limerick, Clare and Galway, have the advantage – using the Nenagh or Holycross roads – of not having to get through the town to reach the stadium. Parking is not a major problem, though entry to the housing estates surrounding the stadium is usually limited on big-match days. Take care not to park too far outside the town: it can be a deceptively long walk to the ground, especially from the east and south. Probably the biggest problem for supporters travelling by car, from the east especially, is that there is only one bridge joining the two sides of the town, which can often cause a long traffic-jam, particularly if the Garda Síochána have blocked off the town centre and are directing cars down side streets.

The town

Thurles was certainly under-used last season, though certain results in the Munster hurling championship meant other venues being chosen for big games. With around 10,000 inhabitants, Thurles is the perfect size for big championship weekends: large enough to accommodate the large crowds, but small enough to give the occasion an intimate festival flavour. Hayes' Hotel – the official birthplace of the GAA – is situated in the heart of the town, Liberty Square, and is always popular with hurling and football fans on match day. A few doors away, Fogarty's and Brennan's and, at the opposite side of the square, the County Bar, are well-known GAA pubs. And, as is increasingly the case, if you are trying to fit in watching a match on television on the same day as actually attending a game, Mackey's pub – located between the train station and the Old Stand – has a big screen at the back of the bar and is within a two-minute dash of the stadium, with Bowe's a little further away, situated beside the train station. Apart from Hayes', the Anner Hotel on the Two-Mile–Borris (Dublin) road and the Horse and Jockey Inn, a few miles outside town to the south, are also usually kept very busy accommodating fans – and often players – on summer weekends. Also in the town is Lar na Páirce, a GAA museum on Slievenamon Road (just off Liberty Square).

Travel distances

Cork city	75 km (46 miles)
Dublin city	145 km (90 miles)
Ennis	136 km (85 miles)
Galway city	142 km (88 miles)
Kilkenny city	64 km (40 miles)
Killarney	166 km (103 miles)
Limerick city	99 km (61 miles)
Mullingar	131 km (81 miles)
Waterford town	104 km (64 miles)
Wexford town	163 km (101 miles)

Tickets

A survey conducted late last season in several Ulster counties revealed just how poorly the GAA is promoting our games to the outside world. Hurling and Gaelic football are uniquely Irish and spectator-friendly spectacles, with club games held every weekend in every county and approximately 1,000 inter-county matches each year. Yet the survey revealed that only 12 per cent of foreign tourists knew about the GAA, though 70 per cent said they would be interested in seeing a sport unique to Ireland. The product exists, the selling agent doesn't.

While attendances at big summer games have reached impressive levels, only the All-Ireland football and hurling finals are guaranteed sell-outs. If, say, in May an American decides to visit Ireland and somehow, accidentally, hears about hurling, surely he or she should be able to purchase a ticket for an All-Ireland quarter-final double-header?

It's true that tickets for championship encounters are now much more widely available and accessible than ever before, to GAA members and non-members alike. While the bulk of match tickets are distributed by clubs to their members, tickets have also become relatively widely available for purchase online, with www.gaa.ie and www.ticketmaster.ie handling several thousand tickets last season. But tickets are still generally only available about a week in advance of the game, which may rule our American tourist out of the game.

On big-match days in Croke Park, any tickets remaining unsold are made available from several outlets surrounding the stadium, including the Matt Talbot Credit Union on Fitzgibbon Street, the Drumcondra Laundrette on Drumcondra Road and a ticket booth opposite Quinn's pub, at the junction of Drumcondra Road and Clonliffe Road. It is advisable to leave plenty of time for queuing if you are planning on buying or collecting tickets from one of these outlets on match day.

Tickets for matches that may attract a full house normally do not go on general sale through the websites or county boards and can usually only be secured through clubs. The All-Ireland football and hurling finals – and a handful of other ties, often involving Dublin – fall into this category.

Ticket prices for this September's All-Ireland hurling and football finals will be €60 for the stands and €30 for the terrace. To attend a semi-final you will have to part with €40 for a seat, or €25 for a place on the terrace. Quarter-final tickets will cost €35 and €20, but if a quarter-final tie is played outside Croke Park the stand ticket will be €30.

Several attempts have been made to better organize the availability and distribution of student tickets – in hope of attracting more students to games as well as stopping non-students from chancing their arms at the €5 stile. The Leinster board have probably led the way in this regard, introducing a rather confusing scheme that appears to have worked, to some degree at least. Under the scheme, students pay full price but may then show student ID and claim back part (usually half) of the cost at the turnstile on the way into the stadium – a system that makes it much more difficult for student tickets to be sold on to non-students. This has resulted in the rather amusing sight of stile operators handing cash to spectators as they enter the stadium.

Championship Diary

May

May 7

Ulster Football Championship, preliminary round

Down v Cavan (Newry or neutral venue)

May 14

Munster Hurling Championship, quarter-final

Tipperary v Limerick (Thurles)

Ulster Hurling Championship, quarter-final

Antrim v London (Ruislip)

Ulster Football Championship, quarter-final

Armagh v Monaghan (Clones)

Connacht Football Championship, quarter-final

New York v Roscommon (Gaelic Park, New York)

Leinster Football Championship, first round

Westmeath v Offaly (Croke Park)

Meath v Louth (Croke Park)

May 21

Connacht Football Championship, quarter-final

Galway v Sligo (Galway)

Leinster Football Championship, first round

Wicklow v Carlow (Wexford)

Ulster Football Championship, quarter-final

Fermanagh v Antrim (Enniskillen)

Munster Football Championship, quarter-finals

Kerry v Waterford (Killarney)

Clare v Limerick (Limerick)

Leinster Hurling Championship, quarter-finals

Dublin v Westmeath (Portlaoise)

Offaly v Laois (Portlaoise)

Ulster Hurling Championship, semi-finals

Down v Antrim/London (Belfast)

Derry v New York (Gaelic Park, New York)

May 28

Connacht Football Championship, quarter-final

London v Mayo (Ruislip)

Leinster Football Championship, quarter-finals
Kildare v Westmeath/Offaly (Croke Park)
Wexford v Meath/Louth (Croke Park)
Ulster Football Championship, quarter-final
Tyrone v Derry (Omagh)
Munster Hurling Championship, semi-final
Clare v Cork

June

June 3

Christy Ring Cup, round 1, Section B

June 4

Ulster Hurling Final
Munster Hurling Championship, semi-final
Waterford v Tipperary/Limerick (Thurles TBC)
Leinster Football Championship, quarter-finals
Longford v Dublin (Pearse Park)
Laois v Wicklow/Carlow (Carlow/Portlaoise)
Ulster Football Championship, quarter-final
Donegal v Down/Cavan (Ballybofey/Cavan)

June 10

Christy Ring Cup, round 2, section B and round 1, section A
Nicky Rackard Cup, round 1
Leinster Hurling Championship, semi-final
Kilkenny v Dublin/Westmeath (Parnell Park/Cusack Park)

June 11

Leinster Hurling Championship, semi-final
Wexford v Offaly/Laois (Kilkenny)
Munster Football Championship, semi-finals
Tipperary v Kerry/Waterford (Killarney TBC)
Cork v Clare/Limerick (Cork/Limerick)
Ulster Football Championship, semi-final
Armagh/Monaghan v Fermanagh/Antrim

June 17

Christy Ring Cup, round 2, section A
All-Ireland Football Qualifiers, round 1
All-Ireland Hurling Qualifiers, round 1

June 18

Leinster Football Championship, semi-final
Kildare/Westmeath/Offaly v Wexford/Meath/Louth (Croke Park)
Ulster Football Championship, semi-final
Down/Cavan/Donegal v Tyrone/Derry
Connacht Football Championship, semi-final
New York/Roscommon v Galway/Sligo (Roscommon)

June 24

Christy Ring Cup, round 3, sections A and B
Nicky Rackard Cup, round 2

June 25

Munster Hurling Championship Final
Connacht Football Championship, semi-final
Leitrim v Mayo/New York (Carrick-on-Shannon)
Leinster Football Championship, semi-final
Longford/Dublin v Laois/Wicklow/Carlow (Croke Park)

July

July 1

All-Ireland Football Championship Qualifiers, round 2
All-Ireland Hurling Championship Qualifiers, round 2

July 2

Leinster Hurling Championship Final

July 8

Christy Ring Cup, round 4, sections A and B
Nicky Rackard Cup, round 3
All-Ireland Hurling Championship Qualifiers, round 3
All-Ireland Hurling Championship, preliminary quarter-final (if necessary)

July 9

Munster Football Championship final
Ulster Football Championship final

July 15

Christy Ring Cup, fifth round, sections A and B
All-Ireland Football Championship Qualifiers, round 3

July 16

Leinster Football Championship final
Connacht Football Championship final

July 22

All-Ireland Hurling Championship, quarter-finals (2)
Christy Ring Cup, semi-finals

July 23

All-Ireland Hurling Championship, quarter-finals (2)

July 29

All-Ireland Football Championship Qualifiers, round 4
(a) Munster runner-up v round 3 winner
(b) Ulster runner-up v round 3 winner
Nicky Rackard Cup, semi-finals

July 30

All-Ireland Football Championship Qualifiers, round 4
(c) Connacht runner-up v round 3 winner
(d) Leinster runner-up v round 3 winner

August

August 5

All-Ireland Football Championship, quarter-finals
Munster winner v round 4 winner (a or b)
Ulster winner v round 4 winner (a or b)

August 6

All-Ireland Hurling Championship, semi-final
Munster champion v quarter-final winner
Christy Ring Cup Final

August 12

All-Ireland Football Championship, quarter-finals (2)
Connacht v round 4 winner (c or d)
Leinster v round 4 winner (c or d)

August 13

All-Ireland Hurling Championship, semi-final
Leinster v quarter-final winner
Nicky Rackard Cup Final

August 20

All-Ireland Football Championship, semi-final

(Munster champ/quarter-final winner v Ulster champ/quarter-final winner)

Tommy Murphy Cup Final

August 27

All-Ireland Football Championship, semi-final

(Connacht champ/quarter-final winner v Leinster champ/quarter-final winner)

September

September 3

All-Ireland Hurling Championship Final (replay October 1)

September 10

All-Ireland Camogie Finals

September 17

All-Ireland Football Championship Final (replay October 8)

October

October 1

All-Ireland Women's Football Finals

October 15

International Rules Series, First Test

Ireland v Australia

October 22

International Rules Series, Second Test

Ireland v Australia